FOOD SECURITY MANAGEMENT
A COMPARATIVE STUDY

FOOD SECURITY MANAGEMENT

A Comparative Study

A. Jayakumar

ANMOL PUBLICATIONS PVT. LTD.
NEW DELHI - 110 002 (INDIA)

ANMOL PUBLICATIONS PVT. LTD.
H.O.: 4374/4B, Ansari Road, Darya Ganj,
New Delhi-110 002 (India)
Ph.: 23278000, 23261597
B.O.: No. 1015, Ist Main Road, BSK IIIrd Stage
IIIrd Phase, IIIrd Block,
Bangalore - 560 085 (India)
Visit us at: www.anmolpublications.com

Food Security Management: A Comparative Study

First Published, 2007

ISBN 978-81-261-3502-8

ICSSR Consultant: Prof. S. Indrakant

[This book is published with financial support from the Indian Council of Social Science Research, New Delhi. However, the responsibility for the facts stated and conclusions reached is entirely that of the Author and the ICSSR bears no responsibility for them.]

PRINTED IN INDIA

Printed at Mehra Offset Press, Delhi.

Contents

Contents

Preface

This book is book about the food security. It provided a preliminary assessment of how food security goals are currently being achieved or thwarted in South Asia, especially in India and Sri Lanka. While there are important issues of food security, it has managed to analyse the assessment, evaluation and comparability of food security in India and Sri Lanka. It has analysed the traditional food security at the macro level, mainly concerning the supply side — access to food through domestic production, buffer stocks, imports or foreign food aid and the demand for food-population growth, changes in income, the proportion of increased income used for purchasing food, foodgrain prices, nutritional requirements and public distribution system.

Many personalities have helped me in writing this research work, and I owe my debt to all of them. First of all I express my deepest gratitude to my supervisor, Prof. I.N Mukherji, whose vision as well constant encouragement has been my greatest source of inspiration and motivation. His kindest co-operatin, sympathetic understanding and faith in me mostly made the completion of this work possible.

I am extremely grateful to ACTIONAID India, which has granted me assistance to complete this research, and without its aid I would have been in a serious financial crisis.

I am also thankful to the library staff of Jawaharlal Nehru University, Ministry of Agriculture, Ministry of Food, NSSO, FAO, World Bank, Indian Institute of Public Administration (New Delhi), and Centre for Development Studies (Thiruvananthapuram) — all in India, and Ministry of Plan and Finance, Ministry of Plan Implementation, Ministry of Food, Department of Census and Statistics, Central Bank of Sri Lanka, Marga Institute, University of Colombo, IIMI, FAO, and World Bank in Sri Lanka. All of them have supplied me with the necessary material and extended full co-operation.

I am also indebted to many others who constantly encouraged me in my academic pursuits especially Dr. Ranaweera Banda, Dr. Chandramani Sharma and Dr. Rajib Nandi. Besides, I express my gratitude to Karthikeyan for his motivation during the crucial days of drafting. Dr. Rajkumar not only encourage me but also readily agreed to edit the manuscript.

Finally, no words are sufficient to express my deep sense of gratitude to my wife Geetha and daughter Gaushika for their live and inspiration.

A. Jayakumar

List of Tables

List of Graphs

Abbreviations

ADP	Agricultural Development Proposals
AIB	Agricultural Insurance Board
BPL	Below Poverty Line
CACP	Commission for Agricultural Cost and Prices
CCIS	Comprehensive Crop Insurance Scheme
CWC	Central Warehousing Corporation
CWE	Cooperative Wholesale Establishment
EAS	Employment Assurance Scheme
FAO	Food and Agricultural Organisation
FCI	Food Corporation of India
FPS	Fair Price Shops
FSS	Food Stamp Scheme
GDP	Gross Domestic Product
GNP	Gross National Product
GPS	Guaranteed Price Scheme
HRV	High Responsive Variety
HYV	High Yield Variety
IADP	Intensive Agricultural District Programme
IRDP	Integrated Rural Development Programme
JRY	Jawahar Rozgar Yojana

LDC	Less Developing Countries
MSP	Minimum Support Price
NREP	National Rural Employment Programme
NSAP	National Social Assistance Programme
NWDPRA	Watershed Development Project for Rainfed Areas
PDS	Public Distribution System
PMB	Paddy Marketing Board
RLEGP	Rural Landless Employment Guarantee Programme
RPDS	Revamped Public Distribution System
RS	Ration Shop
SAARC	South Asian Association for Regional Cooperation
SADCC	Southern African Development Co-ordination Conference
SAP	Structural Adjustment Programme
STF	Samurdhi Task Force
SWC	State Warehousing Corporation
TPDS	Targeted Public Distribution System
USA	United States of America
WFP	World Food Programme
WFS	World Food Summit

1

Introduction

The World Food Conference, convened by the Food and Agricultural Organisation (FAO) in 1974, drew the attention of the world community, for the first time, to the urgent need of devising ways and means to ensure food security for hungry millions of the world in general, and of South Asia in particular. The World Food Summit (WFS) in Rome in November 1996 invited the world's attention towards the chronic problem of hunger and malnutrition, and the potential for increasingly acute food shortages in South Asia. These historic events prompted the academic world to research on the problem of food security, which is an important aspect of human life and suggested ways and means to improve the food scenario in the world. The present research study is just a small endeavour in this process.

Definition

The food security is normally used at macro level, mainly concerning the supply side. A nation enjoys food security when it has enough access to food through domestic production, buffer stocks, imports or foreign food aid, and is in a position to satisfy the needs of its entire population. At the micro level, food security refers to both demand for, and supply of, foodgrains with more emphasis on the demand side. In other words, at the household level, food security essentially implies physical as well as economic access by all the people to enough food for an active healthy life.[1] The definition of food security, as endorsed by the FAO/ World Health Organisation International Conference on Nutrition held in Rome in December 1992, reads: "access for all people at all times to enough food for an active, healthy life." The WFS broadened this definition by stating that "Food security exists when all people, at all times, have physical and economic access to sufficient, safe and nutritious food to meet their dietary needs and food preferences for an active and healthy life." In 1983, the United Nations defined the goal of food security as providing to the entire "population both economic and physical access to a supply of food, sufficient in both quality and quantity, at all times, regardless of climate or harvests, social level or income".[2]

An alternative approach to defining the food security is that of 'entitlements' to food, developed by Amartya Sen. Each person is entitled to food, derived from his or her own production, from exchange through barter, markets or working in non-food production activities, or from transfer (of food) either from the family, the community, civil society or the state. According to Maxwell, food security means a "secure access at all times to sufficient food for a healthy life".[3] M.S. Swaminathan redefines food security as "livelihood security for the households and all members within, which ensures both physical and economic access to balanced diet, safe drinking water, environmental sanitation, primary education and basic health care".[4] The Rome Declaration on WFS reaffirms the "right of everyone to have access to safe and nutritious food, consistent with the right to adequate food and the fundamental right of everyone to be free from hunger".

Thus the term 'food security' suggests sustained supply of appropriate food to everyone in a society to enable their healthy development without serious disruption to the environment, their livelihoods and their culture. Thus, food security has three elements: the availability of food (quantity), the ability of the people to obtain quantity of food (access), and required quality (nutritional value). It can be assessed globally, nationally, locally, and at the level of households and individuals. While various types of risks can generate food insecurity, they can also be temporary, seasonal or chronic. The assessment of food security needs an external agency, which, in turn, should consider how individuals, households and local support systems assess their particular food security risks and respond to them.

Statement of the Problem

In order to understand the concept of food security, one can start by considering the household as a fundamental unit. A food-secure household can be defined as one which has access to enough food for its individual members to lead a healthy life at all times. As regards trends in household food security measured by the percentage of undernourished population, what seems clear is that for India and Sri Lanka, where large section of the population depends on agricultural production as their livelihood, household food security has been closely linked to agricultural production.

What is significant for households and individuals is the availability and adequacy of food intake, i.e., whether or not the quantities actually consumed meet their consumption requirements. This intake can either be produced or procured, but since both production and income/ prices constantly fluctuate, the easy and feasible solution is to evolve a national buffer-stocks policy. The food aid also helps but is not advisable for a long-term basis. Hence, what is required is a national scheme dealing with the delivery of food to the poor, while international food aid can help to stabilise food availability. The poor adjust the expenditure on food because the major share of their income is spent on foodgrains. One solution lies in commercial food imports, but this again involves growing dependency. Huge imports for a long period mean a conflict between national food security and national political security. Another crucial aspect related to imports is whether a food-deficit nation can afford to pay for them.

At all levels, i.e., household, domestic or international – fluctuations in prices often affect food security. But other factors should also be taken into consideration, like developing counties' limited and rapidly diminishing resources; the state of the environment, which suffers from yield increases; and the availability and costs of credit to households. Some other factors include the lack of transportation facilities, markets and infrastructure, which often result from poor management or planning. The lack of off-farm employment opportunities for the poor and women further contribute to food insecurity.

Food security also implies entitlement to food through access to land and other means of production, or through productive employment. When there is no purchasing power, the poor resort to household-level coping strategies which are, in fact, counterproductive. It is also argued that the imperatives of food insecurity arise due to the imbalance between population growth and foodgrain production. Tim Dyson[5] emphasises that population growth will pose the main challenge to food production in the next few decades. The better feeding of the humanity in the years up to 2020 can be really accomplished only by a considerable increase in the volume of inter regional food transfers through trade.

The imbalance between food supply and population growth compels the developing economies to set up an efficient distribution mechanism. An efficient public distribution system, and stable and secure food production are integral parts of food security in the developing countries. A crucial aspect of food security is the efficient management of food economy in a society, which does not have to depend on external assistance to meet the normal shortages occurring in agriculture.

Poverty is the gravest of problems for any nation. Poverty is not only dependent on agricultural production (availability of food) but also income (prices). Poverty, in fact, is the direct outcome of population growth without proportionate increase in agricultural output. The ratio of the people below the minimum standards of nutrition, health, shelter and education has grown in developing countries. Poverty (low or lack of income) cannot be eliminated without the proportionate growth of agriculture. Agricultural growth is needed for poverty alleviation because agriculture is a dominant sector in all the developing economies. Therefore, rapid increase in foodgrain production should be the priority of any development strategy – a factor that depends on rainfall, irrigation, fertilisers and land. In many developing countries the agricultural sector remains one of the important contributors towards the gross domestic product (GDP), employment generation and rural household incomes.

Several factors have contributed, in varying degrees, to the development of agriculture in India and Sri Lanka. However, two key factors stand out – the past policy bias against agriculture and the high degree of distortions in world agricultural markets due to the protection and subsidisation. The traditional policy bias against the agricultural sector, reflected in direct and indirect taxation of agricultural production and exports, arose for a variety of reasons. The second important factor was the socio-political imperative of maintaining low food prices, commonly operated through state-controlled marketing boards. These factors, taken together, had the unintended consequence of depressing farm prices and profitability, thus reducing incentives for investment in the agricultural sector. Agricultural sector policy reforms remain high on the agenda in both India and Sri Lanka. The common objectives of these reforms are enhancing productivity of basic food crops to their potential and diversify production and exports by promoting the development of new crops and the processing of primary products. Agricultural development, thus, is the best advisable solution to help small and marginal poor farmers, so that the rural poor may become productive and thereby improve their living standards.

Significance of the Study

South Asia is emerging as the most deprived region in the world, accommodating nearly one-fourth of humanity. It is the poorest, most illiterate, malnourished and the least gender-sensitive region. The significant question remains as to how long will it take for the poor to gain access to these means and to provide food security for the disadvantaged population facing deprivation and hunger? Food self-sufficiency has been a major goal for India and Sri Lanka since independence. It outlines recent weaknesses in food security and identifies some of the major pressures, tensions and priorities regarding Indian and Sri Lankan food security. Population growth is still outpacing foodgrain production in both the countries.

This research provides a comprehensive assessment of progress in foodgrain output and prospects of the countries in the region, and a clear analysis of the challenges of development faced by them. It attempts a preliminary assessment of how such food security goals are currently being achieved or thwarted in South Asia, especially in India and Sri Lanka. Public distribution system could be viewed either as a tool of macro economic management or as an anti poverty measure. The emphasis is to ensure availability in the face of fluctuations in output and inflation. This research attempts to initiate a comparative study of food security in India and Sri Lanka.

A review of the current literature on food security is given below. A major gap in the literature is that there is no comparative study focusing on the viability of national food security between two nations with similar socio-economic background like India and Sri Lanka. The present study is undertaken on the rationale that the sample countries are following dissimilar distribution mechanisms, i.e. the "Public Distribution System" in India and "Food Stamp Scheme" in Sri Lanka. The reason for selecting food security in South Asia as a subject of study is that it has lately appeared as the principal component of human security.

Survey of Literature

There are diverse sources of literature available on different issues of food security. However, the existing literature can be reviewed under some themes: global, regional and household policies and programmes, agricultural production, food import/aid, food prices, food distribution and insurance/reserves.

The variability in agriculture is caused by the impact of fluctuating weather, showing a differential in the size of harvests in low developed countries (Valdes,[7] 1981). The low level of food stocks in the post-harvest period and their availability during the heavy work period in the rainy season reduces the area sown and also the use of non-household agricultural labour by households in Zambia (Kumar,[8] 1988).

At sub-national level, food security reflects the assured availability of food during a given period for individual households to meet their minimum requirements. A household becomes a fundamental/basic unit of food security of any nation (Alamgir,[9] 1991). Food security depends as much on the lack of purchasing power and entitlement as on variable production and supply. Poverty and starvation cause food insecurity in society mainly due to the lack of entitlements, despite the availability of enough food in the market to procure (Sen,[10] 1982). Hunger is an outcome of prolonged high rates of unemployment, underemployment, growing inequality in wealth distribution, and the declining value of real wages and welfare benefits (Graham,[11] 1997). Innovative policies for rural development and the prosperous small-farmer agricultural economy will reduce poverty and hunger (Wendy and Alex,[12] 1996). Global food surpluses provide the basis for a sustained growth of demand for food. In the short-run, such surpluses can support carefully targeted food subsidies to meet the food needs of low-income households; in a longer term, they can support food-for-work efforts in order to create rural infrastructures needed for a broad-based rural growth strategy (Mellor,[13] 1988). Financial constraints are involved in the rational use of foodgrains in rural wage employment programmes (India's Integrated Rural Development Programme, Jawahar Rozgar Yojana, etc., and Sri Lanka's Samurudhi), community food management, and nutrition programmes (Venugopal,[14] 1992).

The developing countries show little evidence of having efficiently stabilized food consumption through changes in imports and stocks (Valdes and Konandreas,[15] 1981). Trade occupies a more strategic role than the stocks in domestic stabilization policies among members of the Association of South-East Asian Nations (ASEAN), but reliance on imports may well impose an additional burden on the international rice market. A regional commodity agreement on rice may contribute to a significant reduction in the world price stability (Siamwalla,[16] 1981). Food security issues could be tackled through market stabilization in Southern Africa Development Co-ordination Conference (SADCC) countries (Hay and Rukuni,[17] 1988). Malnutrition is due to high transportation costs in Colombia, even though it has adequate food supplies and favorable foreign exchange reserves. The similar situation also persists in India. The uneven income distribution in Colombia and even minor price increase could result in a reduction of food consumption among the poor (Garcia,[18] 1981).

The income of rural households in these countries are dependent on the generation of purchasing power in non-farm occupations, despite greater self-sufficiency in food production and higher aggregate income in Sahelian and Sudanian villages of Burkina Faso (Reardon et al,[19] 1988). The commercialization of agriculture in South Nyanza, Kenya, is not a hindrance to food security at household level (Kennedy,[20] 1988), but according to Vyas, food insecurity in India is due to lack of diversification of agriculture (Vyas,[21] 1996). Besides the diversification of agriculture, major inputs like irrigation, high-yielding varieties of seeds, fertilizers, etc., have a substantial impact on foodgrain production (Sharma and Varant,[22] 1990).

The new technology has substantially increased

household income, which is spent on increased calorie consumption, and has significantly improved children's nutritional status, especially in the rainy season in Gambia of West Africa (von Braun,[23] 1988). The households prefer to buy expensive foodgrains even while having very low levels of income and food security. Marginal farmers with alternative incomes prefer to buy superior foodgrains from the open market, rather than the subsidised low-quality and coarse foodgrains from the public distribution system (Elizabeth,[24] 1995). The semi-subsistence production in urban areas is not marginal, but critical to urban food security and is an important aspect of women's economic strategies (Daniel,[25] 1995).

The important indicators of household food security are: per capita income, total expenditure per capita, food expenditure per capita, and the share of food in total expenditure. The per capita food expenditure provides a stable welfare indicator in the context of a group of households facing homogeneous prices as in Sri Lanka (Sudhir and Harris,[26] 1990). The food stamp programme has not solved the nutrition problem but served reasonably as a food assistance and income supplement programme. The food stamp programme is of considerable value to few countries in view of their own nutrition problems and offers a desirable alternative to food price subsidies, commodity distribution, or direct income transfer (Sexauer,[27] 1977; Bishop et at,[28] 1996 Neville,[29] 1987). The two macro-policy measures – the agricultural price policy and public distribution – are the main instruments of the development policy for the agriculture sector (Tyagi,[30] 1990).

The importance of sustainable environment-friendly food production is that it ensures food and nutrition security (Gopalan,[31] 1996). In South Asian countries the mixed farm operations – food-fed systems i.e., pigs-vegetable-duck-pond system integrated tree cropping system with small ruminants (goat and sheep) would ensure food security (Devendra,[32] 1994).

Food security is not necessarily synonymous with stability in total food supplies. It depends on efficient public distribution system. India has the very large public procurement and distribution system that has been in effect for a long period (George,[33] 1985) and in order to ensure food security there should be an improvement in the efficacy of the public distribution system in transferring food to the poor (Radhakrishna,[34] 1996, Bapna,[35] 1990, Kabra,[36] 1990, Kabra and Ittyerah,[37] 1992, Nawani,[38] 1995). Co-ordination between production, procurement and distribution, and co-operation between consumers or dealers and the government is very important for an efficient and successful public distribution system in India (Suryanarayana,[39] 1985). This school of thought integrates the consumption, production and marketing sectors of the food system into a consistent framework for understanding tradeoffs involved in reaching society's objectives of reducing hunger, improving food security, and raising farm productivity (Peter,[40] 1988). Swaminathan[41] (1996) points to the need for the introduction of a "National Food Security Act" ensuring sustainable food and nutritional security, which can be ensured through scientific and environment feasible agricultural production.

The increasing food imports and food subsidies has resulted in food security in Egypt (Ahmed,[42] 1981). The trade policy can be an efficient stabilization force for most countries (Reutlinger and Bigman,[43] 1981). The beneficial orientation of food aid flows could generally enhance food security and overall economic development in poor countries

(Huddlestan,[44] 1981). Food aid is for vulnerable groups, pregnant and nursing mothers, infants and school children. The feasibility of ensuring food aid has been demonstrated under the food-for-work programme in India (Fonseca,[45] 1983). The understanding between private traders and the government in trading and storing, the promotion of drought-resistant crops such as millets and sorghum, and also farm-level storage and market outlets play an important role in mitigating food insecurity (Lele and Wilfred,[46] 1981). Food insurance schemes deal with food insecurity problem in food-deficit developing countries (Louis,[47] 1981; Huddlestan and Konandreas,[48] 1981; Johnson,[49] 1981).

Food security issues have been studied from both environmental and entitlement/deprivation perspectives. The reduction in input subsidies planned under the Structural Adjustment Programme (SAP) in India may result in aggregate food insecurity, but would ensure individual food security (Mukherjee,[50] 1994).

As evident from the above survey, while many studies have attempted to bring out the multiple aspects of food security, a cross-country comparison has not been attempted so far. Therefore, this study attempts a cross-country comparison of food security in India and Sri Lanka.

Scope and Objectives

The key factors constraining the agricultural sector in India and Sri Lanka are high level of subsidies and protection provided by the government. Domestic support to agriculture encourages over-production, which, in turn, increases supplies to the domestic markets (by reducing import demand or increasing export supply) and depresses domestic prices. This study reviews the current state of food security in India and Sri Lanka and probes how the public distribution system ensures food security in the context of the social, economic and political developments. It outlines weaknesses in food security and identifies some of the major pressures, tensions and priorities regarding Indian and Sri Lankan food security. Improved strategies, policies, and programmes for agricultural and rural development are essential if developing countries are to increase their agricultural output and eradicate hunger in future. In the case of former, the main concern of policymakers is the management of scarcities through buffer stocking, rationing and imports. The emphasis is to ensure availability in the face of fluctuations in output and inflation. As an anti poverty measure, public distribution aims to transfer incomes to low income groups and the programme has become more targeted towards the poor.

The main ***objectives*** of the study are:

(i) To study the national food security of India and Sri Lanka through food production, imports and aid in ensuring food security;

(ii) To examine the food policies in India and Sri Lanka;

(iii) To analyse demand factors with effect on population growth, consumption patterns, etc., and

(iv) To make an assessment of food distribution mechanism in India and Sri Lanka.

Data and Methodology

This study aims to review national food security since independence in India and Sri Lanka.[51] This study utilises secondary data using quantitative methods to assess national food security on the basis of the availability of foodgrains in India and Sri Lanka. The secondary data are from Food and Agricultural Organisation, Ministries of Agriculture, Food and Civil Supplies, Census of India, National Sample Survey Organisation, etc. (India) and Ministries of

Agriculture, Food, Census of Sri Lanka, Central Bank of Sri Lanka, Department of Economics and Statistics, etc (Sri Lanka). The study would also utilise published and unpublished official documents and reports, foreign research reports and related materials. The performance of the agriculture sector, food production, imports, and aid in both the countries since 1961 has been evaluated by estimating the growth rate and index numbers. Indian and Sri Lankan governments' policies and programmes to ensure food security, particularly policies relating to the supply, demand and distribution are analysed qualitatively and quantitatively. The determinants of demand for food are explained by using data from both the countries on population, price indices, income, expenditure and consumption pattern, nutritional intake, etc. In India and Sri Lanka, the data on food production, procurement, stock and distribution, etc are used to discus the distribution aspect of food security.

Chapterisation

The first chapter attempts to examine the issues, concepts, evolution, and state of food security in general. It also documents the literature on food security, different data sources and methodology. Chapter II assesses the performance of food crops, i.e. cereals, rice, wheat, coarse grains, pulses since 1961 in South Asia in general, and in India and Sri Lanka in particular. Chapter III documents the Indian and Sri Lankan government policies and programmes to ensure food security, particularly policies relating to the supply, demand and distribution, and suggests ways to improve them. Chapter IV focuses on the determinants of demand for food since independence. The major determinants of food demand are population growth, rising income, foodgrain prices, and shift in consumption patterns. Chapter V seeks to establish how the households form a central social unit of access to food through the public distribution system both in India and Sri Lanka. The last chapter provides a summary of the main findings and presents some policy recommendations and suggestions.

REFERENCES

1. World Bank, *Poverty and Hunger: Issues Options for Food Security in Developing Countries* (Washington, 1986).
2. Food and Agricultural Organisation, *Food Security: Still Far From the Goal*, (Quebec City, 1995).
3. Maxwell G Daniel, "Alternative Food Security Strategy: A Household Analysis of Urban Agriculture in Kampala", *World Development,* Vol. 23, No. 10, (1995), pp. 1669-1681.
4. M.S. Swaminathan, "Science and Technology for Sustainable Food Security", *Indian Journal of Agricultural Economics,* Vol. 51, nos.1-2, (1996), pp. 60-75.
5. Tim Dyson, Global Environmental Change Programme (London, 1996),
6. Mahbub ul Haq, Wheat, 22, 165, *Human Development in South Asia,* 1997 (Karachi 1997).
7. Alberto Valdes, ed., *Food Security for Developing Countries,* (Colorado, 1981).
8. Subha S. Kumar, "Effect of Seasonal Food Shortage on Agricultural Production in Zambia", *World Development,* Vol. 16, No. 9, 1988, pp. 1051-64.
9. Mohiuddin Alamgir and Poonam Arora, *Providing Food Security for all,* (London, 1991).
10. Amartiya Sen, Poverty and Famines: An Essay on Entitlement and Deprivation, (Delhi, 1982).
11. Graham Riches, ed., *First World Hunger: Food security and Welfare Policies,* (London, 1997).
12. Wendy S Ayres and Alex F McCalla, "Rural Development, Agriculture, and Food Security", *Finance and Development,* Vol. 33, No. 4, (December, 1996).
13. J.W. Mellor, "Global Food Balances and Food Security", *World Development,* Vol. 16, No. 9, (1988), pp. 997-1012.
14. K.R. Venugopal, *Deliverance from Hunger: The Public Distribution System in India,* (New Delhi, 1992).

15. Alberto Valdes and Panos Konandreas (1981), 'Assessing Food Security Based on National Aggregates in Developing Countries', in Alberto Valdes (ed.) *Food Security for Developing Countries,* Westview, Colorado, pp. 25-52.
16. Ammar Siamwalla, Security of Rice Supplies in the ASEAN Region, In Alberto Valdes, ed., *Food Security for Developing Countries,* (Colorado, 1981), pp. 79-100.
17. R.W. Hay and M. Rukuni, "SADCC Food Security Strategies: Evolution and Role", *World Development,* Vol. 16, No. 9, (1988), pp. 1012-1024.
18. Jorge Garcia (1981), 'The Nature of Food Insecurity in Colombia', in Alberto Valdes (ed.) *Food Security for Developing Countries,* Westview, Colorado, pp. 123-142.
19. T. Reardon, P. Matlon and C Delgado, "Coping with Household-level Food Security in Drought-affected Areas of Burkina Faso", World *Development,* Vol. 16, No. 9, (1988), pp. 1065-1074.
20. E. Kennedy and B. Cogill, "The Commercialization of Agriculture and Household-level Food Security: The case of Southwestern Kenya", World *Development,* Vol. 16, No. 9, (1988), pp. 1075-1082.
21. V.S. Vyas, "Diversification in Agriculture: Concept, Rationale and Approaches", *Indian Journal of Agricultural Economics,* Vol. 51, No. 4, (1996).
22. J.S. Sharma and P. Varant Gandhi, *Production and Consumption of foodgrains in India: Implications of accelerated economic growth and Poverty Alleviation,* International Food Policy Research Institute, Research Report 81, (Washington, July, 1990).
23. von Braun, "Effects of Technological Change in Agriculture on Food Consumption and Nutrition: Rice in a West African Setting", *World Development,* Vol. 16, No. 9, (1988), pp. 1083-1098.
24. Elizabeth Oughton, "Targeting foodgrains to the rural poor: A micro level study of India", In Joseph Mullen ed., *Rural Poverty*, (Aldershat, 1995).
25. Daniel Morrow (1981), 'The International Wheat Agreement and LDC Food Security', in Alberto Valdes (ed.) *Food Security for Developing Countries,* Westview, Colorado, pp. 213-240.

26. Sudhir Anand and Christopher Harris, "Food and Standard of Living: An Analysis Based on Sri Lankan Data", In Jean Dreze and Amartya Sen ed., *The Political Economy of Hunger,* (Oxford, 1990), pp. 297-350.
27. Benjamin Sexauer (1977), 'The US food stamp Programme, *Food Policy,* Vol. 2, No. 4, November.
28. John A Bishop, John P Formby and Lester A Zeager (1996), 'The impact of Food Stamps on United States Poverty in the 1980s: A Marginal Dominance Analysis', *Economica,* May, pp. 30-41.
29. Neville Edirisinghe, *The Food Stamp Scheme in Sri Lanka: Costs, Benefits, and Options for modification,* International Food Policy Research Institute, Research Report 58, (Washington, 1987).
30. D.S. Tyagi, "Increasing Access to Food through Interaction of price and Technology Policies - The Indian Experience", In Vijay Shankar Vyas ed., *Increasing Access to food: The Asian Experience,* (Delhi, 1990).
31. C. Gopalan, *Towards India's Food and Nutrition Security,* Keynote address at the National Symposium on "Food Security for the Poor" organised by the FAO and Indian Association for the Advancement of Sciences, (1995).
32. Asian Productivity Organisation, *Sustainable Agriculture Development in Asia,* (Tokyo, 1994).
33. P.S. George, *Some Aspects of Procurement and Distribution of Foodgrain in India,* International Food Policy Research Institute, Working Paper on Food Subsidies No. 1, (Washington, 1985).
34. R. Radhakrishna, "Food Trends, Public Distribution System and Food Security Concerns", *Indian Journal of Agricultural Economics,* Vol. 51, No. 1-2, (1996), pp. 168-183.
35. S.L. Bapna, "Food Security through the Public Distribution System: The Indian Experience", In Vijay Shankar Vyas ed., *Increasing Access to food: The Asian Experience,* (New Delhi, 1990).
36. Kamal Nayan Kabra, *Political Economy of Public Distribution of Food in India,* (New Delhi, 1990).
37. Kamal Nayan Kabra, and Anil Chandy Ittyerah, *The Public Distribution System in India,* (New Delhi, 1992).

38. N.P. Nawani, *Towards Food for all Ideas for a New Public Distribution System,* Ministry of Information and Broadcasting, Government of India, (New Delhi, 1995).

39. G. Suryanarayana, *Public Distribution in India,* (Allahabad, 1985).

40. Peter C. Timmer, "Food Policy and Economic Adjustment", In David E. Bell and Michael R. Reich ed., *Health Nutrition, and Economic Crisis: Approaches to Policy in the Third World,* (Dover, 1988), pp. 177-197.

41. M.S. Swaminathan, "Science and Technology for Sustainable Food Security", *Indian Journal of Agricultural Economics,* Vol. 51, No. 1-2, (1996), pp. 60-75.

42. Ahmed A. Goueli, "Food Security Program in Egypt", In Alberto Valdes ed., *Food Security for Developing Countries,* (Colorado, 1981), pp. 143-160.

43. Shlomo Reutlinger, and David Bigman, "Feasibility, Effectiveness, and Costs of Food Security Alternatives in Developing Countries", In Alberto Valdes ed., *Food Security for Developing Countries,* (Colorado, 1981), pp. 185-212.

44. Barbara Huddleston, "Responsiveness of Food Aid to Variable Import Requirements", In Alberto Valdes ed., *Food Security for Developing Countries,* (Colorado, 1981), pp. 287-306.

45. A.J. Fonseca, *Food Aid for Relief and Development: An Evaluation,* Indian Social Institute, (New Delhi, 1983).

46. Uma J. Lele, and Wilfred Candler, "Food Security: Some East African Considerations", in Alberto Valdes, ed., *Food Security for Developing Countries,* (Colorado, 1981), pp. 101-122.

47. Louis M. Goreux, "Compensatory Financing for Fluctuations in the Cost of Cereal Imports", In Alberto Valdes ed., *Food Security for Developing Countries,* (Colorado, 1981), pp. 307-332.

48. Barbara Huddleston and Panos Konandreas (1981), 'Insurance Approach to Food Security: Simulation of Benefits for 1970/71-1975/76 and 1978-1982', in Alberto Valdes (ed.) *Food Security for Developing Countries* Westview, Colorado, pp. 241-254.

49. Gale D Johnson, "Grain Insurance, Reserves, and Trade:

Contributions to Food Security for LDCs", In Alberto Valdes ed., *Food Security for Developing Countries,* (Colorado, 1981), pp. 255-286.

50. Amitava Mukherjee, *Structural Adjustment Programme and Food Security,* (Aldershot, 1994).

51. The period of study may vary subject to the availability of comparable data on India and Sri Lanka.

2

Food Scenario in South Asia

This chapter reviews the performance of staple food crops of South Asia in general and India and Sri Lanka in particular. It analyses the data on production, area, yield, aid and availability of major food crops. The major cereals, rice and wheat, are supplemented by coarse cereals (barley, maize, millet, sorghum), and pulses. Cereals are the most important ingredients in the human diet and contain significant quantities of protein of variable quantity. The trends in the volume of food production and agricultural inputs, especially land and irrigation in India and Sri Lanka will also be analysed. The chapter also discusses key issues relating to the development of food production, trade and aid for the enhancement of food security in India and in Sri Lanka in the context of their growing population.

Since the Second World War, South Asian nations' strategy has been greater reliance on state planning in the economy. In addition, the Green Revolution, based on the application of Western technology and production models, has stimulated agricultural productivity throughout the region. South Asia's growing self-sufficiency in food provides an insight into the capitalist road to development. An important component of agricultural development process is investment in physical infrastructure i.e., transportation and communication.[1] Development of infrastructure increases aggregate agricultural productivity by increasing the efficiency of resource utilisation at the micro and macro levels.

Although the South Asian economies have had a very sharp contrast from the West in state domination, they have remained mired in poverty. Both India and Sri Lanka are known for promoting social equity through various types of government policies. The role of food crops as the primary item of expenditure by wage earners gives these crops a special importance vis-à-vis the employment-oriented strategies of growth. The following section considers macro data on the economic and social performance of the South Asian economies before analysing the state of food security.

Area Under Cultivation

The harvested area of cereal in general, and paddy in particular, shows an increasing trend in South Asia except Maldives[2], as can be seen in Table 2.1. During the period 1961 to 2000, Nepal has covered more area under cereal cultivation, while Pakistan has succeeded to bring more area under paddy cultivation than all other South Asian nations. India was able to increase 0.17 per cent under cereal cultivation and 0.6 per cent under paddy cultivation annually during the same period, as against Sri Lanka's 1.17 and 1.29 per cent respectively. In India, the area under paddy cultivation in 1961 was 346.94 lakh hectares, which increased to 446.00 lakh hectares in 2000; in Sri Lanka it increased from 4.96 to 8.71 lakh hectares during the same period. In Nepal and Sri Lanka the increase in cereal and paddy production during the post-green revolution period was mainly due to the expansion of area under cultivation.

TABLE 2.1

Harvested Area of Major Food Crops in South Asia (Ha/ lakh)

Year	*Bangladesh*	*Bhutan*	*India*	*Nepal*	*Pakistan*	*Sri Lanka*
Cereals						
1961	86.39	0.68	922.39	17.15	78.59	5.39
1971	95.31	0.90	996.73	20.10	94.74	7.33
1981	111.44	1.12	1055.08	23.13	109.10	8.89
1991	109.55	0.93	1002.43	29.86	117.08	8.31
2000	129.35	1.09	1011.02	33.47	124.63	9.07
GR1	2.47	2.90	0.27	0.92	3.00	-2.49
GR2	0.43	0.69	0.06	1.93	1.05	0.85
GR3	0.61	1.02	0.17	1.90	1.14	1.17
Paddy						
1961	84.84	0.19	346.94	10.88	12.14	4.96
1971	92.98	0.24	377.58	12.01	14.56	6.94
1981	104.61	0.28	407.08	12.97	19.76	8.42
1991	102.45	0.26	426.49	14.12	20.97	7.91
2000	120.00	0.30	446.00	15.50	23.12	8.71
GR1	2.60	2.60	0.66	0.52	4.17	-2.51
GR2	0.20	0.88	0.59	0.89	1.48	0.99
GR3	0.41	1.13	0.60	0.90	1.65	1.29
Wheat						
1961	0.57	0.05	129.27	1.10	46.39	—
1971	1.26	0.07	182.41	2.28	59.78	—
1981	5.91	0.09	222.79	3.92	69.84	—
1991	5.99	0.06	241.67	5.93	79.11	—
2000	8.45	0.13	267.42	6.50	84.63	—
GR1	-1.38	1.98	0.70	-1.80	2.97	—
GR2	8.08	1.69	1.76	4.57	1.35	—
GR3	8.28	1.90	1.95	5.23	1.47	—
Coarse Cereals						
1961	0.99	0.45	446.18	5.17	20.05	0.44

1971	1.08	0.60	436.75	5.81	20.40	0.39
1981	0.92	0.76	425.21	6.24	19.50	0.47
1991	1.11	0.61	334.28	9.82	17.00	0.40
2000	0.90	0.66	297.60	11.47	16.88	0.36
GR1	-7.21	3.12	-0.16	2.26	2.38	-2.61
GR2	0.21	0.46	-1.39	2.54	-0.44	-1.16
GR3	0.33	0.84	-1.16	2.29	-0.40	-0.59
Pulses						
1961	3.65	0.02	238.10	1.73	19.05	0.09
1971	4.74	0.03	222.58	2.13	14.80	0.10
1981	9.49	0.04	222.17	2.69	15.14	0.66
1991	7.25	0.02	246.62	2.73	18.59	0.63
1999	6.68	0.02	239.30	2.98	17.15	0.47
GR1	0.93	3.94	0.00	3.85	-0.97	8.97
GR2	0.87	-1.14	0.11	1.29	0.09	4.96
GR3	1.65	-0.21	-0.01	1.38	-0.13	5.43

Note: GR1 denotes exponential growth rate 1961-1965, GR2 – 1966-2000 and GR3 – 1961-2000.

Source: http://www.apps.fao.org.

The area under wheat cultivation has shown an increasing trend in all wheat producing countries in South Asia during 1961 to 1999. The highest of 8.28 per cent growth was recorded in Bangladesh followed by 5.23 in Nepal, and the lowest of 1.47 per cent reported in Pakistan during the same period. In India, the area under wheat cultivation has increased from 129.27 lakh hectares in 1961 to 267.42 lakh hectares in 1999, a growth of 1.95 per cent annually. The highest increase in the area under wheat cultivation has been reported in Bangladesh, followed by Nepal and the lowest was in India between the pre-and post-green revolution periods. It is interesting to find that the area under coarse cereal cultivation has shown a declining trend in India, Maldives Pakistan and Sri Lanka in South Asia during 1961 to 1999. The highest decline of

12.06 per cent was recorded in case of Maldives followed by 1.16 in India and the lowest of 0.40 per cent in Pakistan during the same period.

In India, the area under coarse cereal cultivation has also declined from 446.18 lakh hectares in 1961 to 297.60 lakh hectares in 1999. The rate of decline in India was higher than in Sri Lanka during 1961 to 1999. The comparative analysis of the pre-and post-green revolution shows that only Bangladesh and Nepal have recorded an increased in the area under coarse cereal cultivation since the introduction of green revolution in mid-1960s. The area under pulse cultivation has shown an increasing trend in all South Asian countries except Bhutan and Pakistan during 1961 to 1999. While Sri Lanka recorded the highest growth of 5.43 per cent, the lowest, i.e., -0.01 per cent was reported in India during the same period. The growth level of area under pulses shows that Maldives, India and Nepal have reported higher level of growth during 1966-2000 than 1961-65.

Harvested Area Per Thousand Persons

The data pertaining to area under cultivation of harvested area of cereals and paddy per thousand persons from 1961 to 2000 has been provided in Table 2.2. India recorded the highest harvested area per thousand persons of cereals, which was 203.85 hectares, followed by Nepal, which had 181.67 hectares. The lowest was reported in Sri Lanka with 59.13 hectares. Even though the total cultivated area of cereals and paddy has been increasing over the period of time, but the increase was not sufficient to cope up with the population growth in South Asia. Consequently there was a decline in harvested area per thousand persons of cereals and paddy in South Asia. In 2000, Nepal has the highest of 139.86 hectares of cereals followed by India.

Similarly, Bangladesh has the highest (92.91 hectares) harvested area per thousand persons of paddy followed by Nepal's 64.77 hectares. The lowest was witnessed in Bhutan with 14.12 hectares. The extent of variations in area under cereal cultivation in Sri Lanka was higher than India.

TABLE 2.2

Per Thousand Persons Harvested Area of Cereals and Paddy in South Asia

(Ha)

Year	*Bangladesh*	*Bhutan*	*India*	*Nepal*	*Pakistan*	*Sri Lanka*
1961	163.86	77.18	203.85	181.67	153.27	53.19
1971	139.11	82.98	175.57	173.37	140.41	57.19
1981	123.09	83.25	149.90	155.47	123.87	59.01
1991	98.41	53.92	115.56	155.10	95.52	48.21
2000	100.15	51.49	99.74	139.86	79.65	48.15
Paddy						
1961	160.90	20.90	76.68	115.25	23.69	48.89
1971	135.70	21.74	66.51	103.58	21.59	54.43
1981	115.55	20.76	57.84	87.16	22.44	55.90
1991	92.03	15.05	49.16	73.32	17.11	45.90
2000	92.91	14.12	44.00	64.77	14.78	46.26

Source: Same as Table 2.1

During the period 1961 to 2000, the per capita area under cereal cultivation in India was higher than Sri Lanka, but the gap has gradually narrowed down by the year 2000. In Sri Lanka, area under cereal cultivation was around 50 hectares per thousand persons from 1961-2000. While in India, it has declined from 203.85 hectares in 1961 to 99.74 hectares in 2000. In the case of India, owing to its higher population growth, per capita cultivated area of cereals has been declining faster than Sri Lanka. The marginal decline in harvested area of cereals in Sri Lanka was due to fact that the Mahaweli Irrigation Project and Settlement Programmes brought more land under cultivation.

Graph 2.1: Per Thousand Person Harvested Area of Cereals in India and Sri Lanka

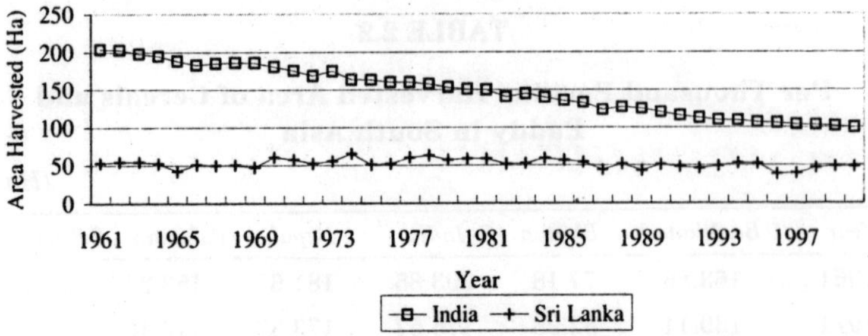

Graph 2.2: Per Thousand Person Harvested Area of Paddy in India and Sri Lanka

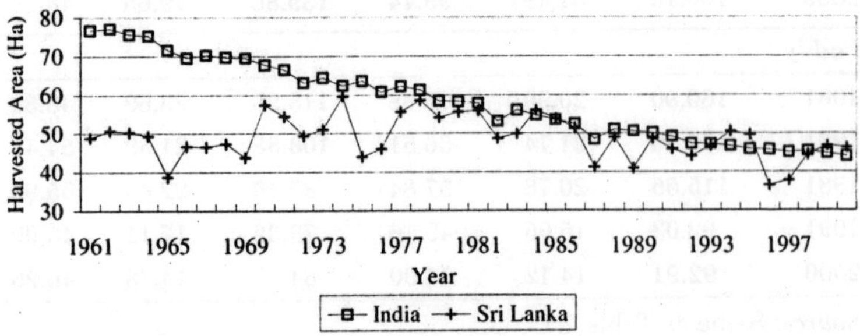

Cropping Pattern

The cropping pattern is also an important element of food security in South Asia. Since the land area is static, the share of area under cereal cultivation had marked an increase from 1961 to 1998. It is a healthy sign of food security. In 1961, Bangladesh had the highest of 66.37 per cent of the land area under cereal cultivation, while Maldives had the lowest with 0.6 per cent. In Nepal, the share of area under cereal cultivation has increased annually at the rate of 1.9 per cent, followed by 1.18 per cent in Sri

Lanka during the same period. The area under coarse cereal had declined from 1961 to 1998 in India, Maldives, Pakistan and Sri Lanka. This has been a matter of concern in view of the fact that coarse cereals are the main food items of the poor people in rainfed areas in South Asia. Similarly, the share of area under pulses production has been declining in Bhutan, India and Pakistan. Only Sri Lanka was able to increase the area under pulse cultivation by 5.43 per cent annually.

TABLE 2.3

Percentage Share of Harvested Area of Cereals, Coarse Cereals and Pulses to Land Area in South Asia

Year	*Bangla-desh*	*Bhutan*	*India*	*Maldives*	*Nepal*	*Pakis-tan*	*Sri Lanka*
Cereals							
1961	66.37	1.45	31.02	0.60	11.99	10.19	8.34
1971	73.22	1.91	33.52	0.31	14.05	12.29	11.34
1981	85.61	2.39	35.49	0.44	16.17	14.15	13.76
1991	84.16	1.98	33.72	0.01	20.88	15.19	12.85
1998	84.62	2.43	33.94	0.03	22.68	16.44	13.39
Coarse Cereals							
1961	0.76	0.96	15.01	0.60	3.62	2.60	0.67
1971	0.83	1.27	14.69	0.31	4.06	2.65	0.61
1981	0.70	1.61	14.30	0.44	4.37	2.53	0.72
1991	0.86	1.30	11.24	0.01	6.87	2.21	0.62
1998	0.73	1.52	9.96	0.03	7.67	2.45	0.56
Pulses							
1961	2.80	0.04	8.01	0.17	1.21	2.47	0.13
1971	3.64	0.06	7.49	0.17	1.49	1.92	0.15
1981	7.29	0.09	7.47	0.18	1.88	1.96	1.03
1991	5.57	0.04	8.29	0.25	1.91	2.41	0.97
1998	5.26	0.04	7.68	0.27	2.02	2.24	0.73

Source: Same as Table 2.1.

The various National Planning Organisations in Sri Lanka have aimed at diversifying the economy and settlement through agricultural modernisation and crop diversification.[3] The government's new agricultural policy aims to diversify some of the rice land into coarse cereals, pulses, etc. in order to enhance the income of the farmers and reduce imports. The yields are generally low with all subsidiary food crops due to low inputs, poor management, and vagaries of weather. At the time of the Census of Agriculture in 1982, the three main export crops (tea, rubber and coconut) covered around 50 per cent of the total cultivated area, while the staple food crop, i.e., paddy covered 37 per cent.[4] The balance of 13 per cent was devoted to the cultivation of other food crops (maize, potatoes, chillies, onions, soyabeans, cowpea, green gram, black gram), vegetables, and fruits.

Graph 2.3: Percentage of Harvested Area of Coarse Cereals to Land Area in India and Sri Lanka

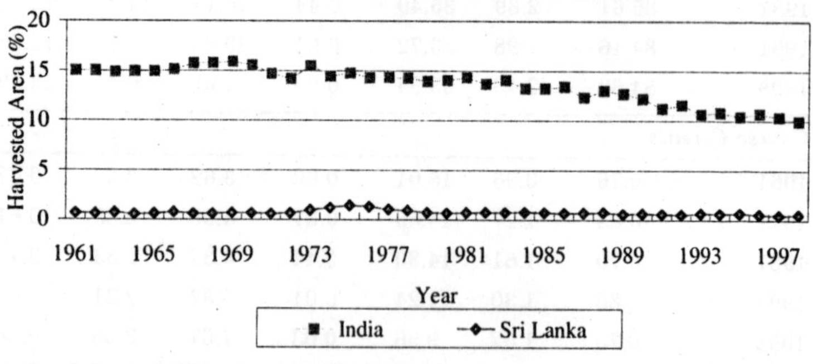

In Sri Lanka efforts towards crop diversification have already been made in the past, especially in the 1980s.[5] However, the expected diversification did not taken due to the fact that the marketing of diversified crops is the main constraint to crop diversification and agricultural growth and, therefore, improving the marketing systems for these products was essential to promote diversification into high-value crops for export, as well as for domestic use.

Food Production

Social objectives, income differentials and subsistence considerations shape the South Asian agricultural policy like in many developing countries. However, agriculture is greatly affected by three major external factors: fluctuations in harvests generated by weather variability, supply-demand relationships in national cereal markets, and their variability in supply-demand conditions. Annual variations in rainfall can be drastic, thus causing cereal yields to vary widely. This, of course, affects the total production and producers' incomes. South Asian agriculture is also characterised by rather large differentials in farm sizes and incomes. It is primarily the smaller farms, often lacking resources that pose problems to the agricultural sector.

TABLE 2.4

Food Production Index in South Asia

(1989-91=100)

Year	*South Asia*	*Bangla-desh*	*Bhutan*	*India*	*Maldives*	*Nepal*	*Pakis-tan*	*Sri Lanka*
1961	45.8	56.3	50.4	46.4	46.6	47.0	34.4	54.0
1971	55.9	63.8	65.9	56.0	66.6	55.4	49.2	71.7
1981	72.7	78.9	89.2	72.4	81.6	70.0	69.2	99.8
1991	101.6	102.0	101.6	101.3	102.8	100.4	103.8	99.4
2000	127.7	128.4	114.4	125.4	130.9	124.2	145.3	115.2

Source: Same as Table 2.1.

The South Asian countries are generally agriculture-oriented in nature and have a considerable farm potential. In normal years agriculture and related activities usually contribute fairly adequate and varied food. The common food of the South Asian nations is mainly rice, and to some extent wheat, which is the staple food in India and Pakistan. The general food security indicators of the SAARC nations have been illustrated in following sections.

The food production index of South Asian countries from 1961 to 2000 is documented in Table 2.4. The data shows that food production index for South Asia as a whole has increased from 45.8 in 1961 to 127.7 in 2000. In 1961, Bangladesh had the highest food production index of 56.3 while Pakistan had the lowest of 34.4. Even though India (46.4) had higher than the South Asia's average, it was less than Sri Lanka's 54.0. The food production index in Sri Lanka had increased to 109.8 in 1986, which is the highest in the South Asia. In 2000, both India and Sri Lanka reported lower than the South Asia's average. Pakistan showed the highest of 145.3 while the lowest of 114.4 was recorded in Bhutan. Graph 2.6 clearly shows the trend of food production index for India and Sri Lanka from 1961 to 2000. In India, food production index was lower than that of Sri Lanka till 1988, but since then onwards it has grown higher than Sri Lanka (Appendix I).

Graph 2.4: Food Production Index in India and Sri Lanka (1989-91=100)

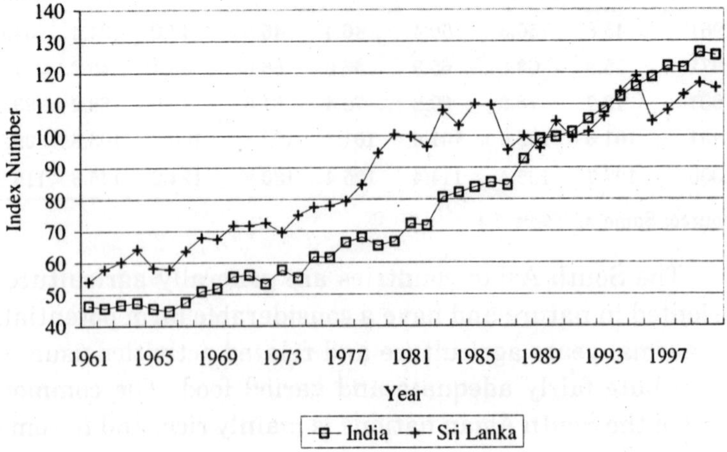

During pre-Green Revolution period, the South Asian nations' main concern was lack of aggregate supply of food. The rising food prices of the 1960s favoured the introduction of fertility-responsive new varieties, intensive usage of subsidised inputs like fertilisers, irrigation, pesticides, and a widespread technological change. The post-Green Revolution period indicates a gradual growth of agricultural production in South Asian countries as they have realised the importance of population and its impact on food security. This realisation has warranted a relatively higher growth of agriculture and food production.

The cereal production has shown an increasing trend in South Asia except Maldives during the period 1961 to 2000 as may be seen in Table 2.5. But the fact is that Maldives is not a cereal producing economy. It manages its food demand by imports from other countries. The highest annual growth of 3.66 per cent in cereal output was reported in Pakistan, followed by Sri Lanka (2.92 per cent). In India, cereal production in 1961 was 873.77 lakh metric tons as against Sri Lanka's 9.52 lakh tons. India has increased its cereal production to 2398.14 lakh metric tons by 2000 at an average annual growth of 2.87 per cent but this was still less than Sri Lanka. Among the major cereals, paddy is the staple food in South Asia. In the case of cereals, Pakistan has reported the highest growth rate of 3.3 per cent, followed by Sri Lanka (2.96 per cent) during the same period. India registered a third position in the growth rate of cereals during the same period. In India, paddy production in 1961 was 534.95 lakh metric tons but it had increased to 1341.5 lakh metric tons by 2000 recording a growth rate of 2.74 per cent annually.[6] Similarly, in Sri Lanka, the major cereal, paddy production was 9.23 lakh metric tons in the year 1961 and it had increased to 27.67 lakh metric tons by 2000 by recording a growth rate of 2.96 per cent per annum. The growth levels of cereals and paddy production during the post -Green Revolution period, i.e. from 1966 to 2000, indicates that India, Nepal and Sri Lanka have reported higher growth rate than the pre-Green Revolution period, i.e. 1961 to 1965.

Wheat also occupies an important position in food production in South Asia except in Sri Lanka and Maldives. The wheat output has increased considerably during the period from 1961 to 2000 in all South Asian nations. The highest growth has been reported from Bangladesh, at 12.29 per cent annually, while Bhutan recorded the lowest of 2.44 per cent. In India, wheat production in 1961 was 109.97 lakh metric tons but it increased to 742.51 lakh metric tons by 2000 at the rate of 5.34 per cent per annum. The impact of Green Revolution greatly reflected on the production of wheat than any other major food crops in all wheat producing countries, except Pakistan (Table 2.5). The growth rate was quite impressive in Bangladesh India and Nepal.

Even though the area under inferior food crops, like coarse cereals has declined during the period from 1961 to 2000, yet in most of the South Asian countries their production has reported an increasing trend, except in Maldives. In India, the coarse cereal production has increased from 228.85 lakh metric tons in 1961 to 314.13 metric tons by 2000, increasing at the rate of 0.72 per cent per annually. Similarly, in Sri Lanka, the supplementary cereal crops production, which was 0.29 lakh metric tons in 1961 increased to 0.34 lakh metric tons by 2000 recording a growth rate of 0.68 per cent per annum. In the case of coarse cereals production, the Green Revolution has made only a marginal impact in Bangladesh, India, Nepal and

Sri Lanka. Other than the cereal, the pulse production has also shown an increasing trend in all countries in South Asia during 1961 to 2000. The highest rate of production of 7.34 per cent has been reported in Sri Lanka as compared to 0.65 per cent in India. The variation in pulse production between the pre-and post-Green Revolution period was witnessed only in India and Maldives. Maldives is the only country where natural climate is highly conducive for production of pulses than any other food crops.

TABLE 2.5

Production of Cereals in South Asia

(Mt/Lakh)

Year	*Bangladesh*	*Bhutan*	*India*	*Nepal*	*Pakistan*	*Sri Lanka*
Cereals						
1961	145.24	0.98	873.77	31.67	67.30	9.52
1971	150.89	1.29	1132.38	34.51	113.36	14.21
1981	215.91	1.64	1475.84	39.34	182.22	22.66
1991	284.62	1.06	1931.01	55.20	211.38	24.30
2000	369.00	1.59	2398.14	69.86	299.23	28.03
GR1	2.47	2.90	0.27	0.92	3.00	-2.49
GR2	0.43	0.69	0.06	1.93	1.05	0.85
GR3	0.61	1.02	0.17	1.90	1.14	1.17
Paddy						
1961	144.26	0.37	534.95	21.08	16.90	9.23
1971	148.97	0.47	646.02	23.44	33.93	13.96
1981	204.46	0.57	798.83	25.60	51.45	22.29
1991	273.77	0.43	1120.42	32.23	48.65	23.89
2000	349.25	0.50	1341.50	40.30	70.00	27.67
GR1	2.60	2.60	0.66	0.52	4.17	-2.51
GR2	0.20	0.88	0.59	0.89	1.48	0.99
GR3	0.41	1.13	0.60	0.90	1.65	1.29
Wheat						
1961	0.33	0.05	109.97	1.35	38.14	—

1971	1.12	0.07	238.33	1.93	64.76	—
1981	10.93	0.09	363.13	4.77	114.75	—
1991	10.04	0.05	551.35	8.36	145.65	—
2000	19.08	0.20	742.51	11.84	210.79	—
GR1	-1.38	1.98	0.70	-1.80	2.97	—
GR2	8.08	1.69	1.76	4.57	1.35	—
GR3	8.28	1.90	1.95	5.23	1.47	—
Coarse Cereals						
1961	0.65	0.56	228.85	9.24	12.26	0.29
1971	0.80	0.75	248.04	9.14	14.68	0.26
1981	0.53	0.97	313.88	8.96	16.03	0.37
1991	0.80	0.58	259.25	14.61	17.08	0.41
2000	0.66	0.89	314.13	17.73	18.45	0.36
GR1	-7.21	3.12	-0.16	2.26	2.38	-2.61
GR2	0.21	0.46	-1.39	2.54	-0.44	-1.16
GR3	0.33	0.84	-1.16	2.29	-0.40	-0.59
Pulses						
1961	2.54	0.01	128.60	0.86	9.34	0.04
1971	3.66	0.01	114.42	1.13	7.88	0.06
1981	5.90	0.02	108.28	1.45	6.91	0.66
1991	5.22	0.02	142.65	1.64	9.90	0.50
1999	5.13	0.02	153.10	2.13	11.23	0.28
GR1	0.93	3.94	0.00	3.85	-0.97	8.97
GR2	0.87	-1.14	0.11	1.29	0.09	4.96
GR3	1.65	-0.21	-0.01	1.38	-0.13	5.43

Note: GR1 denotes exponential growth rate 1961-1965, GR2: 1966-2000 and GR3: 1961-2000.

Source: Same as Table 2.1.

Per Capita Cereal Production

Table 2.6 shows production of per capita cereals and pulses from 1961 to 2000 in South Asia. Nepal reported the highest production of 335.49 kilograms cereal per person while it was the lowest in Bhutan. But in both the countries the per capita production of cereals has declined from

1961 to 2000. The increasing trend in per capita paddy production has been registered only in India, Pakistan and Sri Lanka for the period from 1961 to 2000.

TABLE 2.6

Per Capita Production of Cereals and Paddy in South Asia

(Kg)

Year	*Bangladesh*	*Bhutan*	*India*	*Nepal*	*Pakistan*	*Sri Lanka*
Cereals						
1961	275.47	111.20	193.11	335.49	131.25	93.91
1971	220.22	119.24	199.47	297.65	168.02	111.51
1981	238.50	121.35	209.69	264.44	206.89	150.36
1991	255.69	61.17	222.60	286.66	172.45	141.06
2000	285.70	74.98	236.58	291.95	191.22	148.91
Paddy						
1961	273.62	41.81	118.23	223.31	32.96	91.06
1971	217.41	43.48	113.80	202.18	50.28	109.50
1981	225.85	42.55	113.50	172.11	58.41	147.93
1991	245.95	24.88	129.16	167.36	39.69	138.69
2000	270.41	23.54	132.34	168.41	44.73	146.97

Source: Same as Table 2.1

The per capita production of cereals and paddy was greatly affected in the 1970s in India, due to droughts. In Sri Lanka also, the per capita production of cereals and paddy started declining since 1985, when it had reached its highest point. In India, the per capita output of cereal reached the highest in 1989 (Graph 2.5). The per capita production of cereal was always higher in India in comparison to Sri Lanka. However, in case of paddy Sri Lanka had better per capita production than India during the same period.

Graph 2.5: Per Capita Production of Cereal in India and Sri Lanka

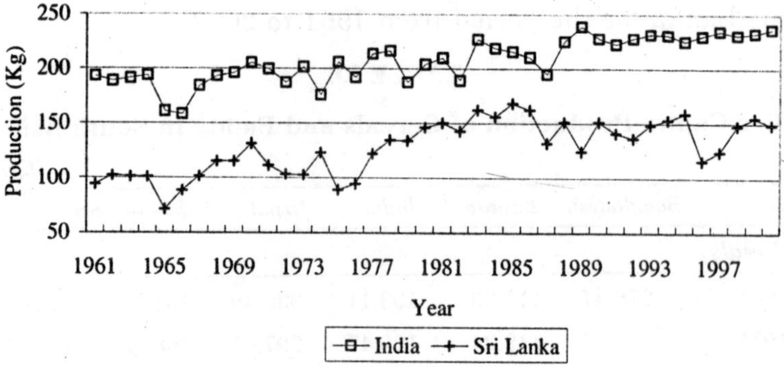

Productivity of Foodgrains

Even though the harvested area of cereals has increased in South Asian countries, the yield has also increased from 1961 to 2000 except Bhutan. India registered a higher growth rate in cereals and paddy production in comparison to all the other countries, but its yield rate of cereal and paddy is less than in Sri Lanka (Table 2.7). The average per hectare production of paddy in Bhutan had come down from 2,000 kilograms in 1961 to 1,667 kilograms by 2000. In India, per hectare paddy cultivation in 1961 was 1,542 kilograms, which had increased to 3,008 kilograms recording the growth rate of 2.13 per cent annually. Similarly, in Sri Lanka, while the yield of paddy was 1863 kilograms in 1961, it had increased to 3,177 kilograms in 2000. Bhutan has reported the highest productivity of paddy in 1961 (2,000 kilograms), while Pakistan reported the lowest of 1,392 kilograms in the same year. But Sri Lanka had improved its paddy productivity to 3,177 kilograms in 2000, the highest in South Asia. The growth levels of cereals output per hectare during the post- green revolution period, i.e.1966 to 2000, indicates that Bangladesh, India, Maldives, Pakistan and Sri Lanka had achieved higher growth rate than during the pre-green revolution period, i.e. 1961 to 1965. Similarly, the green revolution has influenced the per capita output of paddy in Bangladesh, India, Nepal and Sri Lanka.

The average productivity of wheat has shown an increasing trend in all wheat producing countries in South Asia, varying from 3.7 to 0.53 per cent annually. In India, the yield has increased from 851 kilograms per hectare in 1961 to 2,777 kilograms by 2000 at the growth rate of 3.32 per cent. The growth rate during the post-green revolution has been higher than the pre green revolution period, i.e. 1961 to 1965 in Bangladesh, Bhutan, India, Nepal and Pakistan.

As reported, like the increase in the area and production of coarse cereals in South Asian countries, the yield per hectare of coarse cereals tool has shown an increasing trend in India, Maldives, Pakistan and Sri Lanka. In India, per hectare coarse cereal production in 1961 was 513 kilograms, which had increased to 1,056 kilograms in 2000, recording a growth rate of 1.9 per cent annually. Similarly, in Sri Lanka, the yield of coarse cereal was 661 kilograms in 1961, which had increased to 1,022 kilograms by 2000. So far as coarse cereals are concerned the green revolution has supported their growth only in India, Maldives and Pakistan.

Similarly, growth rate of pulses during the post-green revolution has been higher than during the pre-green revolution period in Bhutan, Maldives and Nepal only. The yield per hectare of pulses has increased in South Asia by an average of one per cent annually during 1961 to 2000. In India the growth rate of yield has been reported at 0.66 per cent, which is lower than Sri Lanka's growth rate of 1.37 per cent.

TABLE 2.7

Yield of Cereals and Pulses in South Asia

(Kg/Ha)

Year	*Banglc-desh*	*Bhutan*	*India*	*Maldives*	*Nepal*	*Pakis-tan*	*Sri Lanka*
Cereal							
1961	1681	1441	947	888	1847	856	1765
1971	1583	1437	1136	761	1717	1197	1939
1981	1938	1458	1399	767	1701	1670	2548
1991	2598	1135	1926	1000	1848	1805	2926
2000	2853	1456	2372	2500	2087	2401	3093
GR1	0.98	-0.05	-1.39	1.21	0.44	1.03	-0.72
GR2	1.98	-0.30	2.83	2.69	0.43	2.25	1.74
GR3	1.65	-0.29	2.69	2.06	0.43	2.19	1.71
Paddy							
1961	1700	2000	1542	—	1938	1392	1863
1971	1602	2000	1711	—	1952	2329	2012
1981	1955	2050	1962	—	1975	2604	2646
1991	2672	1654	2627	—	2283	2320	3022
2000	2910	1667	3008	—	2600	3027	3177
GR1	0.89	0.00	-2.02	—	0.83	1.13	-0.81
GR2	2.04	-0.77	2.29	—	0.95	1.12	1.65
GR3	1.70	-0.64	2.13	—	0.91	1.13	1.64
Wheat							
1961	574	1020	851	—	1227	822	—
1971	888	1015	1307	—	847	1083	—
1981	1848	1094	1630	—	1218	1643	—
1991	1677	833	2281	—	1410	1841	—
2000	2259	1539	2777	—	1821	2491	—
GR1	1.23	-0.04	-0.56	—	0.47	1.12	—
GR2	3.32	0.73	3.16	—	1.27	2.63	—
GR3	3.70	0.53	3.32	—	0.90	2.79	—
Coarse Cereals							
1961	656	1256	513	888	1787	611	661

1971	747	1261	568	761	1573	720	652
1981	579	1280	738	767	1436	822	780
1991	722	943	776	1000	1488	1005	1027
2000	734	1345	1056	2500	1546	1093	1022
GR1	6.59	-0.03	-1.21	1.21	-0.50	-0.35	1.90
GR2	-0.18	-0.21	1.99	2.69	-0.32	1.40	1.56
GR3	-0.02	-0.22	1.90	2.06	-0.50	1.44	1.28
Pulses							
1961	695	444	540	600	494	490	457
1971	772	500	514	600	530	533	606
1981	622	600	487	600	537	456	988
1991	720	800	578	627	600	533	804
2000	757	800	618	564	778	729	597
GR1	1.15	1.72	-2.53	0.00	0.59	1.96	4.81
GR2	0.12	1.85	0.83	0.64	0.92	0.45	1.11
GR3	0.12	1.80	0.66	0.51	0.85	0.41	1.37

Note: GR1 denotes exponential growth rate 1961-1965, GR2 : 1966-2000 and GR3 : 1961-2000.

Source: Same as Table 2.1.

The yield per hectare of cereal and paddy in India and Sri Lanka had shown an increasing trend during the period 1961 to 2000. During the pre-green revolution period (1961-65) the yield of paddy has shown a declining trend in India and Sri Lanka. Immediately after the green revolution, due to the introduction of high yielding varieties of paddy in Sri Lanka, and paddy and wheat in India, the output started increasing. The investment in agriculture rose only in a decade following the green revolution, but later declined significantly in the public and private sectors in India.[7] But the yield of cereals and paddy in Sri Lanka was higher than India since 1961. During 1971-79, in Sri Lanka, the yield of cereal in general, and paddy in particular, showed a declining trend. But since 1979 onwards, an increasing trend was witnessed with marginal variations.

Graph 2.6: Yield of Cereals in India and Sri Lanka

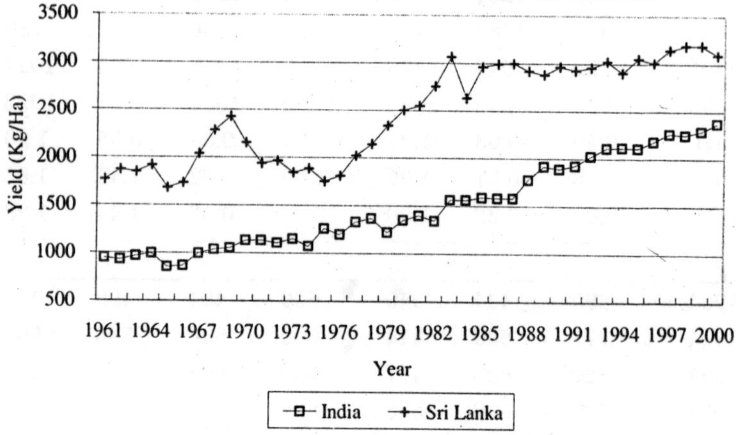

In India, the yield of cereal and paddy has been increasing gradually. During the 1970s, in India the yield has reported ups and down due to severe droughts. However, after 1980, the variation was very marginal due to better monsoon. In the case of India, the increase in productivity has been an important achievement in the post-green revolution period. The variation in the growth rates of total food production over the period of time has largely been accompanied by regional disparities in production across regions.[8]

The following section examines whether over the past 50 years India and Sri Lanka remained self-sufficient economies in so far as the food crops are concerned. It also discusses issues relating to the domestic supply of cereals in both India and Lanka. The wheat production and yield has clearly shown the impact of green revolution since 1968, compared with other crops. In the future the possibilities of further expansion of area under wheat cannot be rated high, as compared with rice. However, changes in the growth rates of rice and wheat production can be one of the major determinants of growth pattern of the agricultural production in India. Moreover, crop diversification can be regarded as an important factor for food security in both India and Sri Lanka. However, in the coming years the area under cereals as a proportion of the gross cropped area may show a decline.

The coarse cereals production faces the risk of fluctuating weather conditions. The fact that 90 per cent of coarse cereals, 90 per cent of pulses and 81 per cent of oilseeds are grown under rainfed conditions highlights the need for upgrading the productivity of these crops to improve the quality of life of the people inhabiting these resource-poor areas in India.[9] However, in India the general trend in per capita output of coarse cereals has been rising, as yield increases have more than offset declines in per capita area harvested. This is in part the result of major agricultural policy reforms followed in the late 1960s. But the total area harvested of coarse cereals remained approximately constant since 1980.

South Asia can marginally increase the land under cereal cultivation in future if it intensifies multiple cropping,[10] because of a realistic increase in the volume of cereal demand - mostly due to population growth. In developing countries as a whole, food production has failed to keep pace with the demand due to faster population growth, the lack of research and technological improvements in food production, deficient agricultural extension services, inadequate investment in rural infrastructure, non-implementation of land reforms, and poor terms of agricultural trade.[11]

In India and Sri Lanka the new wheat and rice varieties were adopted at exceptionally rapid rates in areas where they were technically and economically superior to local varieties. Landowners have gained benefits from the adoption of the higher-yielding grain varieties. Radical political economists argue that the green revolution technology tends to be monopolised by large commercial farmers who have better access to new information and financial resources. Since the advent of the green revolution in 1967-68, food production in terms of yield has increased with the help of triple inputs in agriculture, i.e., seeds, water and fertilisers. Earlier the production increased only by bringing more areas under cultivation.[12] The green revolution is often compared to the "Japanese model" of increase in agriculture productivity by utilising improved varieties of seeds.[13]

In Sri Lanka, rice production remains an important part of food security at the household level. It is clear that Sri Lanka continues to have a comparative advantage in rice production, particularly in the *maha* (wet season) when there are almost no other suitable crop alternatives. The increase in the area of paddy cultivation is mainly due to the establishment of irrigation schemes, and rehabilitation of both major and minor irrigation systems. The yield per hectare has also doubled since Independence, primarily due to the use of improved varieties of seeds, together with the application of fertilisers and agro-chemicals, and the adoption of better management practices.[14]

The high cost of production has led to a low profitability in the case of rice in Sri Lanka. Rice production experienced a drastic fall during the early 1970s. This drop in domestic production gave rise to a sharp increase in the value of imports in Sri Lanka. In the past ten years, the average yield has remained stagnated at around 3,000 kg of paddy per hectare. The uncontrolled surge in the costs of cultivation has been severely discouraging paddy cultivation. By the end of 1990, the biggest Mahaweli Development Project area produced 17 per cent of Sri Lanka's paddy production.[15] The government has placed high priority on the production and availability of the major staple food, i.e., rice. The policy action taken to promote rice production includes large investments in infrastructure, particularly irrigation, land development and settlement, support services involving research, extension and education, input subsidies such as low-priced fertilisers, free irrigation water, rent-free land, consumption subsidies on rice, and floor prices to farmers.

While wheat is not produced in Sri Lanka, it plays a significant role in the food security of the people. At present it has become the second staple diet of the people of Sri Lanka. Maize and millets represent the next largest component of cereal. But while maize production has increased, millet output has declined over the past decade. The Ministry of Agriculture in Sri Lanka has laid considerable focus on certain subsidiary food crops, which fetch high incomes to farmers and have a direct impact on household expenditures. These include a wide range of crops, such as maize, kurrakkan and millets, green and black grams, chillies, onions, oil crops, and tubers.

These crops are mainly grown in the dry and intermediate zones on rain-fed lands under shifting cultivation (chena). Many of these crops are grown for home consumption, as they form part of the regular diet of the Sri Lankan people. The production as well as the productivity level of these crops has been low due to lack of marketing facilities, and the government's poor support for research and development. There are no direct subsidies as such to encourage the production of subsidiary crops although in some areas farmers benefit from free irrigation.

Food Balance Sheet

Millions of people both in India and Sri Lanka do not even have sufficient food for the consumption. However, the problem arises while laying down the criteria to be used to define the population as inadequately fed. Primarily the food problem is defined in terms of total availability at the national level. The total quantity of food available for domestic consumption in a year involves assembling data on food production, trade, aid, and making deductions for quantities of food which are lost in storage, used as animal feed, and seed.

Cereal production data relates to the total domestic production whether inside or outside the agricultural sector, i.e., it includes non-commercial production and production from kitchen gardens. The cereal imports include commercial trade, food aid and granted on specific terms, donated quantities and estimates of unrecorded trade. Export of cereal covers all movements out of the country. In fact, the elements involved in domestic cereal supply are production, imports, exports and change in stocks (increase or decrease). The definition used in domestic supply is as follows:

Domestic Supply = Production + Imports + changes in Stocks (increase or decrease) - Exports.

The growth in share of production of cereal to the domestic supply was the highest in Pakistan (3.71 per cent) followed by Sri Lanka (2.94 per cent) and India (2.91 per cent) during the period from 1961 to 1999. As may be seen in Table 2.8, except Sri Lanka and Maldives, all the other South Asian countries fulfilled more than 90 per cent of their demand of foodgrains from domestic supply during the period from 1961-99. Owing to the low production of cereals, Sri Lanka used to import a reasonable proportion of foodgrains from other countries. The share of cereal import for domestic use has been declining in India (-8.16 per cent) in comparison to all other countries.

TABLE 2.8

Percentage Share of Production, Imports, and Exports of Cereals to Domestic Supply in South Asia

Year	*Bangladesh*	*India*	*Maldives*	*Nepal*	*Pakistan*	*Sri Lanka*
Production						
1961	95.01	95.24	1.85	123.45	91.10	49.51
1971	81.96	100.23	0.59	110.42	92.58	52.07
1981	93.52	98.50	0.38	106.72	117.65	68.90
1991	88.70	97.58	0.01	98.03	106.61	64.36
1999	91.21	108.57	0.07	101.00	96.70	62.22
GR	2.32	2.91	-10.81	2.18	3.71	2.94
Imports						
1961	7.30	5.43	98.15	0.18	16.03	54.33
1971	9.41	2.70	99.41	0.01	2.89	45.26
1981	6.08	0.56	100.00	1.98	2.18	30.19
1991	7.46	0.06	97.10	0.12	5.32	33.71
1999	17.37	1.03	81.47	0.89	12.63	39.48
GR	2.61	-8.16	4.38	16.52	3.63	0.73
Exports						
1961	0.00	0.00	0.00	15.11	2.57	0.03
1971	0.00	0.02	0.00	9.65	1.87	0.01
1981	0.00	0.81	0.00	1.66	9.23	0.06
1991	0.00	0.85	0.00	0.09	6.56	0.05
1999	0.00	1.51	0.00	0.58	6.98	0.09
GR	1.36	22.31	0.00	-13.50	5.81	6.65

Note: GR denotes exponential growth rate (1961-1999). Source: Same as Table 2.1.

Nepal's annual cereal import has increased by 16.52 per cent from 1961 to 1999. In India, the share of cereal import was 5.43 per cent of its domestic supply in 1961 whereas Sri Lanka imported 54.33 per cent. India has been able to reduce its cereal imports by 1.03 per in 1999 and Sri Lanka reduced its imports to 39.48 per cent; its share of imports is highest in South Asia, next to Maldives. So far as export of cereals is concerned, India and Sri Lanka have started exporting cereals, especially rice to other countries whenever they have surplus production. Nepal and Pakistan's export shares were higher than other countries in South Asia during 1961-99.

Graph 2.7 indicates that the cereal import in India and Sri Lanka had come down during the period 1961 to 1999. But Sri Lanka experienced a higher fluctuation in comparison to India's gradual decline. In India, the cereal import has declined sharply from 1977. In the late 1970s, in India, the open market prices of rice and wheat were lower than price under public distribution system. Sri Lanka has imported 70 per cent of the rice requirement in 1964.

In 1961, all South Asian countries, except Sri Lanka, had satisfied their domestic demand of paddy through their domestic production. Sri Lanka was able to meet

Graph 2.7:Percentage Share of Cereal Imports to Domestic Supply in India and Sri Lanka

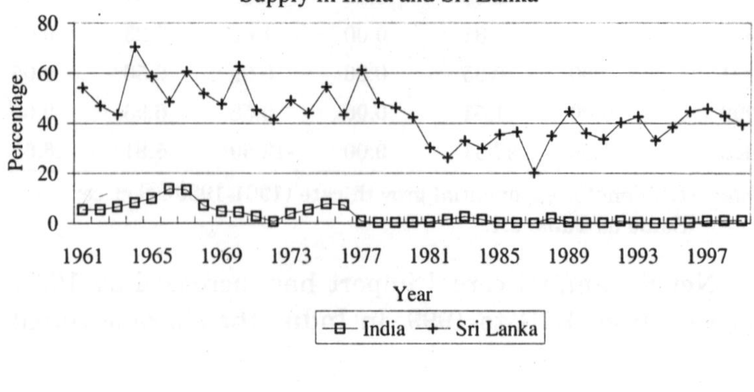

60.02 per cent of its requirement from its production, while the rest were fulfilled by imports. Owing to low level of cereal production Sri Lanka had to rely on substantial food imports. Table 2.9 indicates that all South Asian countries have increased their production during 1961-1996. Pakistan has increased the share of production to

TABLE 2.9

Percentage Share of Production, Imports and Exports of Paddy to Domestic Supply in South Asia

Year	*Bangladesh*	*India*	*Maldives*	*Nepal*	*Pakistan*	*Sri Lanka*
Production						
1961	99.14	99.34	0.00	146.51	117.99	60.02
1971	88.80	100.28	0.00	128.08	108.71	70.92
1981	99.26	97.86	0.00	113.36	156.45	90.75
1991	94.62	99.37	0.00	99.65	158.62	92.47
1996	90.29	101.24	0.00	100.93	158.63	76.01
GR	2.03	2.75	0.00	1.48	3.37	3.24
Imports						
1961	5.05	2.07	100.00	0.00	0.16	44.85
1971	3.09	1.26	100.00	0.00	0.00	25.35
1981	0.57	0.10	107.30	1.59	0.00	9.25
1991	0.09	0.13	91.25	0.15	0.00	7.57
1996	4.98	0.04	119.44	2.95	0.06	15.70
GR	-2.96	-7.80	5.68	5.98	-2.36	-5.75
Exports						
1961	0.00	0.00	0.00	30.93	18.15	0.00
1971	0.00	0.04	0.00	9.13	8.71	0.00
1981	0.00	1.78	0.00	2.01	56.45	0.00
1991	0.00	0.90	0.00	0.00	58.62	0.04
1996	0.00	3.12	0.00	0.00	58.69	0.11
GR	-0.26	26.93	0.00	-16.90	6.35	32.74

Note: GR denotes exponential growth rate (1961-96).

Source: Same as Table 2.1.

domestic supply at a highest rate of 3.37 per cent, followed by Sri Lanka 3.24 per cent, and the lowest was reported in Nepal (1.48 per cent) during the period 1961 to 1999. India was able to increase its annual share by 2.75 per cent during the same period, whereas its imports had shown a negative growth of 7.8 per cent.

So far as the share of imports is concerned, except Maldives and Nepal, in other countries, it has shown a declining trend. In 1961, India imported 2.07 per cent of the paddy whereas Sri Lanka imported the highest of 44.85 per cent. Maldives fulfilled its requirement mainly by imports during 1961 to 1996. Nepal's exports of paddy has declined from 30.93 per cent of the domestic supply in 1961 to none in 1996, whereas Pakistan increased its paddy exports from 18.15 per cent in 1961 to 58.69 per cent in 1996 at an annual growth of 6.5 per cent. India and Sri Lanka also have started exporting rice in 1990s.

Graph 2.8: Percentage Share of Rice Imports to Domestic Supply in India and Sri Lanka

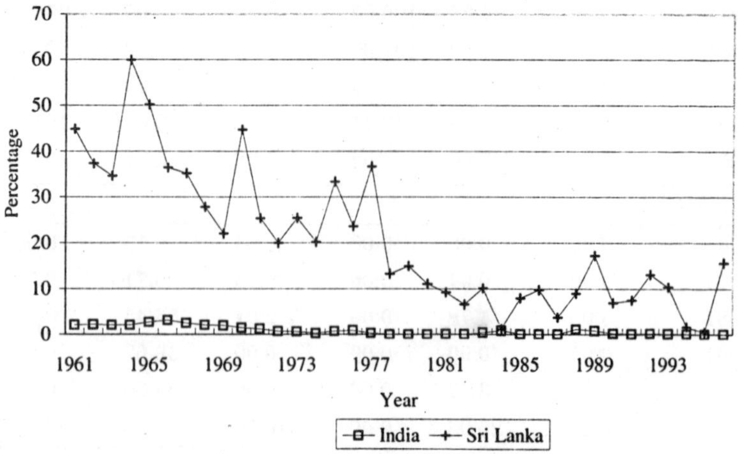

India's rice import remained stable during 1961 to 1996 as against the declining trend in Sri Lanka during the same period. Sri Lanka imported 60 per cent of its paddy requirement in 1964. Since the green revolution, the share of imports in Sri Lanka had declined considerably due to Mahaweli and settlement programmes, fertiliser subsidy, and guaranteed price scheme.

TABLE 2.10

Percentage Share of Production and Imports of Wheat to Domestic Supply in South Asia

Year	*Bangladesh*	*India*	*Maldives*	*Nepal*	*Pakistan*	*Sri Lanka*
Production						
1961	7.07	77.94	0.00	100.07	83.18	0.00
1971	10.27	100.43	0.00	70.17	86.54	0.00
1981	54.42	98.22	0.00	95.30	111.50	0.00
1991	41.35	94.17	0.00	96.85	100.09	0.00
1996	47.13	92.03	0.00	105.47	92.38	0.00
GR	13.38	5.65	0.00	6.47	4.50	0.00
Imports						
1961	55.93	21.93	100.00	0.07	23.56	100.16
1971	75.03	8.07	100.00	0.08	4.18	100.04
1981	43.64	1.58	100.00	6.70	2.96	96.08
1991	66.12	0.00	100.00	0.03	6.68	93.09
1996	41.42	0.92	100.00	0.23	10.75	100.04
GR	3.53	-14.44	8.65	12.77	3.04	2.87

Note: GR denotes exponential growth rate (1961-96).
Source: Same as Table 2.1.

Wheat is an important foodgrain in South Asia. The non-wheat producing countries like Maldives and Sri Lanka satisfy the domestic demand by imports and aid. Only India has been able to reduce the wheat import 14.44 per cent annually during 1961 to 1996. India, Nepal and Pakistan produce an average of more than 90 per cent of their

Graph 2.9:Percentage Share of Wheat Imports to Domestic Supply in India and Sri Lanka

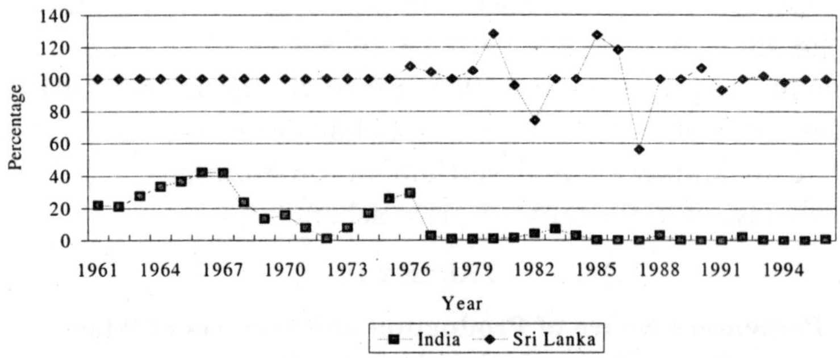

wheat requirements domestically. The growth in the share of wheat production is higher than paddy in wheat producing countries.

TABLE 2.11

Percentage Share of Production and Imports of Pulses to Domestic Supply in South Asia

Year	*Bangladesh*	*India*	*Maldives*	*Nepal*	*Pakistan*	*Sri Lanka*
Production						
1961	100.00	100.05	100.00	104.72	100.05	5.28
1971	100.00	100.18	100.00	100.00	99.85	10.36
1981	99.96	97.94	1.80	103.49	98.51	90.07
1991	84.19	97.67	2.98	104.46	94.38	43.42
1996	93.03	95.08	0.58	108.50	81.05	29.74
GR	2.25	0.58	1.96	2.20	0.13	8.81
Imports						
1961	0.00	0.00	0.00	0.00	0.01	94.72
1971	0.00	0.04	0.00	0.00	0.16	89.64
1981	0.07	2.07	98.20	0.14	1.56	11.58
1991	15.81	2.51	185.80	3.82	8.24	56.96
1996	6.97	5.35	88.42	1.71	21.04	70.28
GR	38.33	27.58	-8.32	8.74	27.45	-0.49

Note: GR denotes exponential growth rate (1961-96).
Source: Same as Table 2.1.

Other than major cereals, rice and wheat, pulses also are an important component of food supply. The share of pulses production to domestic supply in 1961 and 1971 was around 100 per cent in all South Asian countries, except Sri Lanka. In 1961, Sri Lanka produced only 5.28 per cent of its requirements, but in 1981, it could increase to 90.07 per cent with an annual growth of 8.81 per cent during 1961 to 1996. The growth in the share of pulses production in Pakistan was the lowest among the South Asian countries with a mere 0.13 per cent, followed by India's 0.58 per cent. The share of pulses import had continuously declined in Maldives and Sri Lanka by 8.3 per cent and 0.49 per cent respectively, during 1961 to 1996. In India, the pulses import has increased by 27.58 per cent during the same period.

Food Availability

The best indicator of physical access to food is the index of per capita availability of foodgrains. The total quantity of food available for domestic consumption in a given period depends on food production, trade, aid, and food lost in storage, or used as animal feed and seeds. The food availability factor faces uncertainty in the long run in view of continued population growth, increased land scarcity and difficulties with achieving sustainable increases in food crop yields. The increased cereal production variability significantly increases food consumption variability.

TABLE 2.12

Per Capita Availability of Major Food Items in South Asia

(Kg / Year)

Year	*Bangladesh*	*India*	*Maldives*	*Nepal*	*Pakistan*	*Sri Lanka*
Total Cereal						
1961	175	144	85	165	121	123
1971	165	142	94	164	157	139

1981	165	155	157	168	143	140
1991	179	165	148	204	142	137
1999	189	156	116	186	159	150
Rice						
1961	166	72	26	80	17	97
1971	149	69	29	81	30	99
1981	143	71	78	89	23	103
1991	158	81	48	98	16	91
1999	168	74	84	93	15	99
Wheat						
1961	8	28	15	12	84	23
1971	15	36	15	20	109	38
1981	21	46	29	28	109	35
1991	20	59	59	37	116	41
1999	20	56	32	36	136	47
Pulses						
1961	4	23	0	7	12	7
1971	5	16	0	8	8	4
1981	6	13	9	8	5	5
1991	5	14	5	8	6	6
1999	5	13	2	7	7	8

Source: Same as Table 2.1

Although the per capita availability of foodgrains has tended to fluctuate, the underlying trend has been one of increase. In 1961 the highest per capita availability of cereals was 175 kilogram in Bangladesh, followed by 165 kilogram in Nepal, and the lowest was recorded in Maldives at 85 kilogram. The per capita availability of cereals, like rice and wheat has shown an increasing trend, but the pulses have shown a declining trend since Independence in South Asia.

Rice occupies the major share of per capita availability

of cereals in South Asia. The per capita availability of pulses had recorded an increase in Bangladesh, Nepal, Pakistan and Sri Lanka from 1961 to 1999. The comparable data also shows that the per capita availability of rice was higher in Sri Lanka than India during the same period. Similarly, wheat availability in India was higher than Sri Lanka.

Graph 2.10: Per Capita Availability of Cereals in India and Sri Lanka

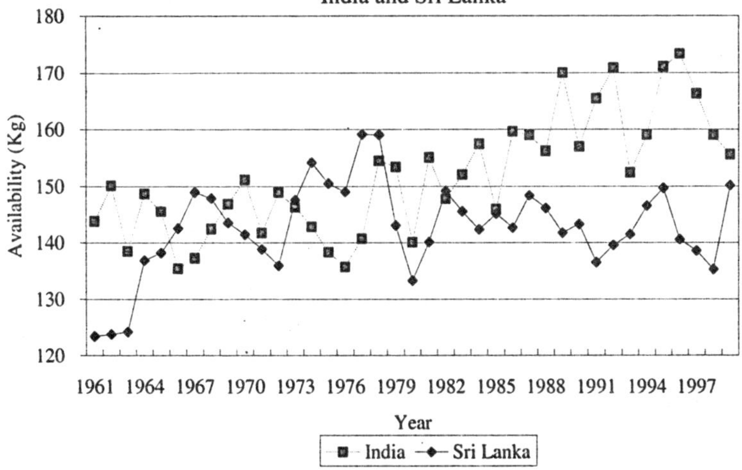

Food Aid

This section documents food assistance to South Asian countries in general and India and Sri Lanka in particular often provided in collaboration with non-governmental organisations and external food aid agencies. In developing countries, food assistance programmes rarely account for less than 5 per cent of the total government expenditure and in many developed countries even larger sums are spent on national food assistance programmes.[16] Asia remained the largest user of food aid under development projects, but these operations were overshadowed by dramatic demands for emergency help, which resulted in the World Food Programme's (WFP) largest emergency operations in 1998.[17]

However, food aid has been declining in the food-deficit countries. Meanwhile, the increase and complexity of relief food aid is done through interventions for enhancing nutrition. In this sense, food assistance is creative for development and fully targets needy individuals in order to ensure food, so that the value of purchasing power is transferred to undernourished people. This should encourage the Indian and Sri Lankan governments to devise cost-effective humanitarian and social welfare schemes for providing food assistance directly to the needy. Feeding mothers and children during critical times in India, and refugees in Sri Lanka are the beneficiaries of the WFP assistance under development projects.[18]

Cereal aid refers to the transfer of cereal from donor to recipient countries either on highly concessional terms or in the form of a complete grant. Data on cereal donations and receipts must be interpreted with particular care, for such flows are motivated by political, economic and other concerns. Donations can change abruptly from year to year usually for reasons unrelated to changes in the food requirements of recipient populations. Table 2.13 presents the statistics on food aid, especially total cereals, rice, wheat, coarse cereals and pulses covering all South Asian countries. The cereal aid from all donor countries has been declining since 1970 in Bangladesh, India, Pakistan and Sri Lanka. But Bhutan, Maldives and Nepal's total cereal aid has shown an increasing trend. Pakistan's cereal aid has declined by 7 per cent as against 5.07 per cent for India and 4.09 per cent for Sri Lanka. India's cereal aid had declined from 25,91,400 metric ton in 1970 to 3,46,959 in 1990, while it declined from 3,38,100 to 69,402 metric ton in the case of Sri Lanka. This reflects that the South Asian countries are marching towards self-sufficiency in cereals.

Among the cereals, wheat occupies the major share for Bangladesh, India, Pakistan and Sri Lanka while rice contributes the major share of food aid for Bhutan, Maldives and Nepal. In 1970, India received 90.14 per cent of the cereal aid in the form of wheat and it had declined to 2.78 by 1999. In Sri Lanka, the cereal aid amounted to 99.26 and 72.22 per cent during the same years. But Pakistan received the whole cereal aid in the form of wheat in 1999.

Measured in terms of the proportion of the total cereal imports of India and Sri Lanka, food aid has declined sharply since independence. The decline, on the one hand reflects the food policy of the successive governments, and on the other the availability of low-priced cereal supplies abroad. The most interesting feature is the declining contribution of cereal aid to total consumption; this is chiefly because both India and Sri Lanka are no longer major recipients of food aid (Graph 2.11).

TABLE 2.13

Food Aid Received by South Asian Countries

(Mt)

Year	*Bangla-desh*	*Bhutan*	*India*	*Maldives*	*Nepal*	*Pakis-tan*	*Sri Lanka*
Total Cereal							
1970	0	0	2591400	0	700	1055622	338100
1980	798399	1188	435378	0	51194	317780	235703
1990	1451974	4208	217069	3189	1345	379719	201437
1999	964084	3436	346959	2718	34100	147645	69402
GR	-1.55	8.69	-5.07	3.42	7.38	-6.95	-4.09

Rice							
1980	88100	100	0	0	8200	0	0
1990	22022	3533	25414	1888	1125	0	2100
1999	6715	2998	15237	2718	27078	0	18796
GR	-12.91	10.95	-1.42	-1.36	5.79	0	0.34
Wheat							
1970	0	0	2335900	0	700	889800	335600
1980	706868	300	71977	0	42194	317780	225901
1990	1429881	0	75643	1301	0	379719	196680
1999	956354	0	9638	0	3970	147645	50123
GR	-0.63	-0.96	-11.71	5.02	1.02	-6.74	-4.72

Note: GR denotes exponential growth rate (1970-1999).
Source: Same as Table 2.1.

Graph 2.11: Cereal Aid in India and Sri Lanka

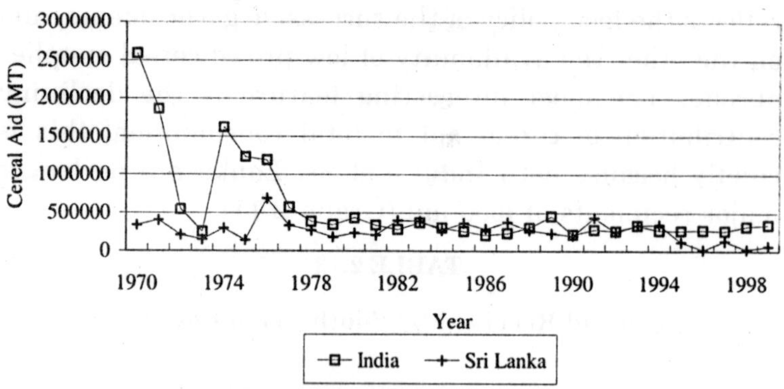

Over the five year period from 1988 to 1993, Sri Lanka received an average Rs1.9 billion or US$39.2 million annually under three categories of assistance: (a) the Programme Food Aid, (b) the Project Food Aid, and (c) the Emergency Assistance. The Programme Food Aid is provided as an outright grant, or on concessional repayment terms. In Sri Lanka this category includes grants or loans from the USA through its PL 480 Title I and III mostly in wheat. It also received wheat under this category from Australia and the European Union. It received around US$39 million worth of food aid annually in this manner. It also received project food aid for specific development purposes. The Project food aid is designed to transfer income to the poor. This is provided on a grant basis in agriculture, and irrigation settlement, especially under food-for-work schemes.

The WFP is the main provider of project food aid in India and Sri Lanka. Emergency food aid is another category under which food assistance is distributed to victims of natural and man-made disasters such as floods, droughts, landslides as well as civil unrest. This assistance helps in alleviating the country's balance of payment problem and releases the scarce foreign exchange to other essential imports. Another advantage of this type of food aid is that the government can generate local currency by the sale of food aid and use it for development purposes.

Cereal aid refers to the transfer of cereal from donor to recipient countries either on highly concessional terms or in the form of a complete grant. Data on cereal donations and receipts needs to be interpreted with particular care, for apart from being influenced by humanitarian consideration, such flows are often motivated by political, economic and other concerns. The quantity donations may change abruptly from year to year, often for reasons unrelated to changes in the food requirements of recipient populations. The data on cereal trade illustrate the important fact that India and Sri Lanka's import, especially wheat and wheat products from the traditional exporting bloc of USA, Canada, etc have remained modest. However, it is clear that cereal import has been declining drastically in India compared to in Sri Lanka.

Irrigation

In an agrarian economy, irrigation plays an important role in generating employment and incomes. The efficient and improved water management ensures an optimum utilisation of scarce land and an increase in agricultural production, especially foodgrains. At the world level average crop yields from irrigated land are roughly three times greater than yields from unirrigated land.[19] The future expansion of the world's irrigation will be slower than in the past because the existing large and medium-scale irrigation systems have been used up extensively.[20]

Irrigation becomes one of the most significant inputs of food production. The area under irrigation has been increasing since Independence, in relative terms, in all South Asian nations. The important indicator associated with the green revolution is land under irrigation as per percentage of cultivated land. The green revolution has induced rational cultivators to bring more land under irrigation. But a reasonable proportion of the cultivated area is still rainfed.

Most of the South Asian countries' growth in food production has come from the irrigated area – where there are distinct opportunities for better utilisation, more multiple cropping and significantly higher yields. As in 1961, Pakistan had the highest percentage of 63.69 per cent (10,751 thousand hectares) of irrigated area to its total cultivated area, followed by 21.78 per cent (335 thousand hectares) in Sri Lanka and the lowest of 3.82 per cent (70 thousand hectares) in Nepal. In 1997, the irrigation covered 81.39 per cent of the area in Pakistan, followed by 44.81 per cent in Bangladesh and the lowest of 25 per cent in Bhutan. India and Sri Lanka covered around one-third of their cultivated land under irrigation in 1997. The average annual growth rate of irrigated area clearly indicates the increasing trend between 1961 and 1997 in South Asia (Table 2.14). During the period from 1961 to 1997, the average growth of irrigated area was the highest of 9.67 per cent in Nepal, followed by 5.76 per cent in Bangladesh and the lowest of 1.35 per cent in Pakistan.

TABLE 2.14

Coverage of Irrigation in South Asia

('000 hectare)

Year	*Bangladesh*	*Bhutan*	*India*	*Nepal*	*Pakistan*	*Sri Lanka*
Irrigated Area						
1961	426	8	24685	70	10751	335
1971	1050	18	31100	117	12986	439
1981	1639	30	38805	584	15300	548
1991	3027	39	47430	1000	16750	530
1997	3693	40	57000	1135	17580	600
GR	5.76	4.42	2.30	9.67	1.35	1.40
Percentage of Irrigated Area to Arable and Permanent Crops						
1961	4.80	8.60	15.33	3.82	63.69	21.78
1971	11.54	17.14	18.91	5.91	67.36	23.11
1981	17.88	24.39	23.04	25.17	75.22	29.30
1991	33.13	29.55	28.01	42.50	79.91	27.85
1997	44.81	25.00	33.56	38.24	81.39	31.78

Note: GR denotes exponential growth rate (1961-1997).

Source: Same as Table 2.1.

In India, the gross area under irrigation has gradually increased since 1961. But in Sri Lanka the irrigated area recorded an increase till 1986, after which the trend has recorded a decline (Graph 2.12). In India, the irrigated area has increased from 26,685 thousand hectares in 1961 (15.33 per cent of the total cultivated area) to 57,000 thousand hectares (33.56 per cent) in 1997. In Sri Lanka, it has increased from 335 thousand hectares in 1961 (27.78 per cent of the total cultivated area) to 600 thousand hectares (31.78 per cent) in 1997. Sri Lanka has made huge investments, in irrigation projects in the dry zone,[21] especially under the Mahaweli Development Programme.[22]

Graph 2.12: Irrigated Land to Arable and Permanet Crops in India and Sri Lanka

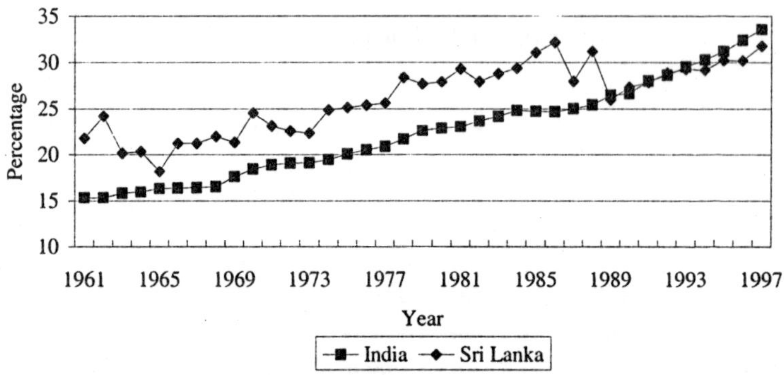

In India, rice consumes much larger quantity of water than needed for wheat, maize, jowar and other cereals. As many as 128 districts in India fall under the category of dry farming, producing most of the coarse cereals, pulses, oilseeds, cotton, and dry fodder.[23] An assured water supply spells prosperity, creates employment potential, increases income and deepens capital formation. The Famine Enquiry Commission of 1945 rightly emphasised that among the measures adopted to increase the area under cultivation and yield per acre, the priority must be given to irrigation projects.[24] India had, then, planned to exploit virtually all of its remaining irrigable capacity by 2000.[25] "By 2013 India's irrigation potential is likely to be fully developed, and one out of every two hectare will continue to rely on rainfall for survival and success".[26] Experts on water resources predict that by 2007 India will experience water famine.[27] In India, about 63 per cent of the cultivated land falls under rainfed areas where the integrated National Watershed Development Project play a vital role to increase the agricultural production in future.

Under European colonial powers, the Dry Zone settlements and the irrigation system declined in Sri Lanka. Irrigation-based agriculture gave place to rainfed crops such as cinnamon and spices.[28] The irrigation development and the introduction of new agricultural technologies, especially after the green revolution have provided the impetus for food crops. In Sri Lanka, the colonisation schemes were initiated generally in combination with irrigation schemes. The stored system of irrigation has been most highly developed in the dry parts of Sri Lanka. Opportunities for the expansion of irrigated area and the benefit/cost ratio for new irrigation schemes have since declined.

This along with increasing competition for water among sectors underlies the need for water conservation in agriculture. The extension of the cultivable land and water resources for large-scale irrigation has reached their limits in Sri Lanka. Growth in agriculture will, therefore, depend largely on an increase in productivity. For example the increase in paddy land since 1977 has been due to the Accelerated Mahaweli Development Project in Sri Lanka.

In the case of Sri Lanka, evidence shows that irrigation development has played a pivotal role in increasing rice production and advancing towards self-sufficiency in rice production. The area under paddy during the period 1952-94 grew at an annual rate of 4 per cent due to the major irrigation schemes. The minor irrigation schemes, and rainfed irrigation grew at a modest 2 per cent and 1.5 per cent, respectively.[29] There has been a marked decline in area under rainfed rice cultivation and output since mid-

1980s. The decline is pronounced in the more urbanised wet zone, where land conversion for non-farm activities has been increasing substantially. Without the investments in major irrigation schemes, Sri Lanka's rice self-sufficiency level would have been at 78 per cent, against 97 per cent it had achieved by 1994.

The provision of financial assistance to farmers to construct agro-wells to augment irrigation facilities is another strategy being adopted to generate sustainable farm incomes. To achieve rural agricultural development, the rehabilitation of minor irrigation schemes is one of the pre-requisites. This programme is being implemented with foreign donor assistance, particularly under the National Irrigation Rehabilitation Project, and the WFP.

The intensification of production in irrigated agriculture has played an important role in achieving and maintaining national food security in the past and it should continue to do so in the future. But the lack of opportunities for further expansion of irrigated area and growing scarcity of water for agriculture and non-agriculture uses add a new problem to the food security. The domestic production of foodgrains has reached the level of self-sufficiency in India, and is about to be achieved in Sri Lanka, with marginal fluctuations that may occur due to weather. Water shortage can increase the predicted gap between the demand and supply of foodgrains in South Asia. Water constraint can lead to major shifts in world foodgrain trade, resulting in increase of their imports significantly. The cereal imports in the case of Sri Lanka are predicted to increase in the future.[30] The participation of a non-governmental organisation in irrigation has resulted in a notable improvement of food security in Eastern Ethiopia.[31] Moreover, the demand for water from the fast expanding towns is widespread in India and Sri Lanka. As such most of the future increase in food demand will have to be met through greater efficiency in the use of current water supplies.

In Sri Lanka, from the early 1950s to mid-1980s the area irrigated rose from approximately 250 to 550 thousand hectares, but remained fairly constant since then.[32] Now the era of major irrigation schemes and irrigated area expansion has come to an end, and output growth in food crops remains stagnant. Oslen argues that the failure to increase crop yield is not due to low prices but due to lack of facilities such as irrigation and extension services.[33]

Producer Price of Paddy

Price relations are amongst the main determinants of the type and volume of agricultural production activities and play a fundamental role in formulation of development of development plans and related decisions. Accordingly, information on price statistics is of great importance. The producer price, as used here, should in theory refer to the national average of paddy comprising all grades, kinds and varieties. The price is determined by the farm gate or first-point-of sale transitions when farmers participate in their capacity as sellers of their own paddy.

Of course, data might not always refer to the same selling points depending on the prevailing institutional set-up in the South Asian countries. Also, different practices prevail in regard to paddy. Methods of arriving at national averages differ from one country to another. Therefore, in order to compare the producer price of paddy among the South Asian countries, in spite of the limitations mentioned above a price index have been constructed. The producer price of paddy per metric ton is shown in local currency (See Appendix II).

Agricultural price intervention has become an important

feature in the food management policy of both India and Sri Lanka in order to ensure food security. The aggregate demand and supply of foodgrains are relatively flexible, causing sharp fluctuations in foodgrain prices, especially paddy, in South Asia. In addition, to a large measure agricultural production is dependent on the monsoons. This, at times leads to unwarranted shortfalls in yields from year to year. Moreover, due to the seasonal nature of output, foodgrain prices have a tendency to continuously increase between the two harvesting periods. The holding capacity of the farmers in South Asia is too low in respect of their output, for them to take advantage of the price rise over the season and, as a consequence, they market most of their produce in the immediate post-harvest period, thereby accentuating the seasonality of price peaks. This leads to a loss of revenue from their marketable output.

TABL15

Indices of Producer Price of Paddy in South Asia

(1966 = 100)

Year	*Bangladesh*	*Bhutan*	*India*	*Nepal*	*Pakistan*	*Sri Lanka*
1966	100	100	100	100	100	100
1971	104	130	130	132	133	131
1976	343	210	210	129	352	339
1981	561	299	299	161	537	610
1986	765	494	328	373	644	749
1991	1141	795	606	504	979	1367
1995	1274	N.A.	677	615	1326	1467
GR	10.36	8.52	6.46	6.78	9.27	10.35

Note: GR denotes exponential growth rate (1966-95).
Source: Same as Table 2.1

Table 2.15 shows the index numbers of producer price of paddy in South Asia. It indicates that during the period 1966-95, Bangladesh has registered the highest growth rate of 10.36 per cent, followed by Sri Lanka with 10.35 per cent. The producer price of paddy in India has gradually been increasing (6.46 per cent) in comparison to other South Asian countries. The producer rice of paddy had been relatively stable in late 1960s in all South Asian countries. There have been several substantial periods of decline in producer price of paddy and several periods of increase.

Summary

In 1997, Bangladesh had a comparatively higher agricultural area of 67 per cent, followed by 60.91 per cent in India, while Bhutan had the lowest of 8.7 per cent. It clearly indicates an added advantage to increase food production to meet the growing demand for food. The annual growth of area under cultivation in Bhutan has been 1.34 per cent, while in Bangladesh it decelerated by 0.15 per cent annually. A comparison of the data on cropped area shows that Sri Lanka has recorded an increase of 0.18 per cent as against 0.15 in India during the period 1961 to 1997. Perhaps the dominant and somewhat intractable factor of food security is the growing marginalisation of holdings under the population pressure. The fragmentation of land holdings is a major factor in India as compared to Sri Lanka. It resulted in lack of gainful off-farm employment opportunities in rural areas, as also the lack of purchasing power, which forced the labour to migrate to urban areas.

The cropping pattern is also an important element in the assessment of food security in South Asia. Since the land area is static, the share of area under cereal cultivation had increased during the period from 1961 to 1998. On the other hand, the area under coarse cereal has shrinked during 1961-1998 in India, Maldives, Pakistan and Sri Lanka. This is a matter of concern since coarse cereals constitute the main food items of the poor people inhabiting the rainfed areas in South Asia. Similarly, the share of area under pulses production has been declining in Bhutan, India and Pakistan. Only Sri Lanka was able to increase the area under pulse cultivation by 5.43 per cent annually.

Almost all the SAARC countries have increased the area under cultivation of food crops between 1961 and 2000. It is quite essential in view of the growing demand for food. However, the growth rates of harvested area are not as impressive as production and yield of major crops in South Asia. Relatively smaller countries Bhutan and Nepal have performed better in comparison to the economically better off nations like India, Pakistan and Sri Lanka. The per capita harvested area of cereals and paddy in South Asian countries is gradually declining due to population growth. The population explosion has had a negative impact on per capita cropland, in all the countries except in Sri Lanka, due to the fact that it has been following better and well-planned family planning programmes.

The traditional food security is determined by the physical access. An assessment of the growth rate between the pre-green revolution period (1961-65) and post-green revolution period (1966 to 2000) had revealed a modest variation in acceleration in area, production and productivity. This shows that the growth rate of foodgrain production has recovered and is being sustained in South Asia. A comparison of the period of 1961-65 with 1966-2000 also shows a sharp decline in the latter period in the growth rate of cropped area, indicating it's declining potential. Yield-based growth, however, has sharply increased in importance, contributing to food production. Analysis shows that most of the yield-based growth came from wheat and rice – particularly wheat, an average yield of which increased between the pre-and post-green revolution periods. At the country level, growth in the yields of individual crops has been of major importance behind the growth in overall yields and production of foodgrains. This indicates the criticality of policies for sustaining yield and technology-based growth in future.

Growth in foodgrain production in the South Asia continues, even though comparatively diverse in output, continues to accelerate, marked by increasing wheat and rice yields, and diversion of area from coarse grains and pulses to wheat and rice. Even though the harvested area of cereals has increased in South Asia, the yield also has increased between 1961 and 2000, except in Bhutan. India registered a higher growth rate in cereal and paddy production in comparison to all the other countries. The increasing trend in per capita paddy production has been registered only in India, Pakistan and Sri Lanka during the period from 1961 to 2000. However, in case of paddy, Sri Lanka has better per capita production than India during the same period. The level of per capita food production has risen significantly in India and Pakistan. India has used its improved cereal production performance to modestly increase levels of per capita consumption, to eliminate its dependence upon imports, and to accumulate sizeable reserve food stocks, which could be utilised to avoid widespread droughts, floods and famines.

The per capita availability of foodgrains for human consumption has fluctuated within South Asia, showing a significant increasing trend. Thus, foodgrain production growth seems to have been largely absorbed by population growth, reduction in imports, and increases in stocks. India has attained food self-sufficiency in cereals as compared to other countries in the sub-continent, depending on smaller volume of cereal imports equivalent to 1.03 per cent of the domestic supply.

As examination of the input, particularly irrigation use level shows large increases since independence. Among the major inputs, irrigation shows a relatively steady increase. Although all the South Asian countries have improved their irrigation potential considerably, but Nepal's growth level of irrigated area during 1961 to 1997 has been quite impressive. Pakistan has better coverage of irrigation than all other SAARC nations since 1961. Better management and utilisation of irrigation would certainly increase the yields greatly in the future, which in turn would enhance the sustained food security in the sub-continent. Sri Lanka is a fairly unique country in South Asia, in the sense that despite its population growth, it has been able to increase supply of cropland per person by opening up large tracts of land for agricultural resettlement and irrigation, e.g. the Mahaweli Scheme which the government viewed as a way to relieve rural population pressures, create employment and increase food production.

The intensification of production in irrigated agriculture has played an important role in achieving and maintaining national food security in the past and must continue to do so in future. But the lack of opportunities for further expansion of irrigated area and growing scarcity of water for agriculture and non-agriculture uses add a new problem to the food security scenario in the South Asian region. The domestic production of foodgrains has reached the level of self-sufficiency in India and is about to be achieved in Sri Lanka, with marginal fluctuations due to weather. Water shortage can increase the predicted gap between the demand and supply of foodgrains in South Asia. The possible solution to ensure and sustain the future food security, can be the development of watershed projects in rainfed areas, which are the best alternative in comparison to the 'high-cost-low-benefit-irrigation projects.

So far as the producer price of paddy is concerned, in South Asia, Bangladesh has registered the highest growth rate of 10.36 per cent, followed by Sri Lanka with 10.35 per cent during 1966-95. India has recorded a gradual increase (6.46 per cent) annually as compared to all other South Asian countries. The producer price of paddy has been relatively stable in late 1960s in all South Asian countries.

This chapter summarises the data on area, cereal production, yield, availability, aid, and producer price of paddy in South Asia. An attempt has been made to project the food scenario by analysing the nature and pattern of growth in food production since 1961, using national data on foodgrains. The difference between production and consumption was quite small in all the South Asian countries, although it was fairly marked in Sri Lanka. In the 1970s, India and Sri Lanka considerably increased their food availability for their population. Since 1980, national food availability has been gradually increasing, and in 1990s it appears to have approached self-sufficiency. This is not to say that every year the food supply has been adequate. Periodically, severe floods or droughts have led to shortfalls in national food availability. During 1994-95, rice and wheat harvest was the best since independence, resulting in an estimated surplus of rice and wheat, which reflected in export data for both India and Sri Lanka. Thus, in normal years these countries can be almost self-sufficient in food supplies, but in some years agro-ecological difficulties can cause significant shortfalls in food availability.

The South Asian countries have shown a fair agricultural

performance since 1961. The increasing shortages and inability to cope with growing food demand at that time gave to occasional marginal surpluses in India and Pakistan. There are however, grave doubts given deceleration trend in the growth of foodgrain production during some periods. This raises questions about the sustainability of the growth and exhaustion of the potential of the "green revolution". There is also concern that the growth in production has had a narrow geographic and crop base and that substantial production growth may not be possible in other crops. Besides, there is concern about the decline of these productivities, and if so, whether the decline would continue, making the future growth both difficult and expensive which may ultimately reflect on the national food security. Yet another puzzle is the emergence of foodgrain surpluses with coexisting hunger, even in the wake of impressive agricultural growth in India.

REFERENCES

1. John M. Antle, "Infrastructure and Agricultural Productivity: Theory, Evidence and Implication for Growth and Equity in Agricultural Development", In Growth and Equity in Agricultural Development ed. Allen Maunder and Kazushi Ohkawa, (London, 1983), p. 181.
2. Since the area under different crops are small in Maldives, the data have not been provided.
3. A. Paul Groves (eds.), Economic Development and Social Change in Sri Lanka: A Spatial and Policy Analysis, (New Delhi, 1996), p. 6.
4. This is the latest available agricultural census in the country. Since then, however, the land use patterns has changed considerably. Various irrigation schemes have brought large land areas under paddy cultivation.
5. R.M. Senanayake: (Marketing Systems for Agricultural Products, (Tokyo, 1997), p. 363.

6. In India, agricultural output has increased at 2.67 per cent per annum during the period 1949-96. It is substantially greater than the insignificant growth rate of around 0.3 per cent per annum in the first half of this century.
7. S.N. Misra, "Capital Formation and Accumulation in Indian Agriculture Since Independence" Indian Journal of Agricultural Economics, Vol. 51, nos. 1 & 2, 1997.
8. G.S. Bhalla and D.S.Tyagi, Patterns in Indian Agriculture Development: A District Level Study, (New Delhi, 1989), G.S. Bhalla and G.Singh, "Recent Developments in Indian Agriculture: A State Level Analysis", Economic and Political Weekly, Vol. 32, No. 13, (1997).
9. The Hindu, Survey of Indian Agriculture 1999, n.18, p. 26.
10. S. Postal, Water for Agriculture: Facing the limits', World Watch Paper 93, (Washington, DC:, 1989), p. 30.
11. Sir. W. Arthur Lewis, "Overcoming the Weakness of Agriculture", In Leading Issues in Economic Development eds. G.M.Meier, (Oxford, 1984), p. 418.
12. P.R. Brahmanand, "The Economy Since Independence", Indian Horizons, Vol. XXXXV, nos..3 & 4, (1998), p. 103.
13. G.M.Meier, Leading Issues in Economic Development, (Oxford, 1984), p. 446.
14. Philip R. Wijewardene, "Sri Lanka", In Sustainable Agriculture Development in Asia, eds. (Tokyo, 1994), p. 446.
15. *Ibid.*, p. 189.
16. Barbara Huddleston, Food Security and Food Assistance, World Food Summit: Technical Background Paper 13, (Rome, 1996).
17. World Food Programme, Annual Report 1998, (Rome, 1999), p. 12.
18. *Ibid.*, p. 12.
19. D. Grigg, The World Food Problem, (Oxford: 1993), pp. 219-24.
20. P. Crosson and J.R Anderson, Resources and Global Food Prospects, (Washington DC, 1992), pp. 45-54.
21. In fact, even in the early period of British rule, the government

paid some attention to the repair of some ancient tanks and canals in the dry zone. But with the emergence of plantations its energies were diverted towards road construction and other activities. The rehabilitation and colonization of the dry-zone was intensified after independence.

22. G.H.Peiris, 'Agrarian Change and Agricultural Development in Sri Lanka', in Paul A. Groves (eds.), Economic Development and Social Change in Sri Lanka: A Spatial and Policy Analysis, (New Delhi, 1996), p. 128.
23. The Hindu, Survey of Indian Agriculture 1999, (Chennai 2000), p. 26.
24. Government of India, The Famine Enquiry Commission, Final report, (New Delhi, 1945), p. 129.
25. S. Postal, Last Oasis, Facing Water Scarcity, (New York, 1992), p. 55.
26. M.S. Swaminathan, "The Agricultural Scene?", Indian Horizons, Vol. XXXXV, nos. 3 & 4, July-December 1998, p. 130.
27. Arabinda Ghose, n.2., p. 139.
28. B.L.Panditharatna, "The Development of the Sri Lankan Settlement System", in Paul A. Groves (eds.), *'Economic Development and Social Change in Sri Lanka: A Spatial and Policy Analysis'*, (New Delhi, 1996), p. 5.
29. *Ibid.*, p. 14.
30. Randolf Barker and M.Samad, " Irrigation Development and Food Security in Sri Lanka", Economic Review, Vol. 23, No. 12, (1998), p. 15.
31. Ole Stage and Peter Rekve, "Food Security and Food Self-Sufficiency: The Economic Strategies of Peasants in Eastern Ethiopia", The European Journal of Development Research, Vol. 10, No. 1, (1998), p. 194. pp. 189-200. Those households under crop mix on irrigated land are able to increase household income reasonably and buy the required foodgrains from the local market in Eastern Ethiopia. "The small and marginal peasants in Eastern Ethiopia are able to acquire twenty times more food than they could produce in their tiny holdings by cultivating cash crops on the lands. It is the only way of obtaining sufficient food and meeting other basic needs".

32. Randolf Barker and M.Samad, " Irrigation Development and Food Security in Sri Lanka", Economic Review, Vol. 23, No. 12, (1998), p. 13.
33. R. O.Oslen, "Impact and Implications of Foreign Surplus Disposal on Underdeveloped Economies," Journal of Farm Economies, Vol. 42, (1960), pp. 1042-51.

3

Food Policy in India and Sri Lanka

Immediately after the Second World War the shortage of food in developing countries necessitated the respective governments to plan appropriate food supply policies through internal adjustments, whether through procurement or imports, or both. In a situation when supplies are less than the market demand, the distribution of the overall short supplies can be done either through market channels, or through controls, or through a judicious combination of both. In India and Sri Lanka, traditionally, the distribution of foodgrains has been the function of traders. In the case of distribution, there are two trends that are generally noticed: first, that the entire marketable or even marketed surplus of foodgrains should be obtained by traders and distributed on demand to consumers; and second, a complete monopoly of foodgrains trade by the government. India and Sri Lanka use this as also various other food policy instruments, e.g., food price subsidy, subsidised rationing, or employment guarantees showing a shift from food availability to food entitlement.

The major policies of demand side are nutritional status and policy instruments. The important component of the nutritional status is the construction of a national food balance sheet through household income-expenditure surveys. The policy instruments on the demand side are to provide entitlements through food subsidies, employment generation, food-for-work programmes, and cash transfers. This chapter focuses on the policy instruments desired to ensure food supply and demand for food, and alleviation of food insecurity in India and Sri Lanka. It also provides suggestions aimed at correcting the imbalances between food availability and the differing people's capability to access the food.

Definition

A working definition of food policy can be stated as "*the integration of state actions affecting the supply, distribution, and consumption of food in order to ensure the continuity of access to enough food for all the people in the country*".[1] It is imperative to analyse food policy in terms of the equation of food availability to food requirements. This can also be stated as the equation of food supply to food demand on the understanding that supply and demand refers to the food needed to satisfy the fundamental nutritional requirements of the population of a county. On the supply side, the food policy is concerned with food production and its rate of growth, in addition to food imports and aid.

The dimensions, causes and consequences of food policies differ widely not only from country to country but even within the same country. Macro economic policies and development strategies of India and Sri Lanka play an important role in influencing food policies through price stability, income generation, employment, and higher production of foodgrains. Policies and programmes for increasing food production and crop output for sale can improve food security if the countries increase or stabilise the real incomes of the food-insecure sections of society.

Agricultural Policy

The agricultural policies of the South Asian countries are shaped by social objectives, income differentials, and subsistence considerations. However, agriculture in the region is greatly affected by three major external factors: fluctuations in harvests generated by weather variability; supply-demand relationships in national cereal markets; and, fluctuations in supply-demand conditions. Farmers in India and Sri Lanka have, over the past five decades, been faced with a greater percentage rise in input costs than in product prices. As such, in recent years, the farmers have become increasingly dependent on purchased inputs, thus becoming more vulnerable to price rises in non-farm sectors.

India and Sri Lanka's medium-term policy strategies in agriculture are aimed at self-reliance in food by upgrading the quality of research and extension support, agricultural seeds and planting materials, rural infrastructure, rural credit markets, storage and marketing facilities and land markets. These reforms are crucial for alleviating rural poverty, assuring food security and getting agriculture moving.

Immediately after Independence, both the Indian and Sri Lankan governments had focused attention more on food production policies. Besides increasing food production, these governments also laid emphasis upon social welfare programmes. The prime aim of these governments was to ensure the availability of stable foodgrains at affordable prices. This means that food production and distribution are the two main instruments of the food policy. Since Independences, these governments introduced subsidy on fertilisers, ensured the guaranteed price for paddy, and took steps for the expansion of land under cultivation. The subsidy element played a vital role in enhancing food production in both countries.

A surge in the production of paddy, wheat and other food crops, which was discernible in the 1960s accelerated in the mid-1970s. In the mid-1960s a greater awareness developed on the part of the governments that the overall food situation could only be improved by enhanced crop production. The difficulties in importing the food items and shortages in rice and wheat created favourable market conditions. The mid-1970s witnessed higher prices for these commodities due to drought condition throughout the world, and shortages of rice and wheat; this acted as an incentive to the production of these two crops. The critical food situation during this period forced both the Indian and Sri Lankan governments to take active measures to encourage the production of these crops. During the 1960s and 1970s the successive governments in India and Sri Lanka experimented and implemented various schemes to ensure food availability and accessibility to it at affordable and subsidised prices to all, especially to the poor.

(i) Agricultural Policy in India

The attainment of Independence created essential preconditions for restructuring the agrarian economy on the path of progress and accelerated development. The Congress Agrarian Reforms Committee made for the first time a detailed survey of agrarian relations in 1949 and made comprehensive recommendations covering almost all the major issues relating to land reforms. It rejected the concept of capitalist farming and disapproved the general extension of State farming. It stressed that there should be a ceiling on the size of holding which a farmer should own and cultivate, and favoured individual peasant farming as the general pattern of agrarian society. The Land Reforms was concretized at the topmost governmental level for the first time in the First Five Year Plan. It acknowledged the achievement in the abolition of intermediaries and emphasized high priority for agricultural production, diversification of agricultural economy and a land policy to reduce disparities in wealth and income, eliminate exploitation, provide security for tenant and worker and promise equality of status and opportunity to different sections of the rural population. The Panel on Land Reforms, which was set up in 1955, marked an important stage in the evolution of land reform policy in India. The Third Five Year Plan stated the idea of setting up a "socialist pattern of society" and "eliminating all elements of exploitation and social justice within the agrarian system".

In India, the agricultural production policy started with the Grow More Food Campaign. The Government of India, on February 8, 1952 appointed a Committee to enquire into Grow More Food Campaign. The Intensive Agricultural District Programme (IADP) was initiated in 1960, as a multi-disciplined and co-ordinated approach to agricultural development, involving the use of a package of practices in optimum utilisation of irrigation potential. The success of IADP brought an advanced Intensive Agricultural Area Programme in 1964-65. These two programmes directed the Government to devise a new development strategy through extensive usage of high-yielding variety seeds, multiple cropping, better utilisation of irrigation, organised provision of inputs (seeds, fertilisers, pesticides and required credit), education and training, and intensification of research. A Special Foodgrains Production Programme was launched during the late 1980s with an objective of enhancing food production. The Planning Commission of India initiated the Agro-climatic Regional Planning in 1988 to focus on developing regionally-differentiated, location-specific development strategies, which maximise the use of land and water resources and reduce regional imbalances through investment and development efforts.[2]

The Green Revolution was introduced in 1966 to boost the cereal production by utilising costly inputs. The high cost-benefit ratio inherent in the use of high yielding variety seeds encouraged the extension organisation to induce the farmers to accept management practices and, therefore, helped in establishing a package approach to agriculture. The area under high-yielding varieties of foodgrains and value of modern inputs of chemical fertilisers, pesticides, insecticides, diesel, and power, showed a phenomenal rise since the Green Revolution. It undoubtedly indicates that Indian agriculture has witnessed radical transformation due to the introduction of technological innovations. The supportive and complementary multiple cropping programme was started in 1967-68. In order to implement successfully such ambitious programmes, and to provide the much needed inputs and services, at an appropriate time such as improved seeds, chemical fertilisers, plant protection, modern implements and machinery, adequate quantities of water and financial assistance a number of public institutions provided with sufficient funds were also set up.

The adoption of a number of modern methods of farming suitable for different kinds of agricultural produce has helped to increase agricultural production in the country. The total foodgrains production shot up to build up sizable buffer stocks. Such technological innovations in agricultural practices mostly helped in raising the production of wheat and rice. It was reported that the area, production and yield of wheat and rice have increased tremendously since 1966-67. A most noteworthy aspect in the radical transformation in Indian agricultural practices was the gradual spread of wheat cultivation to hitherto predominantly rice growing areas.

Under Adaptive Trials Scheme, the technology is tested under actual farm conditions in an effort to shorten the time lag between the discovery of new varieties or practices in the research stations and its adaptation to the farm situation. Adaptive trials pinpoint the reasons for the decline in yield at the farms and guide extension workers in formulating their recommendations suitably, when training the farmers in the new technology. In order to reduce losses as a result of the rusting of wheat crop, a programme was taken up in 1975 for the replacement of rust susceptible local varieties in northern and southern hills where wheat is grown in the off-season.

National Cooperative Development Corporation was launched in 1963, to look after the promotional activities of the farm sector, such as production, marketing, processing and storage of agricultural produce through cooperatives. Similarly, Agro-Industries Corporation was started in 1965 to supply and service agricultural machinery.

The Integrated Rural Development Programme (IRDP), initiated in 1978, was designed to ensure growth with social justice. The Drought Prone Area Programme is one of the area development programmes launched in 1973-74 to tackle the special problems faced by those fragile areas, which are constantly affected by severe drought conditions. These areas are characterised by large human and cattle populations, which continuously put heavy pressure on the already fragile natural resource base for food, fodder and fuel. This continuous biotic pressure is leading to a continuous depletion of vegetative cover, less and less rainfall, increasing soil erosion, and receding ground water levels. The Desert Development Programme was started in 1977-78 to mitigate adverse effects of desertification and adverse climatic conditions on crops, humans and livestock population, and to restore the ecological balance of the area.

A scheme for the Supply of Improved Toolkits to Rural Artisans Scheme was launched as a sub-scheme of the IRDP in 1992. It aims to enable rural artisans (Below Poverty Line) to enhance the quality of their products, increase their production and incomes, and to ensure a better quality of life with the use of improved tools, and also to reduce urban migration. Another scheme known as the Ganga Kalyan Yojana was also launched as a sub-scheme of the IRDP during 1996-97, but it became an independent scheme in 1997. The objective of the scheme was to provide irrigation through the exploitation of groundwater (bore wells and tube wells) to individuals and groups of beneficiaries of small and marginal farmers belonging to sections below the poverty line.

(ii) Agriculture Policy in Sri Lanka

Sri Lanka relies on agriculture as a primary source of surplus for economic growth. Its agrarian policy has been formulated on the basis of a "conservative" and "reform" approach of agricultural development. The provisions of this policy include: protection for domestic production of rice, taxation of plantation crops, food subsidies to consumers, (mostly in the form of rice rations sold in government shops but also in the form of price subsidies for wheat and sugar), and large subsidies for rice production (primarily in the form of public irrigation, and subsidies to and rationing of agricultural inputs, such as fertiliser). The conservative approach emphasises government intervention in the extension services of agriculture. The successive governments sought to strengthen domestic agriculture through land distribution programmes and government-sponsored services in credit, input supply, price support, crop insurance, technical advice, and marketing. The prominent features of the reform approach were reduction in the inequality of agricultural land ownership by redistribution, elimination of tenancy exploitation by regulating share tenancy, promotion of highly integrated types of co-operative farming, and establishment of rural institutions to facilitate the direct involvement of the people in development activities.

The growth of domestic food production as a major shift towards self-sufficiency mainly addresses the problem of aggregate food availability. It has made some impact in averting chronic food insecurity insofar as the employment and income prospects of small and marginal poor farmers and landless labourers have improved. In the future it may also help to overcome some types of transitory food insecurity. A range of policies to increase the productivity of food crops including producer prices, input, credit, irrigation and research promote the focus on domestic food production. The maintenance of self-sufficiency in rice still continues as the main objective of the country's food production programmes.

Immediately after Independence, Sri Lanka's rice imports accounted for nearly two-thirds of total domestic requirements, the reason for which was acute agricultural land scarcity. This situation had warranted new policies for increasing domestic food production. The Paddy Lands Act of 1958 in Sri Lanka gave protection to tenant paddy farmers. Besides, the establishment of agricultural "colonies" with irrigation facilities in the dry zone area of the country played a positive role in increasing food production. The agricultural sector in Sri Lanka consists of two distinct parts: rice and non-rice crops. The two components of paddy cultivation are land settlement and irrigation, and the guaranteed price scheme. The fundamental policy paradigm of Sri Lankan agriculture since Independence in the 1940s was the welfare needs of farmers. A study of five decades of development planning, particularly since 1950 shows that about 15 per cent of plan expenditure computed at constant prices has been spent on agriculture and allied sectors. During the Five-Year Plans different strategies (measures based on the use of improved seeds, chemical fertilisers, pesticides and modern implements, the extension of irrigation facilities, extensive land reclamation) have been applied to accelerate agricultural production.

The Paddy Lands Act (1958) was designed to promote production by giving a permanent and secure title to land to the tenants, to eliminate unlawful eviction and to regulate rents. Also, under the provision of the Act, elected village-level cultivation committees were established to promote the development of paddy cultivation and to secure tenants' rights (Commissioner of Agrarian Services, 1967). Hambantota was one of the first districts in which the Act was implemented.

Attempts had also been initiated to draft an agricultural plan for Sri Lanka's self-sufficiency in rice. It was known as the "Agricultural Development Proposals" (ADP) of 1966-70. A Plan of Development later supplemented the ADP during the same period. The proposals were followed up by annual plan implementation programmes containing specific investment and output targets for paddy production. The ADP represents one of the best attempts at sectoral planning based on a new approach of intensified agriculture, e.g., high yielding varieties of seeds, chemical fertilisers and agro-chemicals, tractors and other agricultural machinery, increased extension services, and agricultural credit. As a result of the ADP, paddy production increased by 55 per cent during the period 1966-70 as compared to 14 per cent increase during 1961-65.[3]

The land reform in Sri Lanka was introduced in the years 1972 and 1975, and large economic reform was introduced in 1978. Sri Lanka's attempts to shift production along the supply curve have been dependent on heavy government intervention in the market, along with control of producer prices and control of input costs. However, in particular areas an attempt has been apparently undertaken to combine land distribution with the "Janasaviya" programme.

Since 1977 the Sri Lankan government had initiated a series of measures - such as extensive capital infusion into irrigation expansion in Dry Zone, enhancing the government's assistance to farmers on new technology in paddy cultivation, and providing price incentives for subsidiary food crops. In the late 1970's, several districts were selected for programmes of the Integrated Rural Development, which encouraged economic planning within the framework of district or sub-district area units.[4]

The government has followed three policy elements to promote rice production: the Guaranteed Price Scheme operated by the Paddy Marketing Board; fertiliser subsidy; and concessional bank credit. The agricultural development process of Sri Lanka accords high priority to government intervention in expanding the agricultural resource base through strategies that have a blend of growth and welfare objectives. The projects and programmes are intended to benefit the farming community by providing equity in irrigation and credit, and to bring more families under settlement schemes.

The popular participation in development, reconstruction and reform policies of the government involved formation of co-ordination committees and community functions. Village self-government provides inputs for agricultural policies. The provision of incentives was for increasing agricultural production and, where possible, diversifying agricultural output for both import substitution as well as export promotion. In fact, the principles of social welfare, equity and popular participation have been considered as consistent and conducive efforts towards increasing the contribution of agriculture in employment generation and overall economic growth. There is, in addition, the need to increase domestic food production, which has always been seen as an economic function of the agriculture sector.

Seed Policy

In India, the National Seeds Corporation was set up in 1963, with the responsibility of seed production and certification. The supply of minikit seed of paddy was started in 1971-72 and that of wheat in 1974-75. These schemes were widely welcomed, particularly by the small farmers. It also resulted in the quick acceptance of some of the latest varieties both in *kharif* and *rabi* seasons; even before the State governments released them. A noteworthy feature of this programme is the adoption by the farming community of the latest varieties, which helped in bridging the gap between the identification of a variety and its spread in the rural areas.

The community nurseries programme has vast potential for raising the extremely low yield rates in some states where most of the farmers have to depend upon rains. The high yielding varieties of rice could not grow quantitatively and to their full potential in these states due to the current practice of raising the nurseries after the break of the monsoons. This late sowing of rice adversely affects the yields. The community nurseries programme seeks to overcome this difficulty by raising nurseries in irrigated areas and distributing the saplings to rain-fed areas at the time of the monsoon. This will not only give sufficient time for the proper growth of the crop, but also enable the farmers to grow a second crop of wheat after harvesting paddy.

The production of rice in India took a spurt after the introduction of high-yielding varieties programme coupled with related essential inputs. The paddy production has increased reasonably in India because of rapid adoption of appropriate high yielding varieties of rice (minikit programme), planting them in time (community nurseries programme), making increased use of balanced fertilisers (fertiliser promotion campaign) and adopting better crop management system and effective transfer of technology (massive training programme).

In India, the area under high-yielding varieties (HYV) of foodgrains, including modern inputs of chemical fertilisers, pesticides, insecticides, diesel oil and power, has shown a phenomenal rise since the Green Revolution. Indian agriculture has witnessed a radical transformation due to the introduction of technological innovations. The Green Revolution was introduced in India in 1966 to boost the cereal production by utilising costly inputs. The high cost-benefit ratio inherent in the use of HYV seeds encouraged the extension organisation to induce farmers to accept management practices and, therefore, helped in establishing a package approach to agriculture.

The Department of Agriculture in India released for the first time HYV seeds of food crops under the Green Revolution technology during late 1960s. In 1970, the HYV covered 71 per cent of the total area under cultivation. After Green Revolution, a breakthrough was made in evolving HYV seeds of a higher potential and a shorter duration to suit different agro-climatic regions. The significance of this was noticed in Indian Punjab.[5] The High Responsive Variety Seeds were found to be more water sensitive and needed sophisticated water management. In India, the area under high yielding paddy seeds had increased from 43.08 million hectares in 1970 to 72.11 million hectares in 1995.

TABLE 3.1

Area under High Yielding Variety Paddy Seeds in India and in Sri Lanka

Year	*India (million hectare)*	*Sri Lanka ('000 hectare)*
1970	43.08	536
1980	60.11	683
1990	64.98	689
1992	65.40	627
1995	72.11	NA

Source: (i) Directorate of Economics and Statistics, *Agricultural Statistics at a Glance 2000,* Ministry of Agriculture, Government of India, New Delhi, 2001.

(ii) Central Bank of Sri Lanka, *Annual Report,* various years, Colombo.

In the 1960s the rate of adoption of HYV was very high in Sri Lanka. By 1970, it was utilised in 70 per cent of paddy areas. The yield potential of the seed varieties has been growing gradually. The willingness and ability of farmers to apply the new technology depends on factors like the size of the land, and the educational level and economic status of the farmers. It is found that small farmers have achieved lower yields than those cultivating lands of more than 2.5 acres in size. The smaller the land size, the stronger was the reluctance on the part of the farmers to adopt these technologies. However, since 1986 there has been a gradual decline in the area sown with improved seed. In 1992, the percentage of land under improved varieties to the total area sown had dropped to 78 per cent. In Sri Lanka, this may be partly due to the privatisation of the paddy seed distribution system. The impact of the HYV seeds was highly responsive to certain key inputs, such as irrigation and fertilisers, pest and weed control, proving more useful than traditional varieties.[7] However, the area under high yielding paddy seeds has increased from 5,36,000 hectares in 1970 to 6,27,000 hectares in 1992.

Irrigation Policy

In India, in view of the water insufficiency to meet the irrigation requirements, the available water resources needs to be utilised with great efficiency and economy. Comprehensive river basin projects had been undertaken for proper development of the land and water resources of the basin. Because of high cost involved in dam construction deep tube wells for ground water development were seen as the best alternative. The National Water Policy was adopted in 1987, and National Water Management Project was implemented during 1987 to improve the irrigation coverage and agricultural productivity, with a view to increase the income of the farmers in the command areas. Water was recognized as a prime natural resource, a basic human need and a precious national asset. Rural Infrastructure Development Fund was started in 1995-96 for financing infrastructure projects including irrigation, soil conservation and watershed management. Another project, known as Accelerated Irrigation Benefit Programme was launched in 1996-97 to accelerate the completion of selected ongoing irrigation projects. Development of integrated farming systems on watershed basis is the main objective under the National Watershed Development Project for Rainfed Areas. Watershed management is one of the crucial areas for improving agricultural production.[8]

In Sri Lanka, the policy emphasis on reviving domestic food crops in dry zone through large public investments in irrigation-cum-land development projects had been initiated way back in the 1930s.[9] The annual equivalent of subsidy to new major irrigation schemes amounts to about Rs.50,000 per hectare, or 20 per cent of the value added per hectare.[10] The Ministry of Plan Implementation in Sri Lanka (1983) points out that about 65 per cent of the additional rice output in Sri Lanka during the 1974-82 period was derived from settlement areas fed by major irrigation schemes. It is argued that the paddy cropping intensity under irrigated settlement schemes was substantially higher than in other areas.[11] This is attributed to more stable conditions of water supply and organised systems of input supplies, which characterise agricultural conditions in the majority of these settlement schemes.[12]

Small village tanks with simple channel systems initially provided water to the early settlers in the Dry Zone. To achieve self-sufficiency in food, investments were made in the restoration and rehabilitation of existing irrigation schemes and the construction of new irrigation schemes. In 1955, a planned irrigation development programme was drawn. Plans and designs were made for the development of the Mahaweli river basin during 1965-70. Stage one of the Mahaweli Project commenced in 1976. During 1977-88 the Mahaweli River Diversion Scheme was accelerated and several Trans Basin Canals diverted to Dry Zone. Being the largest irrigation project, the Mahaweli Development Programme covers nearly 30 per cent of the country's land area, 16 per cent of paddy area and 55 per cent of the Dry Zone. It accounts for 25 per cent of the total paddy production. In Sri Lanka, the largest cost incurred in achieving rice self-sufficiency has been on irrigation. One of the biggest projects in the World, the Mahaweli Irrigation Project was initiated in the late 1960s and accelerated in the late 1970s.[13] The Gal Oya scheme was the first irrigation project to bring new land under paddy by settlement of new colonies to cultivate paddy. The first large-scale irrigation and land settlement project was the Gal Oya River Valley – the Mahaweli Scheme. The marketable surplus of paddy under Mahaweli Development Programme is 88 per cent. Accelerated Mahaweli Programme commenced in 1979 aimed at commercialisation of agricultural production and diversification of the economic base in agriculture and non-farm sectors. There are 535 major irrigation schemes comprising storage schemes, diversion schemes, flood control/drainage schemes and lift irrigation schemes, with a command area of nearly 3,40,000 hectares and 18,000 minor irrigation schemes with a command area of nearly 1,62,000 hectares.[14]

The area under irrigation was increased by rehabilitating the existing, but neglected, irrigation schemes and resettling people in those areas. New irrigation schemes were constructed and new lands were opened up for cultivation, especially in the Dry Zone districts. The area under paddy cultivation had increased from 4,79,000 hectares in 1952 to 9,30,000 hectares by 1994. The highest area cultivated with paddy was in 1984, when it reached 9,90,000 hectares. The paddy lands under irrigated conditions increased from 58 per cent in the 1950s to 68 per cent in the 1990s.

One of the effects of this scheme is that, apart from

new lands, the already cultivated lands too, would be receiving a more assured supply of water. The Accelerated Mahaweli River-basin development programme is a key element of this package, and is to be funded partly by domestic resources released by the elimination of food subsidy, and partly by foreign aid mobilised through World Bank sponsored aid.[15]

Credit Policy

In India, the major policy objective in the sphere of farm credit is its progressive institutionalisation for supporting agricultural development programmes and ensuring larger flows of funds to assist weaker sections of the farming community. The increasing demand for institutional finance from farmers has necessitated a multi-agency approach, involving co-operatives, commercial and regional rural banks in India. The state governments have granted short, medium and long-term crop loans to farmers under different credit programmes with subsidised interest rates.[16] The Agricultural Refinance Corporation was started with the objective of providing refinancing facilities to land development banks and commercial banks for financing schemes of agricultural development. Besides, Food Corporation of India for marketing of agricultural products and for providing remunerative prices to the produce of the farmer has been started.[17] Government programmes to facilitate structural improvements in agricultural production include different type of agricultural credit at the state level, e.g., through the Small Farmers Development Agency.

In India, the role of agricultural credit and credit institutions is imperative for increasing agricultural production, productivity and profitability. After the nationalisation of commercial banks and establishment of Regional Rural Banks and Co-operative Banks, more attention has been paid to agricultural credit delivery system, which is more responsible to the needs of small and marginal farmers. The increasing demand by the farmers for institutional finance has necessitated a multi-agency approach involving co-operatives, commercial and regional rural banks.[18]

The major policy objective in the sphere of agricultural credit in India is it's progressive institutionalisation to ensure larger flow of funds to weaker sections of the farming community. Co-operatives are an integral part of the country's agricultural system because its major customers are rural agricultural labourers and marginal and small farmers. Nearly 60 per cent of short-term loans and 35 per cent of the investment credits are provided by co-operatives, even though rural non-farm credit markets play a substantial role in rural credit.

In Sri Lanka, agricultural credit was being provided under a variety of schemes since before independence. The comprehensive rural credit scheme began in 1973 and was designed to meet in a consolidated manner all the requirements of the rural sector. In 1973, Rs 80.1 million were loaned for paddy cultivation. During the Maha season of 1973-74 there was an appreciable increase in the number of people utilising institutional credit. In Sri Lanka, the New Comprehensive Rural Credit Scheme gives interest subsidy ranging from 7.5 per cent to 10 per cent per annum to increase the credit support to domestic agriculture. The Comprehensive Fund Credit Scheme utilises co-operatives as dispersion and collection agencies. The credit may be short term for food production, and from medium and long term for agricultural implements and land developments. The loan recovery rate for paddy was 94.1 per cent in 1988-89, which declined to 62.3 per cent, perhaps due crop failures in Sri Lanka. However, of the total loans advanced on an average 69.8 per cent credit is in respect of paddy; the balance was spent towards subsidy for food crops during the 1988-98 period. Of the total loans, 60-65 per cent of the amount was granted during only in the Maha season during the same period.[19] The loan recovery rate declined for all crops in general, and paddy in particular, during 1988-98.

There are two types of agricultural credits in Sri Lanka: formal (commercial banks) and non-formal (money-lenders, landlords, merchants). The formal credit is available at subsidised interest rates from government lending institutions. Even though the concessional credit facility is available in the rural sector, the demand for non-institutional credit has remained high.[20] During the immediate post-independence period, there was no credit available to the agriculture sector from the formal sector.

TABLE 3.2

Percentage Distribution of Loans by Source in Sri Lanka

Sources	*Survey Period*					
	1963	*1973*	*1978-79*	*1981-82*	*1986-87*	*1996-97*
Number of Loans						
Institution (%)	7.6	11.5	10.7	9.7	16.6	43.1
Non-Institution (%)	92.4	88.5	89.3	90.3	83.4	56.9
Amount of Loans						
Institution (%)	14.3	20.3	25.3	37.7	39.8	67.3
Non-Institution (%)	85.7	79.7	74.7	62.3	60.2	32.7

Source: Report on Consumer Finances and Socio Economic Survey, 1996-97, Part I, Central Bank of Sri Lanka, Colombo, 1999.

It may be observed in Table 3.2 that in 1963 non-institutional sources provided 92.4 per cent of the total loans obtained by the household sector. But it has gradually declined to 56.9 per cent in 1996-97. In 1996-97, the institutional sources become the main source and provided

67.3 per cent of the total value of loans. In recent years, formal credit is a very important source of finance for agricultural purposes in Sri Lanka.

Agricultural Insurance Policy

In India, the fluctuating weather conditions have forced the government to provide indemnity to farmers whose produce gets damaged. The growth in the crop insurance programme has been an important aspect of food security, providing relief against natural calamities, and pest attacks. In India crop insurance was introduced as a pilot scheme in 1979-80 in limited areas. Later a Comprehensive Crop Insurance Scheme (CCIS) was launched in 1985. The CCIS covers all farmers including small and marginal farmers in all regions susceptible to natural calamities like drought and floods. All are eligible to avail of the crop loans, which are disbursed, with a ceiling of Rs.10,000 per farmer. The premium is 2 per cent of the amount insured for rice, wheat and millets, and one per cent for oilseeds and pulses. Since its inception in 1985, about 58.2 million farmers have been covered over an area of about 99 million hectares insuring a sum of Rs.16,524 crore, of with claims of over Rs.1,454 crore had been paid to the farmers till March 31, 1998, although the premium income is only Rs.268 crores. The CCIS and the Experimental Comprehensive Crop Insurance Scheme have been merged together and a new scheme known as the Modified Comprehensive Crop Insurance Scheme has been subsequently launched. This progressively covers all the farmers.

In Sri Lanka, the Ceylinco Insurance Company Ltd insured an extent of 1,000 hectares of paddy land and collected premia to a value of Rs.0.74 million.[21] Crop insurance was inaugurated on a pilot basis in 1958-59 and, since higher cover without increased premium was afforded to those who followed specified practices, it has been used to popularise improvements such as row sowing and transplanting. In 1977-78, approximately 40 per cent of the Maha season crop was insured, but this was largely attributed to compulsory insurance in some areas. Farmers are still unsure of the value of the insurance programme.[22] In Sri Lanka, the Agricultural Insurance Board (AIB) provides agricultural insurance coverage for paddy and subsidiary food crops. The AIB has also introduced an agricultural insurance scheme for maize on an experimental basis. During 1998, the insurance premia collected under paddy amounted to Rs.9.25 million, against an indemnity payment of Rs.1.55 million.

Food and Fertiliser Subsidy in India

A subsidy refers to a specific good, the price of which is lowered by the subsidy vis-à-vis other goods.[23] Cash payments to producers or consumers are an easily recognisable form of subsidy. In India, the national food assistance programmes generally suffered reductions during the late 1980s and 1990s.

Policies associated with macro economic stabilisation have resulted in higher food prices due to exchange rate realignments and reduction in food subsidies. The foodgrain subsidy borne by the Central Government rose from Rs.47 crore in 1971-72 to Rs.8,100 crore in 2000-01 (Table 3.3). The factors responsible for the continued rise in food and fertiliser subsidy could be increase in the quantum of procurement, public distribution and stocks of foodgrain over the years. It also could be increase in the unit cost of operation of the government agencies at a faster rate than the revenues obtained through sale in the public distribution system. The decline in expenditure on social services has affected the poor who are most dependent on public support.

TABLE 3.3

Explicit Subsidies in Central Budget in India

(Rs. / Crore)

Year	*Food*	*% Change*	*Fertiliser*	*% Change*
1971-72	47	—	0	—
1972-73	117	148.9	0	—
1973-74	251	114.5	0	—
1974-75	295	17.5	0	—
1975-76	250	-15.3	0	—
1976-77	506	102.4	60	—
1977-78	480	-5.1	266	343.3
1978-79	570	18.8	342	28.6
1979-80	600	5.3	603	76.3
1980-81	650	8.3	505	-16.3
1981-82	700	7.7	381	-24.6
1982-83	711	1.6	603	58.3
1983-84	835	17.4	1042	72.8
1984-85	1101	31.9	1928	85.0
1985-86	1650	49.9	1924	-0.2
1986-87	2000	21.2	1898	-1.4
1987-88	2000	0.0	2164	14.0
1988-89	2200	10.0	3201	47.9
1989-90	2476	12.5	4542	41.9
1990-91	2450	-1.1	4389	-3.4
1991-92	2850	16.3	5185	18.1
1992-93	2800	-1.8	5796	11.8
1993-94	5537	97.8	4562	-21.3
1994-95	5100	-7.9	5769	26.5
1995-96	5377	5.4	6735	16.7
1996-97	6066	12.8	7767	15.3
1997-98	7500	23.6	7426	-4.4
1998-99	8700	16.0	7598	2.3

1999-00	9200	5.7	8750	15.2
2000-01	8100	-12.0	—	—

Source:(i) Department of Economic Affairs, *Government Subsidies in India, Discussion Paper,* Ministry of Finance, Government of India, New Delhi, 1997.

(ii) Economic Division, *Economic Survey 2000-2001,* Ministry of Finance, Government of India, New Delhi.

Graph 3.1: Food and Fertiliser Subsidy in India

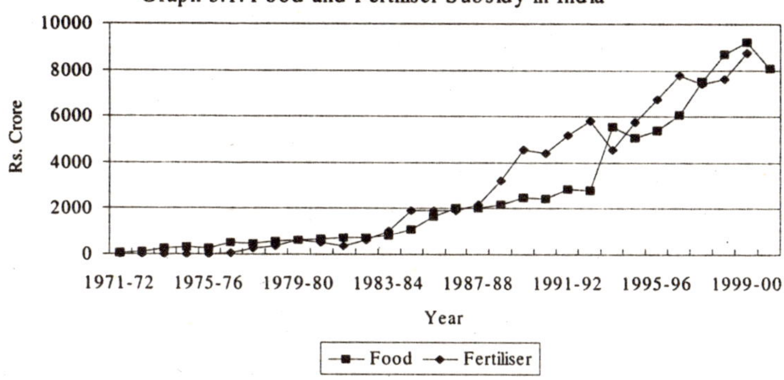

The input subsidies on fertilizer, irrigation, electricity and credit formed one-third of total plan expenditure on agricultural irrigation in India. The fertilizer subsidy has increased from Rs.60 crore in 1976-77 to Rs.8,750 crore in 1999-2000. The fertilizer subsidy has increased faster than food subsidy from 1987-88 to 1996-97 (Graph 3.1). The government should, in fact, reallocate a reasonable share of subsidies for the development of infrastructure to reduce fiscal and budget deficits. The reduction in subsidies is also crucial for stepping up public investment in Indian agriculture. In place of providing subsidies, the government should deploy a part of these funds for capital formation in agriculture. This will result in increased income for the farmers which in turn would enable them to modernise their farming practice through use of improved seeds, required quantities of fertilizers and pesticides, and installing drip irrigation system, etc. The burgeoning input subsidies on fertilisers, canal waters, electricity, rural credit, etc., lead to inefficient use of scarce resources and also cause environmental degradation besides escalating fiscal deficits. If subsidies have to be given, they should be directed to low-consumption areas where response is the highest.[24]

Food and Fertiliser Subsidy in Sri Lanka

In Sri Lanka, the principal element of the government's social policy concerning food supply took shape during the Second World War and has been continuing till date. Its most important feature is the so-called "food subsidy", which has been inherited from the British and entails the rationed supply of a specified quantity of rice at subsidised prices to every person, regardless of income variations in the population. The Korean War (1951-53) and the subsequent boom in worldwide commodity prices left Sri Lanka richer.[25] The wealth obtained from tree crops exports was seen as a justification for and the basis of, food subsidies. The food subsidies started accelerating during the period 1956-60. It accounted for 19.4 per cent of government revenue in 1964.[26]

The increase of expenditure on food subsidy can be attributed primarily to the price increases of subsidised commodities. The rice subsidy, which commenced during World War II and continued till September 1978, proved to be a heavy burden on the government budget.[27] Rice was provided to all at subsidised price since 1942, and free of cost in 1965 under the rationing scheme in Sri Lanka. Wheat flour was also brought within the purview of quantity rationing and price subsidisation, while their availability in the open market was curtailed through the regulation of wholesale and retail trade.

Over a greater part of this period the majority of food

commodities in the open market remained subject to price controls. The end of Korean War[28] (1949-51) has forced the Sri Lankan Government (1952-53) to reduce the subsidy. Consequently, the price of rice was increased and free meals for school children were cut.[29] In 1966, an attempt was made to limit food subsidies by excluding income tax payers from benefits. Taxpayers with taxable income of over Rs.1,000 were required to pay a tax equal to the subsidy, unless they handed back their ration books. The amount of rice given at the subsidised price was also reduced.

Although subsidised rice quota was reduced, but some part was given free. The system of rice rationing was abolished, and the Floor Price Scheme and Fertiliser Subsidy Scheme were withdrawn during 1977-88.[30] The grant of universal eligibility for food subsidies was restricted only to low-income families in 1978.

In 1979, the Ration Book Scheme was abolished and the Food Stamp Scheme (FSS) was introduced for needy families, while food subsidy for the higher income groups was withdrawn, it was extended to the poor through FSS. During this period, several food items were removed from the list of price controlled consumer items. A wheat-flour subsidy was introduced in 1994, but it was gradually phased out in 1996-97.

Table 3.4 indicates that the food subsidy in 1955 was Rs. 101.9 million. It has increased to the highest of Rs.2,414.7 million in 1979 but the highest per cent change was reported during 1977-78, just before the commencement of Sri Lanka's economic liberalisation. Even though the percentage food subsidy had shown an increasing trend since 1955, the steep increase was reported during 1976-79. The food subsidy has been reduced drastically immediately after the introduction of economic liberalisation through targeting the food distributing system (Graph 3.2).

TABLE 3.4

Budgetary Subsidies and Transfers of Sri Lanka

Year	*Food Subsidy (Rs.in Million)*	*Percentage Change*
1955	101.9	—
1961	357.2	25.7
1965	421.3	1.6
1971	616.8	23.3
1972	714.6	15.9
1973	703.4	-1.6
1974	929.2	32.1
1975	1019.7	9.7
1976	771.6	-24.3
1977	1407.5	82.4
1978	2171.7	54.3
1979	2414.7	11.2
1980	125.0	-94.8
1981	125.0	0.0
1982	100.0	-20.0

Source: Nutrition and Janasaviya Division, *Food and Nutrition Statistics 1950-90,* Ministry of Policy Planning and Implementation, Sri Lanka, Colombo, 1992.

A fertiliser subsidy scheme for paddy was introduced in 1951. The fertiliser subsidy was re-introduced, but subject to an overall ceiling. A subsidy of 50 per cent was given to cultivators who purchased seed paddy from the Department of Agrarian Services.[31] Fertiliser consumption increased from 14,000 tonnes in 1957 to nearly 90,000 tonnes in 1971. Fertiliser subsidy between 1978-85 was three times higher than the average 1971-77 levels. It has reached to Rs.782 million in 1980 and declined to Rs.369 million in

Graph 3.2: Food Subsidy in Sri Lanka

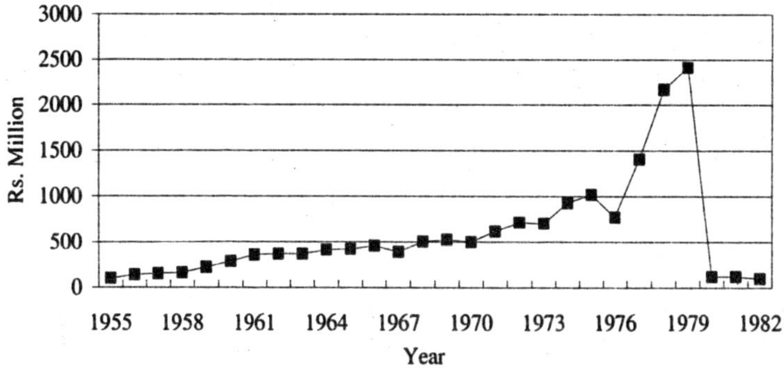

1986.[32] The fertilizer subsidy was revised and adjusted several times depending on the international prices of fertiliser. In 1990 the subsidy was removed completely and was reintroduced in 1994 to encourage the application of inorganic fertiliser.[33] In Sri Lanka, since the 1950s, the government has provided subsidy to popularise the use of chemical fertilisers among paddy farmers. The rate of subsidy ranged from 33 to 75 per cent from 1951 to the time of its elimination in 1989.[34]

The fertiliser price fluctuations became one of the main factors behind the fertiliser usage and paddy output in Sri Lanka. The subsidy rates are 40 per cent for urea, 15 per cent for ammonium sulphate, 9 per cent for nitrate of potash, and 22 per cent for triple super phosphate.[35] In Sri Lanka the successive governments did not increase the fertiliser prices according to the world prices, but rather continued to grant subsidy, which resulted in a rapid increase in government expenditure. In 1983 the subsidy was given an overall annual allocation of Rs.1,000 million triggering pressure for its removal in the second half of the 1980s. In spite of subsidisation, the fertiliser consumption in paddy cultivation greatly depended upon the land tenure and land size. Small and tenant cultivators have not been able to apply fertilisers in reasonable quantities, as done by large farmers, due to lack of adequate incomes. The reintroduction of fertiliser subsidy in 1994 and the relief package offered to farmers failing to repay their loans, paved the way for increased paddy production to a record level of 2.6 and 2.8 million metric tons in 1994 and 1995 respectively.

Foodgrain Price in India

The main objective of the foodgrains price policy in India has broadly been more concerned with the stabilisation of consumer price than with ensuring maximum price to producers. During the first three Five-Year Plan periods, there was no definite policy. The Government of India was generally safeguarding the interests of consumers more than producers. Several studies on aggregate supply response suggest a weak association between agricultural price and production.[36] In reality, it is evident that agricultural production reacts more favourable to certain types of governmental activity in rural areas.

(i) Commission for Agricultural Costs and Prices

The Government of India set up the Agricultural Prices Commission in 1965 on the recommendation of the Jha Committee, and later renamed it as the Commission of Agricultural Costs and Prices (CACP) with the task of recommending a balanced and integrated price structure in the interest of both the consumers and producers. The CACP keeps the following factors in view: the need to provide incentives to the producer for adopting improved technology and for maximizing production; the need to ensure rational utilization of land and other production resources; and, the likely effect of price policy on the rest of the economy, particularly on the cost of living, level of wages, and industrial cost structure before recommending the procurement prices.[37] The foodgrains for which the CACP has responsibility include paddy, wheat, jowar, bajra, maize, ragi, barley, gram, and other pulses. An amendment in March 1980 made it incumbent upon the Commission to take into account the changes in the terms of trade between the agricultural and non-agricultural sector while recommending procurement/support prices.[38]

The CACP considers procurement prices of the previous year, the trends in open-market prices, cost of production, input prices, interstate price dispersion, cost of living, and general price level before fixing the procurement prices. The most important of these criteria is the cost of production because unless prices cover the costs, there will be no incentive to increase production. The CACP is generally guided by the average cost, which would induce the farmers to improve their efficiency and would discourage production in inefficient farming areas and on inefficient farms.[39]

The CACP is guided by several concepts of parity, such as inter-commodity price parity, inter-sectoral price parity, input-output price parity, and parity between prices received and prices paid by farmers, though these different parities are not formally synthesized into a composite parity index. The inter-sectoral price parity arises when the prices of cash crops are determined. The input and output price parities reflect the changes in the overall cost of production of a crop and as such are a relevant factor in price determination. It is believed that any automatic linkage between the prices received by the farmer and the prices paid by him will only feed the vicious circle of cost-price inflation.[40]

The CACP also considers the terms of trade while fixing prices. The concept is based on the ratio of indices of prices received and prices paid by the agricultural sector. During the period 1964-65 to 1974-75 the terms of trade had generally remained in favour of the agricultural sector compared to the late 1960s and early 1970s but moved against it during 1975-76.[41] However, according to some authors "an effective approach for correcting the distortions resulting from terms of trade becoming adverse to the agricultural sector would seem to be in adopting all such measures which result in increases in productivity, although some improvements in terms of trade could be effected by adjusting the output prices."[42] Some others observed that the various criteria listed above were applied and emphasized in an uncoordinated way. They were never integrated into an objective model to compute the price to be recommended.[43] According to another critic there was no direct relationship between the prices recommended and any of the considerations listed above.[44]

Agricultural commodity prices show large spatial, varietal, and quality differences as well as variations over time. Spatial differences can be explained partly by transport costs and partly by imperfections in the market. The approach to quality differences is to fix the price of a well-specified fair average with differentials for other qualities. A similar approach is used for varietal differences. Prices are determined for standard varieties, and prices for all others are indicated in terms of price differentials based on past relationships. The government of India fixes a single price for a specified variety of each cereal. However, state governments fix different prices for different varieties, particularly in the case of rice.

(ii) Minimum Support Prices

The minimum support price (MSP) is generally announced just before the sowing season in India. These prices guarantee to the farmer that in the event of excessive production leading to a glut in the market, prices of his produce will not be allowed to fall below the minimum economic cost. These prices generally influence indirectly farmers' decisions regarding crop diversification. It not only covers the production cost but also provides an adequate incentive. The areas to be sown, however, depend upon the actual prices the farmers realize for the previous crop, as also upon their expectations for the coming season. The government agrees to buy all grain at a predetermined fixed price to protect farmers' income in good crop years. In effect, the public agencies have been buying all available food grain stocks in the market at procurement prices, which have been much higher than the support prices.

The MSP serves as a long-term guarantee for investment decisions of producers with an assurance that the prices of their commodities would not be allowed to fall below the level, even in the case of a bumper crop. The MSP for rice and wheat was proposed as a consumer-oriented food policy. Even though foodgrains production in 1964-65 had increased the food position in 1965 remained precarious because of drought in that year.

During 1977-78, the MSP of rice and coarse cereal was Rs.85 per quintal and Rs. 115 for wheat. By 1999-2000, the prices had increased to Rs. 490 per quintal of rice, and Rs. 415 for coarse cereals. Wheat's price was fixed at Rs.550 in 1998-99. In general, the MSP of wheat has been higher than rice and coarse cereals since 1978-79. But the price difference between rice and coarse cereals are marginal. The percentage change in prices of rice, wheat and coarse cereals was continuously more than 10 per cent during 1989-93.

TABLE 3.5

Procurement/Minimum Support Prices of Paddy, Wheat and Coarse Cereal in India

(Rs. / Quintal)

Year	*Paddy*	*% Change*	*Wheat*	*% Change*	*Coarse Cereal**	*% Change*
1978-9	85	—	115	—	85	—
1979-80	95	11.8	117	1.7	95	11.8
1980-81	105	10.5	130	11.1	105	10.5
1981-82	115	9.5	142	9.2	116	10.5
1982-83	122	6.1	151	6.3	118	1.7
1983-84	132	8.2	152	0.7	124	5.1
1984-85	137	3.8	157	3.3	130	4.8
1985-86	142	3.6	162	3.2	130	0.0
1986-87	146	2.8	166	2.5	132	1.5
1987-88	150	2.7	173	4.2	135	2.3
1988-89	160	6.7	185	6.9	145	7.4
1989-90	185	15.6	215	16.2	165	13.8
1990-91	205	10.8	225	4.7	180	9.1
1991-92	230	12.2	250	11.1	205	13.9
1992-93	270	17.4	330	32.0	240	17.1
1993-94	310	14.8	350	6.1	260	8.3
1994-95	340	9.7	360	2.9	280	7.7
1995-96	360	5.9	380	5.6	300	7.1
1996-97	380	5.6	475	25.0	310	3.3
1997-98	415	9.2	510	7.4	360	16.1
1998-99	440	6.0	550	7.8	390	8.3
1999-00	490	11.4	—	—	415	6.4

Note: * Coarse cereal includes Jowar, Bajra and Ragi.

Source: Directorate of Economics and Statistics, *Agricultural Statistics at a Glance 2000,* Ministry of Agriculture, Government of India, New Delhi, 2001.

It is important to note that the general principle underlying commodity price support programmes in India is to protect the cost of cultivation from a severe price decline, while permitting the market system to determine commodity prices. Thus tariffs are set at relatively low levels, so that the use of effective quantitative restrictions on imports remains very limited. However, the government aims to maintain flexibility in production and encourage farmers to make adjustments in changing economic conditions. The central government has started a number of programmes, in order to provide assistance in storage, transportation, and exports. The MSP becomes the floor price in periods of good harvest and hence they indirectly influence the farmers' decisions regarding the allocation of land and other resources among crops. The minimum support price plays a dual role as it supports the farmer when the market price of food crops is lower (during bumper harvest), and as a procurement price (an element of tax) when market price is higher.

The MSP of rice, wheat and coarse cereals during the period 1978-2000 has been presented in Graph 3.3. Since 1991, the MSP has started increasing at a faster rate for rice, wheat and coarse cereal. The liberalisation resulted in removal of subsidies on agriculture, which in turn tends to increase the cost of cultivation. It finally forced the government to increase the MSP. Though the government generally accepts the procurement prices recommended by the CACP, yet during certain years the prices announced by them were higher. For example, for wheat, the prices fixed exceeded those recommended by the CACP by Rs.2.5 to Rs.5.0 per quintal in three out of eleven years. For crop year 1983-84, however, the price announced by the government was lower by Rs.3.0. In the case of paddy, higher prices ranging from Rs.2.0 to 50 were announced for four out of eleven years. The differences between the two sets of prices were larger, at Rs.7.0 to 10.0 a quintal for coarse grains.

Graph 3.3: Minimum Support Prices in India

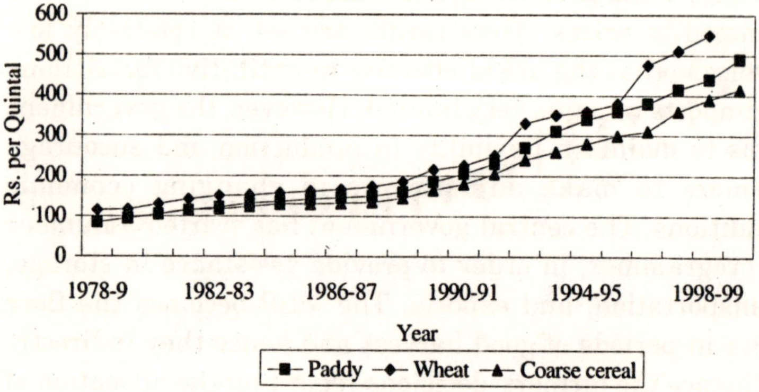

The procurement at average harvest tends to increase the open market price of foodgrains. The procurement price affects market price because the farmers' lobby is involved in fixing the MSP. The relationship between procurement and market prices seems to be strong. Hence, any excess demand in the open market due to stock build-ups or any rise in procurement prices is likely to result in a self-perpetuating price spiral and will have far-reaching consequences in food security for the poor.

When the price difference is higher, it plays a role of production incentive to increase production and investment in agriculture. The price policy had a favourable impact during the early post-Green Revolution period. However, even though a price support policy may have existed on paper for all cereals, its operation has almost been entirely non-existent for coarse cereals, and even for major cereals, in some food-deficit states due to institutional failures. In fact, market prices are found to have been lower than support prices for coarse cereals. The continuing uncertainty and sharp variability of foodgrain prices, as well as competition from imports result in the wide fluctuation in the incomes of farmers. The MSP policy has been introduced to safeguard against price fluctuations of food crops.

(iii) Procurement Prices

The Food Corporation of India (FCI) was established on January 1, 1965 as the sole agency of the Central Government to purchase, store, transport and distribute foodgrains. But, since 1980, the FCI has confined its activities to rice and wheat, and the National Agricultural Co-operative Marketing Federation handles coarse cereals. The importance of building up a buffer stock of foodgrains to stabilise the food economy of the country was recognised after the great Bengal Famine in 1943. In a good crop year, purchases by the FCI are substantial whereas in a poor crop year when market prices are high their purchase remains small.

The procurement prices are generally fixed and announced by the Government of India, in consultation with the state governments at the start of the marketing seasons in order to enable the FCI and the state government agencies to procure foodgrains from the farmers directly or in the market. It represents the price at which FCI / Central Warehousing Corporation or State Warehousing Corporations procure foodgrain from farmers directly, or in the market, depending upon the system of procurement adopted, including compulsory levy. The quantity to be procured is not only determined by the government's needs for disbursements under the public distribution system, but also depends upon the grain offered for sale by farmers at the prices fixed by the government. These prices are generally higher than the support prices but lower than the free market prices in normal years. In a good crop year in surplus states, free market prices would have been lower but for government purchases; after the surplus is mopped up, market prices tend to run higher than procurement prices.

Foodgrain Price in Sri Lanka

The Guaranteed Price Scheme (GPS) was introduced in 1948[45] with the objective of raising farmers' incomes by offering an assured price to protect them from middlemen, to enhance the national food production, and to ensure the procurement of supplies for distribution under the government's rice ration scheme at fair prices.[46] The Paddy Marketing Board (PMB) established the guaranteed price scheme in 1971 to purchase directly from farmers. Co-operatives and Agrarian Service Centres, which acted as purchasing agents of the PMB, then transferred the supplies to the Food Commissioner after the milling for ration at fair prices. In Sri Lanka the GPS is one of the important price stabilisation policies. The guaranteed price was fixed at Rs.8 per bushel (40 paise per kg) in 1948; it was Rs.7.42 in 1998. The average annual percentage change is more than 10 points during 1948-98.

TABLE 3.6

Guaranteed Prices for Paddy in Sri Lanka

Period		*Price*		*% Change*
From	*To*	*Rs./kg*	*Rs./bushel*	
1948	July 1951	0.38	8.0	—
August 1951	August 1952	0.43	9.0	13.2
September 1952	October 1967	0.57	12.0	32.6
November 1967	October 1972	0.67	14.0	17.5
November 1972	14th February 1972	0.72	15.0	7.5
15th February 1973	30th September 1973	0.86	18.0	19.4
1st October 1973	28th March 1974	1.20	25.0	39.5
30th March 1974	10th July 1974	1.44	30.0	20.0
11th July 1974	15th November 1977	1.58	33.0	9.7

16th November 1977	5th November 1980	1.92	40.0	21.5
6th November 1980	28th January 1981	2.40	50.0	25.0
29th January 1981	14th September 1981	2.52	52.5	5.0
15th September 1981	7th March 1983	2.76	57.5	9.5
8th March 1983	13th November 1986	2.99	62.5	8.3
14th November 1986	9th August 1988	3.35	70.0	12.0
10th August 1988	5th February 1990	3.83	80.0	14.3
6th February 1990	10th March 1991	5.27	110.0	37.6
11th March 1991	9th May 1993	6.47	135.0	22.8
10th May 1993	1998	7.42	—	14.7

Note: One bushel equals 20.87 kg.

Source: Nutrition and Janasaviya Division, *Food and Nutrition Statistics 1950-90,* Ministry of Policy Planning & Implementation, Sri Lanka, Colombo, 1992.

In 1973, paddy purchase becomes a government monopoly; inter-regional transport of rice and paddy was curbed and fertiliser was issued only to those selling to the PMB. However, in 1975, these restrictions were relaxed. Since the inception of GPS in 1948 till 1978, the guaranteed price remained higher than imported price of rice.[47] It became an effective floor price when the market price was lower. The GPS, originally conceived to set domestic producer prices above the world prices cannot be considered basically as a stabilising policy, although its indirect effect on stabilising domestic supplies is evident. The GPS is still in force, but its role is marginal. In the past the GPS had been extended to other food crops[48] (termed the Floor Price Scheme) to dampen the domestic price fluctuations. The output pricing policies act as a price support mechanism for producers, and trigger the government involvement directly in procuring the excess supplies.

Since 1977, under the economic liberalisation, the agricultural policies have included the removal of restrictions on the import of inputs such as seeds and fertilisers. The

Graph 3.4: Guaranteed Price of Paddy in Sri Lanka

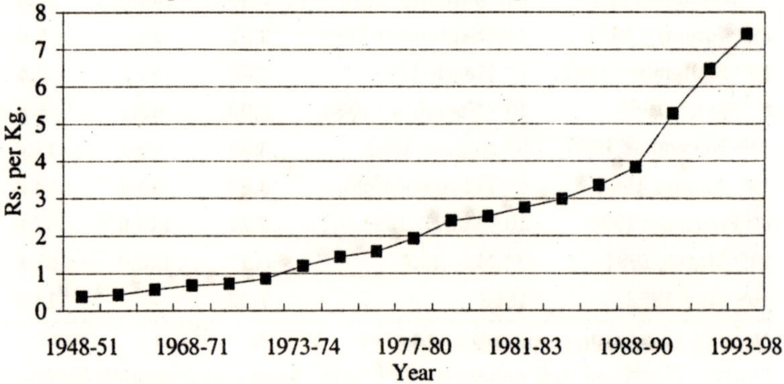

marketing of farm output was made competitive by encouraging private sector participation in local production and marketing, reducing agricultural trade restrictions. These events laid a strong emphasis on the competing private sector, which started to dominate trade. The only function of the GPS was to provide an assurance to farmers that they would receive at least the guaranteed floor price. This was thought to prevent private traders from depressing the prices by offering rates below a certain level, especially in peak production periods. Apart from this regulatory and stabilising role, the administered price plays only a passive role, especially in the case of procurement. The private sector now plays a larger role in purchasing, storage, milling of rice for wholesale and retail trade. The number of traders in the rice market has increased reasonably after the liberalisation.

The GPS has been theoretically planned to be a mark-up on the estimated cost of domestic paddy production and to be higher than the world market price for paddy. Generally the GPS was kept in line with the open market foodgrain prices, revised frequently to ensure adequate procurement of paddy for the government's ration scheme. Paddy production has increased since 1977 due to improved prices, greater availability and subsidisation of fertilisers, and improved agricultural extension services which have enabled a larger area to be cultivated under improved seed varieties and better water management practices.[49]

There are vast differences between the open market price, the ration shop price, and the effective consumer price. The difference suggests that consumer subsidy plays a major role in fixing the prices. According to one scholar the producer prices were more favourable to producers during 1951-55 and 1978-85, and the consumer received large subsidy, especially in 1960s. In Sri Lanka, consumer subsidies for the entire 1951-85 period were about 14 per cent. The consumer cost of rice was 78 per cent of the import price in 1970, and increased to 100.6 per cent in 1972.

External shocks, low domestic production due to adverse weather, and the lack of imported fertiliser made it more difficult to provide subsidy to the consumers. As a result, consumer prices averaged 20 per cent above the import prices during 1973-77.[50] The procured paddy from the local market is distributed to consumers under the rice ration scheme reducing the income inequality between the farm and the non-farm sector.

During 1948-66, even though the government changed the guaranteed price of paddy per bushel thrice, the GPS found it difficult to compete with the private sector, because the guaranteed price was lower than the open-market price in the face of a nexus between farmers and traders. The GPS was highly successful during 1967-1971. Rs.2.0 has increased the guaranteed price of paddy, but by 1971 the government was able to purchase as much as about 49 per cent of the total paddy production under the GPS.[51]

The main reasons for this success were the efficiency of co-operatives in rural areas, commercialisation of paddy, and adequate supply of agricultural inputs. The domestic agricultural sector has benefited from investment in agriculture, guaranteed prices, and subsidies.[52]

The Co-operatives and Agrarian Service Centres which acted as purchasing agents of the PMB then transferred rice to the Food Commissioner after milling for ration scheme to consumers at fair price. During 1971-76, the steep decrease in paddy production forced the government to import rice in sufficient quantity. The cost of a bushel of imported rice increased five times from Rs.7.77 to Rs.38.37 during the 1971-74 period.[53] In 1975, the restrictions on paddy marketing were removed and the paddy sector had since started growing by 10 per cent per annum.[54] As a result of the withdrawal of marketing restrictions and better harvest due to better conditions of weather, rice prices declined sharply and were in the range of Rs.2.50-3.50 per measure.[55]

The guaranteed price schemes are operated by both the PMB and the Co-operative Wholesale Establishment (CWE) for eight subsidiary crops - maize, kurakkan, groundnuts, soybean, gingelly, cowpea, green, and black grams. The average annual purchase of the CWE was around one per cent of annual output and hence its effect on the market prices was insignificant. The GPS has been virtually inactive since the abolition of the PMB monopoly in the procurement of paddy in the mid-1980s. As a result, the PMB could manage to procure only 2 per cent of the total paddy production.[56]

Since 1977 the PMB's role under the liberalised economy has been reduced to stabilise the paddy price. The government has often changed the guaranteed price in accordance with the rising open-market prices of paddy and rice. Currently the GPS operates impartially as a floor price scheme for paddy. In general, the GPS can be considered as an important factor in adopting new cultivation technologies for the commercialisation of paddy.

Agriculture Research and Extension

In India, any attempt at radical changes in the people's socio-economic conditions must therefore, need to be directed towards rural communities. With a view to attaining all-round rural development, the Community Development Programme was launched as early as in 1952. Its objective was to ensure substantial improvement in rural life through the adoption of a new agricultural technology for maximising production and rural incomes. The country was divided into approximately 5,000 development blocks to enforce a systematic planning and utilisation of human and material resources. Each block, comprising nearly 100 villages, was subdivided into ten circles, and each circle is manned by a Village Level Worker who is the extension functionary at the grassroots level. A team of specialists in agriculture, animal husbandry, co-operatives, panchayats, social education, and public health assists the Village Level Workers. The Block Development Officer acts as a team leader and is responsible for the co-ordination of block development activities. The programme has resulted in the establishment of a viable infrastructure in rural areas right from the village level to the State level with a mix of governmental and non-governmental agencies.[57] An important aspect of the development programme is that extension workers and farmers are included, along with research personnel, in taking final decisions about the suitability of a crop variety or practice under actual farming conditions. Such an involvement is important and is of great value to the extension workers, farmers and also research workers insofar as it provides feedback information.

In many states large landowners monopolise the services of the extension agencies. A study in Uttar Pradesh shows that since 70 per cent of the family heads were completely illiterate, access to literature remains primarily the prerogative of the better-educated and wealthier landowners.[58] Moreover, with the spread of commercialised agriculture, government extension services, credit and marketing co-operatives are now overwhelmingly geared to men, not to women.[59] There are, however, agricultural extension services to educate the farmers on improved methods of production. Since 1973 the District Agricultural Extension Officer were given a free hand to concentrate on extension work in India. The entire service has been progressively streamlined and has no doubt played an important role in the spread of new practices.

In Sri Lanka, agricultural extension services focus on three important factors: education in agricultural technology; helping the people develop an understanding and reasoning ability to enable them to think through and arrive at solutions to their own problems; and action to help not only in the implementation of farm business but also improvement of farm households.[60]

Extension services in Sri Lanka have mainly been directed towards educating the farmers in the use of new agricultural technologies for improvement in productivity, increase in the income level of farm households, and the achievement of self-sufficiency in the country's foodgrains. Public investment in agricultural research appears to be a very profitable undertaking and the average rate of return for India was 48 per cent and might be comparable with Sri Lanka.[61]

At the village level, Extension Officers (Krushi Vyapthi Sevaka) provide the updated information on new technology to the farmers as per directions from the divisional level. A Training and Visit System approach was introduced in the early 1980s. The social aspect of the farmers is an important factor for their active participation in the extension services in the paddy sector. "People in Sri Lanka are receptive and willing to adopt new practices provided they are sound and introduced to them in a convincing and friendly way".[62] However, the rural infrastructure contributes to the slow progress of agricultural extension activities. For example, in the early 1990s performance of the agricultural extension services had deteriorated considerably in Sri Lanka due to fact that the services of the village-level extension workers were absorbed into the general administrative services, and their agrarian services were discontinued.

In Sri Lanka the integrated farming approach and co-ordination between state agricultural related agencies at different levels provide extension and other services to farmers under '*Govisevan*' and '*Govikendra*' programmes. Nearly 1,22,000 farmers in 1995, and another 43,000 farmers during the first half of 1996, received technical know-how on improved agricultural practices. Agrarian Service Centers, which were almost abandoned in the past, have begun to be reactivated as co-ordinating centres for input supply and marketing of farm produce. Of the total of 540 centers, 59 have so far been rehabilitated.

Demand Policy in India

In India, the demand policy instruments in general emphasis disaggregated access of the people to food. The major instrument of demand-side food policy is nutritional status. The important components of the nutritional status are the construction of a national food balance sheet in order to obtain an overall picture of the nutritional status of the country, household income-expenditure, and more specific investigations of vulnerable groups to assess the degree, nature and intensity of their inability to acquire sufficient food. It is observed that malnutrition may still be widespread and a number of households food-insecured, even though the total food supplies are adequate to meet nutritional needs in the country.

Poverty Alleviation Programmes in India

To ensure economic access to food, the Indian Government has launched various employment programmes. The basic purpose of these programmes is to transfer incomes to weaker sections to enable them to purchase the major foodgrains, i.e., rice and wheat. In addition, foodgrains are allocated from the central pool for relief works and additional employment-generation programmes undertaken particularly during the off-season periods, and during droughts, and floods. Under these programmes a part of the wage is paid in the form of subsidised foodgrain. During the abnormal years (for example in 1979-80 and 1987-88) the government had increased the supplies through both the public distribution system and employment generation programmes to prevent the outbreak of a famine. However, due to lack of awareness among the weaker sections, and rampant corruption in the administration these programmes have not been successful to the desired extent.

In so far as the economic access to the public distribution system is concerned, it is amply clear that the weaker sections of society are solely dependent on wage incomes. The availability of employment opportunities during peak agriculture seasons is not enough in the wake of increasing labour force.

The policy instruments seek to either lower the price of foodgrains to improve entitlements (food subsidies) or increase command over food (by employment creation, food-for-work programmes, or cash transfers). In India, the employment provision has been used extensively as a tool for protecting entitlements by initiating different government-sponsored programmes. The high incidence of poverty in rural India is directly related to the prevalence of unemployment and under-employment on a large scale. The majority of rural population is landless and depends entirely on wage employment.

The strategy and policy of direct attack on poverty by way of target approach for the rural poor came into operation in the Fourth Five-Year Plan. With the main objective of improving the asset base of the poor and involving the poor in the production/income generation processes of the economy, the IRDP was initiated. The IRDP was launched initially in 2300 blocks and has been extended to all the blocks of the country since 1980. The Development of Women and Children in Rural Areas was launched as a sub-scheme of the IRDP during 1982-83. It enables rural women to actively participate intensely in skill training and infrastructure programmes for self-employment.

One of the major programmes planned in this direction is the JRY, which was started in 1989 by merging the National Rural Employment Programme (NREP), and the Rural Landless Employment Guarantee Programme (RLEGP). Table 3.7 depicts that the funds available under JRY has drastically declining from 1989-89 to 1997-98. It also shows declining trend in fund utilisation, target and achievement. Even the fund and target has been declining over the years the percentage of utilisation shows a increasing trend and the percentage of achievement shows a mixed trend during the same period respectively.

TABLE 3.7

Performance of Jawahar Rozgar Yojana in India

(Rs. in crore)

Year	*Funds Available*	*Funds Utilised*	*% Utilisation*	*Target*	*Achievement*	*% Achievement*
1989-92	9576.37	7709.83	80.51	25402.64	25481.47	100.31
1992-93	3594.63	2709.59	75.38	7537.95	7821.02	103.76
1993-94	4767.63	3878.71	81.36	10383.26	10258.40	98.80
1994-95	5418.22	4268.33	78.78	9865.45	9517.07	96.47
1995-96	5791.90	4466.91	77.12	8480.05	8958.25	105.64
1996-97	2583.38	2163.98	83.77	4141.37	4006.32	93.24
1997-98	2872.03	2451.65	82.82	3864.90	3960.79	102.48

Source: Ministry of Rural Areas and Employment, *Annual Report, 1998-1999,* Government of India, New Delhi, 2000.

The Training of Rural Youth for Self-Employment Scheme (TRYSEM) was started in 1979. It aims to provide basic technical and entrepreneurial skills to the rural youth from families "below the poverty line", enabling them to take up self-employment in agriculture and industry, services, and business activities. The major self-employment programme, the Integrated Rural Development Programme (IRDP), and the wage employment programmes of the National Rural Employment Programme (NREP) and the Rural Landless Employment Guarantee Programme (RLEGP) were introduced at different periods of time to combat poverty.

One of the short-term strategies for the alleviation of rural poverty is the Employment Assurance Scheme (EAS) introduced in 1993 in 1778 blocks of 261 districts across the country in which the Revamped Public Distribution System was in operation. The principal objectives of the EAS were to provide gainful employment during lean agricultural seasons, and to create economic infrastructure and community assets for sustained employment and development. Unlike JRY, the allotment of funds available for EAS has been increasing from 1993-94 to 1997-98. The funds utilisation indicates a steady improvement during the same period. Table 3.8 shows a better performance on funds utilisation and man-days generated under EAS during the same period respectively.

TABLE 3.8

Performance of Employment Assurance Scheme in India

(Rs. in crore)

Year	*Funds Available*	*Funds Utilised*	*% Utilisation*	*Man-days generated**
1993-94	548.77	183.75	33.48	494.74
1994-95	1775.27	123.45	69.59	2739.56
1995-96	2671.45	1720.61	64.41	3465.27
1996-97	3383.34	2160.41	63.85	4030.02
1997-98	3425.32	2904.97	84.81	4717.74

Note: * in Lakh.

Source: Ministry of Rural Areas and Employment, *Annual Report, 1998-1999,* Government of India, New Delhi, 2000.

The National Social Assistance Programme (NSAP) was launched in 1995, in the form of a national policy for providing social assistance benefit to poor households in the event of old age, death of primary bread-winners and maternity. The three sub-schemes of the NSAP are: the National Old Age Pension Scheme; the National Family Benefit Scheme; and, National Maternity Benefit Scheme.

The Millions Wells Scheme (MWS) was launched as a sub-scheme of the NREP and the RLEGP during 1988-89; it has become an independent scheme since 1996. It provides open wells free of cost to poor, small and marginal farmers living below poverty line. Table 3.9 provides the performance of MWS in India. The percentage of utilisation of fund allotted under MWS has increased from 19988-89 to 1997-98.

TABLE 3.9

Performance of Million Wells Scheme in India

(Rs. in crore)

Year	*Allocation*	*Utilisation*	*% Utilisation*	*No. of Wells*
1988-89	271.40	132.90	48.97	50345
1990-91	524.63	279.74	53.32	56433
1991-92	524.63	495.19	94.39	172328
1992-93	605.33	534.05	88.22	180995
1993-94	954.37	639.74	67.03	151673
1994-95	1049.61	776.18	73.95	158780
1995-96	559.07	538.29	96.28	142685
1996-97	559.07	502.33	89.85	108897
1997-98	559.07	495.61	88.65	103499

Source: Ministry of Rural Areas and Employment, *Annual Report, 1998-1999,* Government of India, New Delhi, 2000.

Poverty Alleviation Programme in Sri Lanka

In Sri Lanka, since Independence, plans were initiated to address the question of poverty which led to a package of special programmes of land distribution, rural works, supplementary feeding for mothers and school children. This was in recognition of the need to have more far reaching intervention programmes for the poor, while growth-oriented strategies were being pursued for the economy.

(i) Janasaviya

In Sri Lanka a programme for addressing the problem of rural poverty known as "*Janasaviya*" (strength of people) was started in 1989. The perception that poverty and malnutrition are growing had brought about more direct state intervention and thereby the launching of *Janasaviya*. The major thrust in terms of social policy, however, began after the outbreak of ethnic violence. The *Janasaviya* programme was designed to re-orient the State's political, economic, social and administrative machinery to serve the poor.[63] The beneficiary coverage of the *Food Stamp Scheme* and *Janasaviya* programme touched 69.3 and 45.3 per cent of the estimated total families during the second round (3.12.1990 to 3.12.1992) respectively.[64]

TABLE 3.10

Beneficiary coverage of the Janasaviya Programme in Sri Lanka

Category	*First Round (2.10.89 to 2.10.91*	*Second Round (3.12.90 to 3.12.92)*
Estimated Total Families	1336426	237253
No. of Food Stamp Families	201458	164397
No. of Janasaviya Families	141360	107924
Estimated Total Expenditures*	5611.5	3776.2

Note: * Rupees in million.

Source: Nutrition and Janasaviya Division, *Food and Nutrition Statistics 1950-90,* Ministry of Policy Planning & Implementation, Sri Lanka, Colombo, 1992.

The monthly grant was fixed at Rs.1,458, comprising a cash "consumption" transfer of Rs. 1,000 released every month, and a "savings" component of Rs.458 that the households got in lump sum at the end of the two-year period, which was to be used for investment projects. The monthly grant was a fairly large amount by local standards; it was about nine times higher than the average household payment under the Food Stamp Scheme (FSS), which was Rs.167 in 1992. Janasaviya beneficiary households were also supposed to get an additional lump sum grant of Rs.25,000 at the end of the two-year period. The Janasaviya accounted for 0.7 per cent of the GDP in 1992, aiming to provide poor households with fixed monthly cash grants for a period of two years. The Janasaviya has been planned for 11 rounds, of which four have already been launched and the remaining seven will be launched within the next several years. Once the Janasaviya programme is started in an area, the FSS is phased out, except that the households receiving public assistance can retain their food stamp scheme benefits.

(ii) Samurdhi

According to the government, although 1.2 million families in the country need welfare assistance, only 0.5 million families have received the welfare package of Rs.1,458 per month under the Janasaviya. This is the main reason for introducing a new welfare programme – the "Samurdhi". Sri Lanka launched the Samurdhi (prosperity) package (combination of all social welfare programmes in Sri Lanka) in August 1995 to promote self-employment in rural areas and to alleviate poverty, benefiting about 1.5 million families. The scheme envisages welfare payments, saving schemes, self-employment projects, banking societies, insurance schemes, and vocational training.

TABLE 3.11

Cash Grants Given Under the Samurdhi in Sri Lanka

Category	*Number of beneficiaries*
Rs. 1,000 per month	31,360
Rs. 500 per month	931,069
Rs. 200 per month	309,914
Rs. 100 per month	231,951

Source: Samurdhi Authority, *Samurdhi: Poverty Alleviation Programme,* Ministry of Policy Planning and Implementation, Sri Lanka, Colombo, 1998.

As of October 1996, 1,504,294 families in 14,509 Grama Niladhari Divisions received benefits, based on Samurdhi Family Profile Survey results, totalling Rs.613 million per month. A beneficiary family will have to exit from the programme when the income of a beneficiary exceeds Rs.2,000 per month for a continuous period of six months, or when at least one member of the family finds employment. As beneficiaries exit from the programme, others who fall below the poverty line (Rs.2,000 per month) will be able to join the programme. A total of 19,80,162 families received benefits under this scheme at the end of June 2000, covering twenty districts in Sri Lanka.[65] This indicates that about 46 per cent of the total population receive benefits under this scheme.[66] The total cost of the *Samurdhi Income Supplementary Programme* for the first six months of the year 2000 increased marginally to Rs.4,069 million, compared to the corresponding period of the previous year. There were 1,67,286 households that received Rs. 951 million for the first six months of 2000 under the Dry Ration Programme. Similarly, 1,04,755 families received benefits to totalling Rs.79 million during the same period under Nutrition Allowance Programme.

TABLE 3.12

Number of Beneficiaries and Value of Grants under Samurdhi Welfare Programme in Sri Lanka

Cash Grant	*Number of Beneficiaries*			*Total Value (Rs. In Million)*	
	June 1999	*Dec 1999*	*June 2000*	*Jan-Jun 1999*	*Jan-Jun 2000*
Samurdhi	1968744	1987653	1980162	4066	4069
Dry Ration	155293	154932	167286	850	951
Nutrition	154388	80718	104755	40	79
Total	2278425	2223303	2252203	4956	5099

Source: Central Bank of Sri Lanka, *State of the Economy – 2000,* Government of Sri Lanka, Colombo, 2001.

The *Samurdhi* Task Force (STF) is planned for the Samurdhi beneficiaries. Small-scale development projects such as irrigation, water supply, road and building construction, are undertaken by the STF. By mid-October 1996, 11,640 such projects have been started with Rs.10,000 each from the government. The *Samurdhi* Programme also aims to improve saving habits of the poor in order to generate the required capital for self-employment. All beneficiaries are encouraged to save a part of the income supplement – Rs.200 per month by the poorest (i.e., those receiving Rs.1000 per month from the programme), and Rs.100 per month by the rest (those receiving Rs.500 per month). Approximately 1.5 million passbooks have already been distributed to beneficiaries, and about Rs.870 million saved up to June 1996.

An insurance scheme has been introduced by the Sri Lankan Insurance Corporation to protect the beneficiaries in the event of accidents, natural disasters, etc. Up to June 1996 about 8,80,000 *Samurdhi* beneficiaries and 26,000 Samurdhi Niyamakas have become members of the insurance scheme. Since 1995, the *Samurdhi* has become the main delivery mechanism[67] for social welfare, especially for poverty alleviation in Sri Lanka. However, it accounts for almost one per cent of the GDP and retains a considerable potential for further consolidation without jeopardising assistance to the poor. The *Samurdhi* covers more than 50 per cent of the population, while the proportion of the population below the poverty line is estimated at 22 per cent.[68]

In Sri Lanka major income transfer programmes together dispersed the equivalent of about 2.5 per cent of the GDP in 1992. The Poor Relief Food Stamp Programme accounted for 0.7 per cent of the GDP in 1992 aiming to improve the nutritional status of poor households by increasing their disposable incomes with monthly coupons that can be exchanged for food at special co-operative stores. The Assistance to Displaced Population, accounting for 0.6 per cent of the GDP in 1992, is part of the assistance programmes for families and individuals displaced by the civil war in the North and East providing dry food rations to the displaced populations.

Mid-Day Meal Scheme

In India, the School Mid-Day Meal Scheme, perhaps the earliest measures of nutritional relief programme, was launched in 1925 when the Corporation of Madras initiated it for the about 500 poor school children. The Government of Tamil Nadu was the first to sponsor it in 1957 to cover all children throughout the State. Later, several states followed suit. In 1995-96 the Government of India launched it as an all-India programme for the benefit of students in primary schools (in Revamped Public Distribution System and EAS blocks of 2,368) all over the country in areas where low female literacy rates persisted. The scheme had been extended to all other Low Female Literacy blocks (2,005) during 1996-97, and to all primary schools (825 blocks) and 3,000 Nagar Palikas during 1997-98. Foodgrains (rice and wheat) are supplied by FCI free of cost.

In Sri Lanka, the school mid-day meal, a supplementary food security programme was introduced in 1989 after 16 years of planning in view of the evidence that nutrition levels among school children were low and possibly declining. It was initially conceived as a community effort to feed its children, utilising locally grown foodstuffs and thereby generating additional demand and income for cultivators. However, in 1990, due to managerial difficulties it was converted into a cash transfer of Rs.3 per day per child, which was given on condition that a child brought a wholesome meal from home to be eaten at mid-day. In 1989, the mid-day meal cost Rs.1,514 million; it was Rs.1,644 million in 1990, Rs.1,402 million in 1991, Rs.1739 million in 1992, and Rs.1,995 million in 1993. In September 1993 the scheme was converted into a food stamp, worth Rs.50 per month, to a school child aged between five and 18 years, to be given on request.[69] This programme accounted for 0.4 per cent of the GDP in 1992. It is a universal programme for all children attending primary and secondary schools.[70] The programme provides a subsidy of Rs.3 per day per child to families of students bringing a nutritious and non-wheat flour-based meal to school. The subsidy is given in the form of monthly coupons, which can be redeemed at special co-operative stores. Teachers make a note of students who either fail to attend school or bring a suitable meal, and the corresponding amounts are deducted from the entitlement at the end of the month. Mid-day meal facility was abolished in 1996.

Integration of Policy Instruments

Finally, the supply, demand and distribution policy instruments should be integrated in order to form a coherent and synthesised food policy. The integration is necessary not only because of different components of the overall agriculture, food and nutrition programmes, but also due to the presence of central and state governments. It indicates a theoretical co-ordination of different ministries in India and Sri Lanka to ensure food security.

Summary

There are different sets of policies to ensure food security both in India and Sri Lanka. The agricultural supply policies are related to food production, which include subsidised inputs – seeds, irrigation, fertilisers, and credit. The demand factor includes poverty alleviation and income generation programmes. The food policy in India, evolved since the Bengal famine of 1943, and in Sri Lanka since the introduction of rationing scheme in 1942, has proved successful and has enhanced national food security.

The Green Revolution, based on the application of western technology and production models has considerably stimulated agricultural productivity in India and Sri Lanka. Besides, in both these countries, comprehensive crop insurance schemes have been enacted to reduce the adverse effects of weather on farm incomes to assist small and marginal farmers to continue with agriculture.

India has many irrigation projects as compared to Sri Lanka. In Sri Lanka, the major irrigation project, Mahaveli benefits a large number of people in settlement as well as irrigation coverage due to its geographical advantage.

With respect to credit policy in India commercial banks, regional rural banks and the co-operative banks play a vital role in providing finance to increase food production unlike only the commercial banks in Sri Lanka.

Incentive prices in the form of MSP in India, and GPS in Sri Lanka, are essential for the success of agricultural production programmes based on HYV technology. But the MSP is still very important instrument to control the open market prices and to ensure food security. In Sri Lanka the GPS's importance has declined considerably due to liberalisation. In India, institutional support for implementation of price policy is provided by the CACP and the FCI. The CACP plays an advisory role to the government in price determination and the FCI assists in co-ordinated implementation of procurement, distribution, and buffer stock policies. In Sri Lanka, PMB played an important role in implementing the price policy till liberalisation. To maintain a steady food supply, to determine the quantity and to protect the rice producers, Sri Lanka had fixed the producer price higher than import price. Thus Sri Lanka was able to achieve some flexibility only through arrangements involving free rice, subsidised rice, and market-priced rice.

Even though India has IRDP, DPAP, JRY, EAS, etc. as the income generating programmes, in Sri Lanka the *Janasaviya* (up to 1995) and *Samurdhi* programmes directly help the poor sections of the society in the form of cash payments.

The Mid-Day Meals Scheme, as a supplementary food security scheme also provides individual (school children) food security in India but Sri Lanka has discontinued the programme.

Many programmes with regard to irrigation, HYV seeds, land intensification, extension and research, employment guarantee schemes and rural work or food for work programmes, which are pursued both in India and Sri Lanka have proved to be beneficial to the landless and marginal farmers to enhance food security.

Both the Indian and Sri Lankan agricultural policies must be able to cope with the problems of small farms, which pose various problems of farm structure, income and human adjustment, and the large commercial farms, which provide maximum output. In this direction, India and Sri Lanka should develop research on promotional and regulatory services and economic programmes to ensure household and individual food security rather than national food security.

National food policies are pursued not only through

agriculture, but also through a combination of food assistance and development assistance for agricultural and infrastructure/institutional development. Development assistance interventions in the areas of economic growth, nutrition, health, family planning and other poverty alleviation interventions also contribute to food security, as do the programmes aimed at women. The problem of augmenting the people's incomes, particularly of the vulnerable sections of society, can be tackled only through long-term solutions in the socio-economic spectrum of a nation's activity. Market-oriented policies provide such an environment for economic growth, which is the major source of poverty alleviation and increased food security. It can perhaps be an intensification of the "food for work" programmes, targeted programmes, and emergency relief to cover only urban non-farm labourers, small and marginal farmers and landless agricultural workers.

Essential elements of the enabling economic environment include food and agricultural policies that operate in the context of a market-oriented national trade system. The governments of India and Sri Lanka need to conduct an in-depth study of the eligibility criteria and amounts of the entitlements before drafting their food policies while taking into account all the other sources of public assistance for households. The household usually acts in a community-level action.

REFERENCES

1. Ellis Frank, Agricultural Policies in Developing Countries (Cambridge, 1992,) p. 27.
2. Pradeep Chaturvedi (ed), Sustainable Agriculture in India (New Delhi, 1990), pp. 1-4.
3. W.D. Lakshman, ed., Dilemmas of Development; Fifty Years of Economic Change in Sri Lanka (Colombo, 1997), p. 114.

4. Central Bank of Ceylon, Review of the Economy 1985 (Colombo, 1986), p. 35.
5. Francis Moore Lappe and Joseph Collins, Food First: The Myth of Scarcity, (London, 1980), p. 104.
6. Kurt Finsterbusch, "The Contribution of Agricultural Research Centres to Sri Lankan Agriculture", in Paul A. Groves eds., Economic Development and Social Change in Sri Lanka: A Spatial and Policy Analysis (New Delhi, 1996), p. 189.
7. People's Bank, "Peasant Agriculture", Economic Review, Vol. 3, No. 10 (Colombo, 1978), p. 9.
8. Government of India, Ninth Five Year Plan, 1997-2002, Vol. II, p. 464.
9. Premachandra Athukorala and Sisira Jayasuriya, Macro Economic Policies, and Growth in Sri Lanka 1969-90 (Washington D.C., 1997), p. 9.
10. World Bank, Sri Lanka: Nonplantation Crop Sector Policy Alternatives (Washington, 1996), p. 13.
11. W.Gooneratne and Gunawardena.P.L.J, "Poverty and Inequality in Rural Sri Lanka", In W.Gooneratne and P.L.J. Gunawardena, ed., Poverty and Inequality in Rural Asia (Bangkok, 1984), p. 26.
12. R.D.Wanigaratne, Intra-Regional disintegration effects of Frontier Land Settlement in Sri Lanka, (Colombo, 1987), p. 26.
13. Surjit Bhalla, "Sri Lanka", In Anne O.Krueger, Maurice Schiff and Alberto Valdes, ed. The Political Economy of Agricultural Pricing Policy: Asia, Vol. 2, (Washington, 1991), p. 211.
14. Central Bank of Sri Lanka, Economic Progress of Independence Sri Lanka, (Colombo, 1998), pp. 157-159. A Major Irrigation Scheme irrigates more than 80 hectares of land area and a Minor Irrigation Scheme provides water less than 80 hectares.
15. *Ibid.*, p. 155.
16. Government of India, Technical Cooperation Among Developing Countries, What India can offer, (New Delhi, n.d.), p. 55.
17. *Ibid.*, p. 3-6.
18. *Ibid.*, p. 55.
19. Central Bank of Sri Lanka, n.14, p. 47.

20. N. Sanderatne, "A Profile of the Informal Rural Credit Market in the Mid-Seventies", Staff Studies Vol. 11, nos. 2&3 (1981), p. 3.
21. Central Bank of Sri Lanka, Annual Report 1998 (Colombo, 1999), p. 179.
22. Kurt Finsterbusch, "The Contribution of Agricultural Research Centres to Sri Lankan Agriculture", in Paul A. Groves eds., Economic Development and Social Change in Sri Lanka: A Spatial and Policy Analysis (New Delhi, 1996), p. 183.
23. Government of India, Government Subsidies in India, Discussion Paper, 9, Department of Economic Affairs, Ministry of Finance, (New Delhi, 1997), p. 3.
24. C.H.Hanumantha Rao and Ashok Gulati, "Indian Agriculture: Emerging Perspectives and Policy Issues", In Uma Kapila ed., After 4 years of Economic Reforms (New Delhi, 1995), p. 359.
25. Surjit Bhalla, n.13, p. 200.
26. *Ibid.,* p. 198.
27. Central Bank of Sri Lanka, n.14, p. 94.
28. Sri Lanka had an export boom during Korean War (1949-51); the price of rubber has increased.
29. Central Bank of Sri Lanka, n.14, p. 14.
30. *Ibid.,* p. 22.
31. *Ibid.*, p. 40.
32. Surjit Bhalla, n.13, p. 211.
33. Central Bank of Sri Lanka, n.14, p. 96.
34. W.D. Lakshman, n.3, p. 270
35. Premachandra Athukorala and Saman Kelegama, "Agricultural Trade Liberalisation in the Uruguay Round: Implications for Sri Lanka", in ed. Benoit Blarel, Garry Pursell and Alberto Valdes, Implications of the Uruguay Round Agreement for South Asia: The case of Agriculture (New Delhi, 1999), p. 208.
36. S.L.Bapna, "Food Security Through the PDS: The Indian Experience", In D.S.Tyagi and V.S. Vyas, ed., Increasing Access to Food: The Asian Experience (New Delhi, 1984), p. 119.

37. Government of India, Report of the Agricultural Prices Commission on Price Policy for Kharif Cereals for 1965-66 Season (New Delhi, 1965).
38. Government of India, Annual Report 1979-80 (New Delhi, 1980).
39. A.S.Kahlon and D. S. Tyagi, Agricultural Price Policy in India, (New Delhi, 1983).
40. Government of India, Interim Report on Agricultural Price Policy, (New Delhi, 1975).
41. D.S. Tyagi, "Domestic Terms of Trade and their effect on Supply and Demand of Agricultural Sector", Economic and Political Weekly, Vol. 22 (Bombay, 1987).
42. A.S.Kahlon and D. S. Tyagi, n.39.
43. Raj Krishna and Raychaudhuri, Some aspects of Wheat and Rice Price Policy in India (Washington, D. C. 1980).
44. P.S.George. Some aspects of Procurement and Distribution of Foodgrains in India (Washington, D.C., 1985).
45. The Marketing Commission from 1948 to 1957 when the Department of Agrarian Services undertook the function administrated GPS. The paddy Marketing Board took over the Scheme from 1971.
46. Central Bank of Sri Lanka, n.14, p. 40.
47. *Ibid.,* p. 95.
48. The other food crops are kurakkan, maize, gingelly, sorghum, mustard, chillies, green gram, tamarind, black pepper, and coffee.
49. P. Alailima and N. Sanderatne, Trends and Future Prospects for Food Supply and Consumption: Implication for Food Policy in Sri Lanka, (Colombo, 1982).
50. Surjit Bhalla, "Sri Lanka", In Anne O.Krueger, Maurice Schiff and Alberto Valdes, ed. The Political Economy of Agricultural Pricing Policy: Asia, Vol. 2, (Washington, 1991), p. 207.
51. Central Bank of Sri Lanka, Annual Report 1980, (Colombo 1981), p. 31.
52. Erick Thorbecke and J.Svejnar, Economic Policies and Agricultural Performance in Sri Lanka 1960-84, (Paris, 1987), p. 45.

53. Central Bank of Sri Lanka, Annual Report 1978, (Colombo 1989), p. 24.
54. N.L.Sirisena, "An Evaluation of Agricultural Policy on the Paddy Sector, 1950-85", Sri Lanka Economic Journal, Vol. 1, No. 1, (1986), p. 77.
55. N.A.Fernando, The Political Economy of Agricultural Pricing Policies in Sri Lanka Since Independence (Colombo, 1987), p. 44.
56. Premachandra Athukorala and Saman Kelegama, n.35, p. 208.
57. Government of India, n.40, p. 59.
58. Francis Moore Lappe & Joseph Collins, n. 5, p. 114.
59. P.A.S. Dahanayaka, "Disincentive effects of food aid on food production in Sri Lanka", Staff-Studies, Vol. 8, No. 2 (1978), p. 29-38.
60. P.C.Bansil, Ceylon Agriculture: A Perspective (Delhi, 1971), pp. 106-7.
61. Per Pinstrup-Anderson, Agricultural Research and Technology in Economic Development (London, 1982), p. 102.
62. Davut Aris, Guide to Agricultural Extension in Sri Lanka (Peradeniya, 1976), p. 16.
63. The programme implementation has been planned for 11 rounds. The divisions having the largest concentration of food stamp holders being considered the poorest and to be taken up first. The first round started in October 1989 with a total of 2,10,000 food stamp holders. After scrutiny, the number to receive Janasaviya was reduced to 1,57,800; an additional 40,000 who were identified as being in poverty but were not on the food stamps programme were given food stamps. The second round, which started in December 1990, covered 1,04,000 households.
64. Ministry of Policy Planning & Implementation, Food and Nutrition Statistics 1950-1990, (Colombo, 1992), p. 97.
65. Dry ration Scheme is being implemented in Jaffna, Mannar, Mullaitivu, Vavuniya and Killinochchi, where Samurdhi for the benefit of displaced families.
66. Central Bank of Sri Lanka, State of the Economy – 2000 (Colombo, 2001), p. 53.

67. Samurdhi is consolidation of different social transfer programmes including food stamps and emergency assistance, and elimination of the mid-day meal.
68. World Bank, Sri Lanka: Recent Economic Developments and Prospects, Poverty Reduction and Economic Management – South Asian Region, Report No. 17761-CE, (New York, 1998), p. 11.
69. W.D. Lakshman, n.3, p. 162.
70. World Bank, Sri Lanka Country Economic Update FY93: Public Sector Rationalisation for Private Sector Development and Poverty Alleviation, Report No. 11862-CE (New York, 1993), p. 30.

4

Determinants of Demand for Food

The demand for food is influenced by many factors including population growth, changes in income, the proportion of increased income used for purchasing food, foodgrain prices, and nutritional requirements. The main feature of food security is the population's capacity to obtain adequate quantities of food with a reasonable degree of assurance. Since the Second World War the per capita food availability has increased gradually in India and Sri Lanka, even though the minimum nutritional level could not be attained. As Meier observes, "the basic problem seems to be the effective demand, ensuring how to get purchasing power to the undernourished. Even when large supplies of food are available in one area, distant and scattered rural communities often do not receive their share."[1]

Today several million people probably do not have sufficient food for daily consumption in India and Sri Lanka. However, the problem arises from population growth. Grigg writes that a reasonable number of people are considered to be suffering from insufficient protein consumption.[2] Primarily the food problem is defined in terms of dietary energy deficiency or under-nutrition. It constitutes the principal criterion for a recent definition of hunger.[3] It is significant that all cereals contain sufficient quantities of protein, albeit of variable quality.[4]

People's food preferences change in accordance with changes in their income.[5] During the period 1950-90, approximately two-thirds of the total increase in world cereal production can be attributed to population growth. The interactions between demographic growth and food demand will be more complex and subtle than the population increase in the future. The demographic growth can indirectly influence the quantum of food demand through its effects on national income distribution.

Demography Profile of India

Between 1952 and 1972, approximately 86 per cent of the total world population lived in underdeveloped countries, where food output kept pace with or exceeded the rate of population growth.[6] The annual population growth rate between 1950-98 was 2.15 per cent.[7] The urban bias strategy of developing countries actually discriminated against the agricultural sector, resulting in the inefficiency and inequity of the sectors.[8]

TABLE 4.1

Demographic Indicators of India

Year	*Population (crore)*	*Growth Rate*	*CBR**	*CDR**	*Urban Pop %*
1951	36.11	—	—	—	17.3
1961	43.92	2.2	—	—	18.0
1971	54.82	2.5	36.9	14.9	19.9
1981	68.33	2.5	33.9	12.5	23.3
1991	84.63	2.4	29.3	9.8	25.7
1996	94.33	—	27.5	9.0	—

Note: CBR denotes crude birth rate, CDR refers crude death rate, and * indicates per thousand population.

Source: Central Statistical Organisation, Selected Socio-Economic Statistics: India 1999, Ministry of Statistics and Programme Implementation, Government of India, New Delhi, 2000.

Table 4.1 provides a profile of population growth and urbanisation in India. The annual rate of population growth was 2.2 per cent during 1951-61 but it has increased to 2.5 per cent annually during 1961-81. Since 1981 population growth has started declining in India. The significant demographic feature of India has been the declining rate of growth since 1980 due to successful family planning programmes.

The crude birth rate and death rate were reported declining trend since independence in India. The rate of urbanisation is increasing due to the fact that the growing rural migration. Insofar as urbanisation is concerned, India is progressing more rapidly than Sri Lanka. In India, other than rural to rural migration other types of migration increased from 1961-91 due to variety of reasons, but the important one was unemployment. It may be seen in Table 4.2 that migration from rural to rural areas has declined from 74.7 per cent in 1961 to 64.5 per cent in 1991 while urban to urban migration has increased from 8.1 per cent in 1961 to 11.2 per cent in 1991. The migration from rural to urban areas showed an increasing trend during the period 1961 to 1991. The migration from urban to rural

TABLE 4.2

Percentage Distribution of Migrants in Different Migration Stream in India

Year	*Rural to rural*	*Rural to urban*	*Urban to urban*	*Urban to rural*
1961	73.7	14.6	8.1	3.6
1971	70.3	15.3	8.9	5.5
1981	65.2	17.6	11.2	6.0
1991	64.5	18.4	11.2	5.9

Source: Central Statistical Organisation, Selected Socio-Economic Statistics: India 1999, Ministry of Statistics and Programme Implementation, Government of India, New Delhi, 2000.

areas has increased from 1961 to 1981 and declined during the period 1981-91.

The population in areas of low agricultural potential, which amounts to two thirds of India's cropped area, is dependent on rains; moreover, the weak market infrastructure often forces reliance upon local food production. This leads the people to migrate to more fertile areas or to urban centres for gainful non-farm economic activities. In this regard the watershed management programme in rainfed areas in order to increase food production would check the out migration.

Demography Profile of Sri Lanka

Table 4.3 provides a profile of population growth and urbanisation in Sri Lanka. The annual rate of population growth in India has been higher than that of in Sri Lanka. The high rate of population growth during the 1946-63 period averaged 2.8 per cent due to a fall in mortality rates and high birth rates in Sri Lanka. The significant demographic feature of Sri Lanka has been the declining rate of growth since independence due to successful family planning programmes. The international migration has played a positive role in bringing a demographic transition in Sri Lanka. As expected the crude birth rate and death rate were reported to be higher in India than in Sri Lanka.

One of the important factors of urbanisation has been access to convenience foods, especially when there is less leisure time for urban families to prepare time-consuming traditional dishes. Urbanisation in Sri Lanka brought the shift towards wheat products like bread. The considerable economic progress as manifest in per capita income and urban growth are the non-demographic factors for the growing demand for cereals in future. Nevertheless, population growth will be an even more dominant determinant of the growth in cereal demand in the coming years. The rise in per capita income is unlikely to create much additional demand for cereals. The urbanisation has slowed down since the 1970s due to increasing land prices, rents, the high cost of living, and also the inadequacy of housing facilities in Sri Lanka.

TABLE 4.3

Demographic Indicators of Sri Lanka

Year	*Population (crore)*	*Growth Rate*	*CBR**	*CDR**	*Urban Pop %*
1946	0.67	—	37.4	20.2	15.4
1953	0.81	2.8	38.7	10.9	15.3
1963	1.06	2.7	34.4	8.5	19.5
1971	1.27	2.2	30.1	7.7	22.4
1981	1.48	1.7	28.2	5.9	21.5
1991	1.72	1.4	20.0	5.8	—
1996	1.83	1.2	18.6	6.5	—

Note: CBR denotes crude birth rate, CDR refers crude death rate, and * indicates per thousand population.

Source: Central Bank of Sri Lanka, Economic Progress of Independent Sri Lanka, 1998.

The growing urban migration probably plays a significant residual role in pursuing a change in composition of food basket of consumers in urban areas in Sri Lanka. The pattern of migration changed between 1978-79 and 1996-97. The migration from rural to urban areas is not showing any definite trend. However, there is a decline compared to 1978-79. Table 4.4 depicts that the rural to rural and urban to rural areas migration had declined from 1978-79. The main reason for migration within the urban sector was search for better facilities while rural to urban was for employment and education.

TABLE 4.4

Percentage Distribution of Migrants in Different Migration Stream in Sri Lanka

Year	*Rural to rural*	*Rural to urban*	*Urban to urban*	*Urban to rural*
1978-79	76.4	23.1	32.2	63.0
1981-82	84.9	7.2	52.8	43.0
1986-87	84.8	13.2	58.7	39.5
1996-97	89.1	8.9	59.3	37.0

Source: Central Bank of Sri Lanka, Report on Consumer Finances and Socio Economic Survey 1996-97, Part – I, Colombo, 1999.

The future rate of growth of population in India and in Sri Lanka will depend in large measure on the actual change that takes place in fertility rates. The main factors, which have a strong influence on fertility rates, are rapid urbanisation, along with education and greater extent of employment opportunities for women. The population migration from rural to urban areas in Sri Lanka shows a declining trend while in India it is increasing. In addition, declines in fertility rates have been facilitated by the expansion of more effective policies and programmes for family planning and improving women's reproductive health.

The demographic trends in India and Sri Lanka, in combination with their continuing low levels of per capita food consumption would require strong growth in their food supplies to significantly close the gap with consumption levels. The implications of the demographic and overall development prospects together with the assessments of agricultural production, consumption and trade are that per capita food supplies for direct human consumption in both the countries would continue to grow. But, the absolute numbers and proportion of poor people living in cities and towns are expected to grow rapidly in future as people continue to leave rural areas in search of employment. These people, both in India and Sri Lanka, will be at great risk of malnutrition unless food is affordable.

Household Size in India and Sri Lanka

The household size is an important factor in determining household expenditure. In 1961, the average household size was 5.2 persons in India while in Sri Lanka it was 5.8 persons in the same year. The data for India showed the trend of increase in household size during the period 1961-91, while in Sri Lanka it showed a declining trend during 1961-91 (Graph 4.1). In Sri Lanka, the average household size during the period 1961-91 was lower than India. According to the Central Bank of Sri Lanka, the average household size was 4.6 persons in 1996-97.[9] In Sri Lanka the average household size has shown a continuous decline, mainly an outcome of the marginal drop in population growth, following the family planning programmes launched in the late 1960s. The declining trend in average household size in Sri Lanka tends to reduce the household and per capita expenditure on food.

Graph 4.1: Average Household Size in India and Sri Lanka

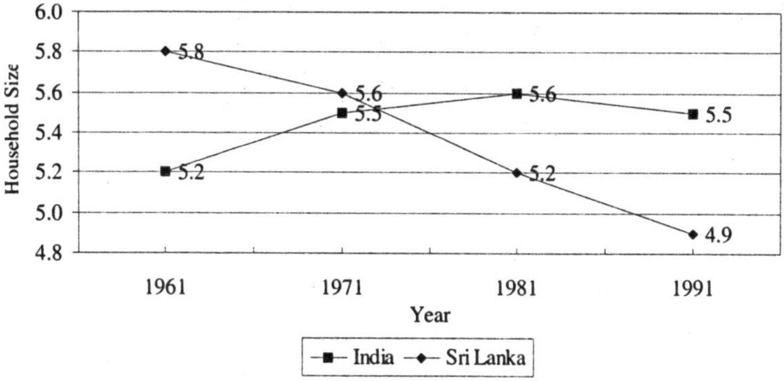

Household Income in India

In India, demand for food increases as economic growth

leads to changes in consumers' income. The increase in income leads to an increase in per capita demand for food. As incomes rise, demand will also rise, but it will increase at differential rates depending on the levels of income of consumers. The well-established fact is that low income households spends a larger portion of the increased income on additional purchases of food than higher-income households, i.e., the income elasticity with respect to the demand for food is higher for the poorer consumers than the rich. Income elasticities are high for cereals at the bottom and top levels of the income profile because at the bottom level the desire to increase consumption and at the higher group a strong demand for livestock products, which are cereal intensive. There will be a range of income elasticities for demand for food, depending on the levels of the income and growth of the income in the coming years. The combined effect of population growth and increases in income will account for the bulk of changes in demand for

TABLE 4.5

Percentage Distribution of Households by Annual Household Income by Sector in India

Annual household Income	*Percentage of households*	
	Rural	*Urban*
< 1000	7.0	5.7
1000 – 2999	31.5	13.9
3000 – 4599	27.4	16.3
5000 – 7499	15.5	16.6
7500 – 14999	14.4	26.8
15000 – 29999	3.4	15.6
30000 >	0.7	5.1

Source: National Sample Survey Organisation, Report of the Pilot Survey of Income, Consumption and Savings – Part II, Report No. 398, Government of India, New Delhi, 1993.

food. According to Yudelman, "the growth of per capita income from 3.0 to 5.5 per cent during the 1991-2020 period would accelerate the growth rate of demand for food grains".[10]

In India, income is not necessarily a good indicator of living or welfare. Besides reliable data on income distribution is not available. The highest number of households receives average annual income between Rs.1,000-2,999 in rural areas, whereas the highest, i.e., 36.8 per cent households receive Rs.7,500-14,999 in urban areas. The higher income receivers concentrated mainly in urban areas, while the maximum number of lower income households remains in rural areas. "The mean household income for rural India as a whole was Rs.25,653 per year which corresponds to a per capita income of Rs.4,485 in 1994".[11]

Sources of Income in India

The contributions of different components to total household income are estimated in Table 4.6. India has avoided direct enquires on household income in view of the inherent difficulties of the task. In contrast, the National Sample Survey Organisation, for the first time, computed the average monthly household income by using consumption data along with estimates of savings and income tax data.[12]

According to the *Report of the Pilot Survey of Income, Consumption and Savings*, the highest percentage of income from agricultural and allied activities in rural areas is 46 as against wages and salaries (57 per cent) the highest source of household income in India in urban areas. The income from non-agricultural enterprises is 10 per cent in rural areas and 27 per cent in urban areas. According to National Council of Applied Economic Research, agriculture and allied activities contribute to 55 per cent of the total household income in rural India. This is followed by income from salaries and professional services which amounts to 16.5 per cent.[13]

TABLE 4.6

Percentage of Household Income by Source and Sector in India

Source	*Percentage of total income by sector*	
	Rural	*Urban*
Agriculture and allied activities	46.0	3.0
Wages and salaries	33.0	57.0
Non-agricultural enterprises	10.0	27.0
Rent, dividend and interest	0.5	3.0
Other sources	11.5	10.0

Source: National Sample Survey Organisation, Report of the Pilot Survey of Income, Consumption and Savings – Part II, Report No. 398, Government of India, New Delhi, 1993.

Household Income in Sri Lanka

In 1995-96, urban households were reported to have the highest average household income i.e., Rs.10,067; and lowest average household income i.e., Rs.4,005 was reported from the estate sector in Sri Lanka as may be seen in Table 4.7. The average monthly household income of the country was estimated at Rs.6,463 in 1995-96. In 1995, Sri Lanka's per capita income had reached Rs.36,418, which was the highest among the South Asian countries.[14] During the period following Independence, Sri Lanka was among the relatively high-income countries in the region, but has since lagged behind in economic performance. However, recent economic growth has been quite satisfactory and a still better performance is expected in the future.

TABLE 4.7

Average Monthly Household Income by Sector in Sri Lanka

(Rs. in Current Prices)

Sector	*Survey Period*			
	1980-81	*1985-86*	*1990-91*	*1995-96*
All	881	2012	3506	6463
Urban	1274	3176	6783	10067
Rural	795	1725	2724	5982
Estate*	753	1551	2399	4005

Note: *The Estate sector consists of the households in tea, rubber and coconut estates with 20 or more acres and with 10 or more resident workers.

Source: Department of Census and Statistics, Household Income and Expenditure Survey – 1995-96, Preliminary Report, Ministry of Finance and Planning, Sri Lanka, Colombo, 1999.

Sources of Income in Sri Lanka

Changes in income influence the demand for food. The most important component in the food basket in the developing countries is cereals. According to the *Household Income and Expenditure Survey – 1995-96*, the percentage of monetary income to the total income in Sri Lanka was 81 per cent. In 1996-97, the income in cash accounted for 82 per cent of the total income, whereas the income in kind accounted for 18 per cent.[15] In Sri Lanka 44.1 per cent of income for rural households came from wages and salaries while in the case of urban households, this percentage was 49.4. Of the total household income, 2.9 per cent has come from the *Janasaviya* and *Samurdhi* programmes in rural sector and while in case of urban sector, this percentage was 0.6. The share of agricultural activities was also very nominal, being 9.5 per cent and 0.8 per cent in rural and urban areas respectively. The value of transfer payment made by the government under the *Janasaviya* and *Samurdhi* programmes was considered as money income.[16]

TABLE 4.8

Percentage of Household Income by Source and Sector in Sri Lanka

Source	*Percentage of total income by sector*	
	Rural	*Urban*
Agriculture and allied activities	9.5	0.8
Wages and salaries	44.2	49.4
Non-agricultural enterprises	16.2	17.8
Rent, dividend and interest	1.0	1.8
Janasaviya/Samurdhi	2.9	0.6
Other sources	26.2	29.6

Source: Department of Census and Statistics, Household Income and Expenditure Survey – 1995-96, Preliminary Report, Ministry of Finance and Planning, Sri Lanka, Colombo, 1999.

According to Central Bank of Sri Lanka, income from occupations accounted for 63.3 per cent in 1996-97 and this was marginally lower than the 1986-87 level of 65.8 per cent of the total income. The income derived from property and transfer accounted for 18.7 per cent and 17.6 per cent of the total income respectively.

Of the money transfers, the food stamps, and the *Janasaviya/Samurdhi* grants accounted for 1.7 per cent of the income in 1996-97, an increase of 0.4 per cent over 1986-87 level.[17] Of the government money transfer income the major component was the targeted *Samurdhi* package started in 1996-97, which was more important for the low-income groups. A major setback to the welfare schemes implemented in Sri Lanka since Independence was that the really deserving poor could not be targeted effectively, the reason being that these schemes covered a large segment of the population. It has become difficult to finance the increasing expenditure on such welfare programmes through budgetary resources. Therefore, in the 1980s, the government decided to improve efficiency mainly through better targeting.

Foodgrain Prices in India

The demand for different cereals is influenced by a number of factors that include everything from the relative prices of foodgrains to social customs and preferences. Foodgrain prices play an important role in ensuring food security in the low agricultural productive economies, as well as in distributing income between farm and non-farm sectors, across the geographical regions: The continuous increase in the prices of all commodities will reduce the real income of households. The Cairns Group[18] reiterates the choice of a market-oriented and commercially viable agricultural trade and favours the elimination of all agricultural subsidies that distort prices, production, and trade.[19]

Oslen stated that since most farmers' marketable surplus was quite small, the response to prices might be to retain more for their own consumption when food prices rise.[20] Dodla argued that prices received by farmers in developing countries were relatively higher than those received by producers of manufactured products in these countries. The producer prices have not been suppressed to the extent suggested by the conventional World Bank analysis of border prices and the alleged discriminatory nature of government interventionist policies in developing countries.[21]

Table 4.9 provides the structure of wholesale price indices of food items during 1986-1995 in India. The relative price variation has been comparatively higher in the case of pulses and rice than wheat. The variations were due to the market availability of pulses and rice. During 1986-95, the wholesale price for rice has increased at 10.16 per cent, 9.16 per cent for wheat and the highest, i.e., 13.32 per cent for pulses. The introduction of economic liberalisation in India had an impact on the foodgrain prices, especially cereals. For example during 1990-92 the price of rice has grown at 19.94 per cent while for wheat the rise was 21.10 per cent. But the prices of pulses did not have any direct impact of liberalisation.

TABLE 4.9

Wholesale Prices Index Numbers of Major Foodgrains in India

(Base: 1981-82=100)

Year	*Rice*	*Wheat*	*Cereals*	*Pulses*	*Foodgrains*
1986	132.1	126.0	128.3	130.2	128.6
1987	141.2	130.3	134.9	144.8	136.3
1988	159.1	148.5	152.2	190.5	157.5
1989	167.7	154.9	161.0	206.0	167.2
1990	172.6	156.9	162.5	218.6	170.3
1991	203.2	193.7	197.5	244.8	204.0
1992	248.2	230.0	242.5	254.7	244.2
1993	259.7	242.5	245.2	286.3	250.9
1994	286.9	272.0	275.6	356.5	286.8
1995	311.6	271.0	296.8	391.7	309.9

Source: Directorate of Economics and Statistics, Bulletin on Food Statistics, 1994-95, Ministry of Agriculture, Government of India, New Delhi, 1996.

Another important criterion to study food security is the comparison between international and domestic prices. India has been able to reach self-sufficiency in foodgrains and insulate the domestic economy from very large fluctuations in the world market. In view of the rupee devaluation, tariff reforms and withdrawal of restriction on agricultural exports, the agricultural sector may gain *vis-à-vis* the manufacturing sector. The comparison of Minimum Support/Procurement Prices with international price may not be appropriate because the Minimum Support Prices may be higher than open-market prices. The role of agriculture is even more significant in the matter of price stability in developing economies because of the dominant position of food as a wage good. The adverse impact of increase in food prices is far too severe in developing countries.[22] It may be seen that after 1993 the wholesale prices of pulses are increasing faster than the wholesale prices of major cereals like rice and wheat which is a concern for national food security in India (Graph 4.1).

The Consumer Price Index (CPI) captures the retail price movement for different sections of consumers. There are at present three important consumer price indices covering different socio-economic groups in India. The Consumer Price Index for Industrial Workers measures monthly movement of retail prices of various goods and

Graph 4.2: Wholesale Price Index in India

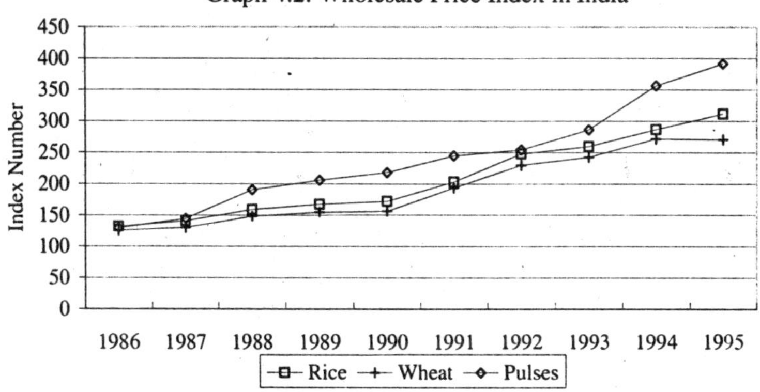

services in various industrial townships. The Consumer Price Index for Urban Non-Manual Workers monitors prices of goods and services in various cities on a monthly basis. The Consumer Price Index for Agricultural Workers is utilised for fixation and revision of minimum wages in agriculture. Among the CPI Numbers, Consumer Price Index for Industrial Workers has been widely used in India. Table 4.10 depicts the annual trend in Wholesale Price Index and Consumer Price Index Numbers.

TABLE 4.10

Wholesale Price Index and Consumer Price Index Numbers in India

Year	*Wholesale Price Index**	*Price Index of Ag. Prod.**	*Price Index . of Mfg Prod.**	*Consumer Price Index@*		
				Agricultural Labourer	*Industrial Workers*	*Urban Non-Manual Workers*
1980-81	N.A.	N.A.	N.A.	100.0	100.0	100.0
1981-82	100.0	100.0	100.0	112.4	112.5	111.9
1982-83	104.9	107.3	103.5	118.2	121.2	120.9
1983-84	112.8	121.4	109.8	131.6	136.4	133.3
1984-85	120.4	129.2	117.5	131.9	145.1	144.2
1985-86	125.4	129.1	124.4	138.2	154.6	153.9
1986-87	132.7	142.8	129.2	144.8	168.1	166.1
1987-88	143.5	161.8	138.5	159.2	183.5	181.0
1988-89	154.2	170.9	151.6	179.2	200.0	196.2
1989-90	165.7	174.4	168.6	188.9	212.7	209.2
1990-91	182.7	198.3	182.8	203.2	237.2	232.3
1991-92	207.8	236.8	203.4	242.5	269.3	264.0
1992-93	228.7	255.5	225.6	272.4	295.0	291.4
1993-94	247.8	271.4	243.2	282.0	317.2	311.6
1994-95	274.7	307.7	268.8	315.0	349.2	341.9
1995-96	295.8	330.5	293.1	N.A.	N.A.	N.A.
1996-97	312.4	355.9	303.6	N.A.	N.A.	N.A.

Note: * Denotes Base: 1981-82=100 and @ denotes Base: 1980-81=100.

Source: Planning Commission, Data and Statistics, Government of India.

One can derive from the Table 4.10 that the consumer price index for industrial workers and urban non-manual workers was increasing faster than agricultural workers during 1980-81 to 1993-94. The index of agricultural prices was moving faster than price indices of wholesale and manufacturing production during 1981-82 to 1996-97. These could be due to the restriction on movements in respect of foodgrains (wheat, rice, coarse cereals, etc.).

TABLE 4.11

Average Price of Cereals, Rice and Wheat in India

(Rs. per Kg)

Item / Sector	*Cereal*	*Rice*	*Wheat*
RURAL			
1972-73	1.17	1.39	1.03
1977-78	1.48	1.78	1.31
1983	2.45	3.17	2.00
1987-88	2.86	3.53	2.32
1993-94	5.08	6.19	4.17
URBAN			
1972-73	1.31	1.56	1.10
1977-78	1.69	1.99	1.47
1983	2.83	3.49	2.32
1987-88	3.30	4.00	2.74
1993-94	6.05	7.23	5.03

Source: P.D. Joshi, Changing Pattern of Consumption Expenditure in India and Some Selected States, Sarvekshana Analytical Report No. 2, National Sample Survey Organisation, , Government of India, New Delhi, 1998, pp.85-86.

The retail prices of major cereals are a significant determinant of food security at household level. Table 4.10 presents the average price of cereals, rice, and wheat per kilogram in rural and urban areas in India. As expected, an average price per kilogram of rice is higher as compared to wheat in rural and urban areas in all NSS Rounds[23]. Further the retail prices of cereals, rice and wheat in urban areas are higher than the rural areas.

The ratio of urban price to rural price varies between 112 per cent to 117 per cent for rice, between 107 per cent to 121 per cent for wheat, and between 112 per cent to 119 per cent for cereals. As such the urban food security primarily depends on the food production in rural areas and the efficient food marketing systems in India.

Foodgrain Prices in Sri Lanka

Stability in the prices of foodgrains is always preferred as it provides food security. The movement of the foodgrain price level is generally measured by consumer price index, which is more often referred to as the cost living index. In Sri Lanka, price level remained stable during 1952-66, while during 1967-76 a moderate acceleration in prices was witnessed. During 1952-66, after independence, shortages in domestic supply of foodgrains were met through imports to stabilise foodgrain prices. Sri Lanka had followed price controls, rationing, subsidisation of foodgrain, domestic purchase and distribution of foodgrains. The post-liberalisation period was characterised by a sharp acceleration in prices.[24]

During the 1990s the average growth of foodgrain prices was 11.47 per cent, while Colombo Consumer Price Index (CCPI) was 10.79 per cent and Wholesale Price Index (WPI) was 9.63 per cent. The foodgrain prices continued to remain high in Sri Lanka despite improvement in domestic food supplies resulting from good harvests as well as the increased availability of imported food. The good harvest of rice and other subsidiary crops during 1993-94 and 1994-95 has decelerated the increase in foodgrain prices. The foodgrain price index has started increasing since liberalisation and has been higher than CCPI (Graph 4.2). The high inflation recorded in 1996 shows that the price increases for foodgrains remain a specific concern.[25]

TABLE 4.12

Colombo Consumers Price Index and Wholesale Price Index in Sri Lanka

(Base 1952=100)

Year	*Food Index*	*CCPI*	*WPI – Food**
1955	105.1	100.5	—
1960	100.8	103.5	—
1965	107.3	112.5	—
1970	136.6	138.2	—
1975	204.3	198.3	—
1980	339.7	318.2	—
1985	598.4	561.2	—
1990	1090.9	1008.6	599.2
1991	1220.3	1131.5	649.1
1992	1366.0	1260.4	720.0
1993	1519.4	1408.4	770.4
1994	1654.1	1527.4	760.4
1995	1768.1	1644.6	800.0
1996	2107.6	1906.7	1040.7
1997	2336.9	2089.1	1132.2
1998	2592.1	2284.9	1223.2

Note: CCPI denotes Colombo Consumer Price Index and WPI denotes Wholesale Price Index.

denotes 1974=100. The Index Numbers are computed by Department of Census and Statistics.

Source: Department of Census and Statistics, Statistical Profile of Sri Lanka, Ministry of Finance and Planning, Sri Lanka, Colombo, 1998.

Graph 4.3: Price Index in Sri Lanka

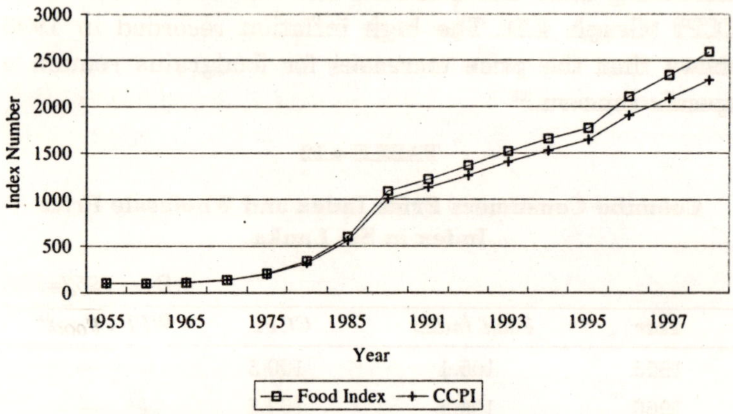

The prices of cereals are determined by the government and are fixed below the world prices in most years though Sri Lankan farmers have to pay more than the world prices for machinery and pesticides. The retail price of par-boiled rice was 79 cents in 1948 and in increased to Rs. 22.44 in 1996. The price of bread was also raised from 29 cents in 1948 to Rs.5.99 in 1996. During the 1967-76 period, the international oil price hike forced Sri Lanka to initiate administrative measures including subsidies, rationing and distribution of foodgrains including rice and wheat flour. The economic liberalisation had a substantial impact on foodgrain prices. In 1979, food subsidy for the higher income groups was withdrawn and the food stamp scheme for the poor was introduced. The price of wheat flour and bread was raised in the 1980s. The paucity of rain and civil disturbances contributed to the increase in foodgrain prices including Guaranteed Price of paddy. Sri Lanka has reduced the administered prices of wheat flour and bread in the 1990s.

TABLE 4.13

Retail Prices of Rice and Bread in Colombo

Year / Item	*Rice: Par-boiled (Rs. / Kg.)*	*Rice – Raw (Rs. / Kg.)*	*Bread (Rs. / 450gm / loaf)*
1948	0.79*	—	0.29
1952	1.94	1.89	0.25
1967	2.49	2.40	0.30
1976	6.74	6.60	0.89
1996	22.44	22.93	5.99

Note: * Rationed.

Source: Central Bank of Sri Lanka, Economic Progress of Independent Sri Lanka, Colombo, 1998.

Food Expenditure in India

Ever since attaining Independence, India has been making continued efforts through development plans for a socio-economic transformation of society to minimise economic disparities. It will, therefore, be of interest to examine how far the level of consumption expenditure, an indicator of the level of living in the rural and urban areas, has improved or deteriorated over the past 50 years.

This section is confined to analyse the share of expenditure on different items of consumption in both the rural and urban areas. The food items continue to dominate household budgets implying that food security should be the major focus of policies concerned with welfare. The most important components in the food basket in India are major cereals which include rice, wheat and coarse cereals viz., maize, jowar, bajra, etc., and pulses. The monthly mean per capita expenditure for rural India was Rs.287 in 1995.[26] The average monthly consumer expenditure as a percentage of total expenditure on some broad items in rural and urban areas of India is presented in Table 4.13.

The percentage of expenditure on food to total expenditure showed a substantial fall from 72.8 per cent in 1972-73 to 65.6 per cent in 1983 and 63.2 per cent in 1993-94 in rural areas.

TABLE 4.14

Percentage of Monthly Expenditure of Food and Non-Food Items to Total Expenditure in India

Item/Year	*1972-73*	*1977-78*	*1983*	*1987-88*	*1993-94*
Rural					
Rice	20.7	18.4	18.7	15.7	15.4
Wheat	9.1	7.7	7.9	7.2	6.5
Coarse Cereal	10.8	6.7	5.7	3.2	2.3
Total Cereal	40.6	32.8	32.3	26.1	24.2
Pulses	4.3	3.8	3.5	4.0	3.8
Total Food	72.8	64.3	65.6	63.8	63.2
Non-Food	27.2	35.7	34.4	36.2	36.8
Urban					
Rice	12.2	11.4	11.3	8.6	8.3
Wheat	8.4	7.4	6.8	5.5	5.2
Coarse Cereal	2.7	1.7	1.3	0.8	0.5
Total Cereal	23.3	20.4	19.5	14.8	14.0
Pulses	3.4	3.6	3.2	3.4	3.0
Total Food	64.5	60.0	59.1	55.9	54.7
Non-Food	35.5	40.0	40.9	44.1	45.3

Source: P.D. Joshi, Changing Pattern of Consumption Expenditure in India and Some Selected States, Sarvekshana Analytical Report No. 2, National Sample Survey Organisation, Government of India, New Delhi, 1998, pp. 29-30.

In respect of non-food items, the percentage expenditure increased from 27.2 per cent in 1972-73 to 34.4 per cent in 1983, and further to 36.8 per cent in 1993-94 in rural areas. Similar pattern has been observed in the urban sector also. During the same period, rural and urban households have diversified their consumption patterns into higher expenditure on nutritious items like milk products, eggs, and meat. The urban households' expenditure on food declined from 64.5 per cent in 1972-73 to 59.1 per cent in 1983, to 54.7 per cent in 1993-94.

In the rural areas in India, 22.8 per cent of the household expenditure is spent on major foodgrains, and another 22.8 per cent on other food items. In 1995, the estimated monthly per capita expenditure on foodgrain in rural India was Rs. 87.5 while other food items cost Rs.95.8.[27] It is found that the percentage share of expenditure food items has declined over the years in both the rural and urban areas, which was, in fact, expected due to the rise in foodgrain prices. The reasons for decrease in share of food is because of Engel Law and change in taste.

Food Expenditure in Sri Lanka

While adequate food supply is a necessary condition for food security the main cause of food insecurity is not the lack of supply or even high prices, but the weak purchasing power of some households. In Sri Lanka, a large number of households have low income, which severely limits their purchasing power. The *Household Income and Expenditure Survey – 1995-96* recorded the average monthly household expenditure as Rs.6,385. The same data for households in urban sector were Rs.10,202 per month.

The lowest monthly household eexpenditure was reported from households in estate sector, the average expenditure amount being Rs.4,676.[28] Table 4.14 reveals that in 1995-96 an average household in Sri Lanka spent about 53.6 per cent of its income on food. In rural and urban areas, 55.9 per cent and 43.9 per cent of household's income was spent on food items, respectively. Similarly the rural and urban households spent 44.1 per cent and 56.1 on non-food items respectively. In the estate sector, the percentage of food expenditure, i.e., 65.4 per cent, was the highest in comparison to the other sectors because of low income.

TABLE 4.15

Percentage of Monthly Expenditure of Food and Non-Food Items to Total Expenditure in Sri Lanka, 1995-96

Item	*All Sectors*	*Rural*	*Urban*	*Estate*
Rice	10.65	6.29	11.69	14.97
Wheat flour	2.72	2.27	2.65	9.13
Pulsed	2.00	1.28	2.10	3.85
Food	53.60	55.90	43.90	65.40
Non-Food	46.40	44.10	56.10	34.60

Source: Department of Census and Statistics, Household Income and Expenditure Survey – 1995-96, Preliminary Report, Ministry of Finance and Planning, Sri Lanka, Colombo, 1999.

The share of expenditure on the major staple food e.g., rice has been declining since 1980-81 among all sectors in Sri Lanka as may be seen in Table 4.15. The share of wheat (wheat flour and bread) consumption has been gradually declining due to the government's increasing subsidy on wheat.

The share of expenditure on rice in rural sector was 33.9 per cent, which gradually declined to 21 per cent in 1995-96; a similar pattern was reported in urban and estate sectors also. The share of expenditure on other cereals, excluding pulses has also been declining. Such an inequality in the distribution of expenditure, however, does not necessarily enhance food security.

TABLE 4.16

Percentage Share of Different Food Items to Total Food Expenditure in Sri Lanka

Item	*1980-81*	*1985-86*	*1990-91*	*1995-96*
Rural				
Rice	33.9	27.9	23.9	21.0
Wheat	5.8	6.8	4.6	4.8
Pulses	2.4	3.6	4.2	3.8
Urban				
Rice	23.2	18.5	17.6	14.4
Wheat	9.1	8.6	7.1	5.2
Pulses	2.3	3.3	4.4	3.2
Estate				
Rice	33.5	25.7	23.6	22.8
Wheat	14.4	16.4	11.3	14.0
Pulses	3.0	4.9	5.4	5.9

Source: Department of Census and Statistics, Household Income and Expenditure Survey – 1995-96, Ministry of Finance and Planning, Sri Lanka, Colombo, 1999.

Per Capita Food Expenditure in India

The current consumption expenditure as a proxy of permanent income is considered more appropriate for welfare measurement in India. The factors accounting for the shift in the pattern of consumption expenditure are the rise in the prices of cereals, or changes in per capita production/ net availability of cereals, leading to changes in tastes, habits and preferences. The consumption of cereals in terms of quantity and calorie intake in different food groups has thus undergone a change.

The average monthly consumer expenditure on major food items to total food expenditure in the rural and urban areas of India is presented in Table 4.17. It reveals that in the rural sector the percentage expenditure on cereals had declined from 55.7 per cent in 1972-73 to 49.2 per cent in 1983, to 38.3 per cent in 1993-94. Similar pattern has been observed in the urban areas also, where the proportion of expenditure on total cereal has declined from 36.2 per cent in 1972-73 to 33.0 per cent in 1983, and further to 25.7 per cent in 1993-94. The expenditure has increased over the years on all the items in both rural and urban areas due to the price rise in general.[29] In 1995, the total food expenditure was 63.9 per cent of which expenditure on foodgrains was 30.5 per cent in rural India.[30] The proportion of expenditure on rice and rice products had declined from 28.4 per cent in 1972-73 to 24.4 per cent in 1993-94 in rural areas, and from 18.9 per cent in 1972-73 to 15.3 per cent in 1993-94 in urban areas respectively. A similar pattern has been noticed in respect of wheat in rural and urban areas during the different NSS Rounds. But the coarse cereal consumption has declined comparatively from 1972-73 to 1993-94 in rural and urban areas. However, a mild increase in percentage expenditure has been observed in respect of pulses in both the sectors.

The per capita consumption of foodgrains averages 14 kilogram per month for rural India, which corresponds to 467 gram per day.[31] This is marginally less than the nutritional norm of intake for the rural population. However, only 33.2 per cent of households utilised the PDS regularly and only about 23.5 per cent of their requirements were met through this system in India. The per capita consumption of foodgrain met from PDS was 14.3 per cent while the quantity of cereals bought from PDS in a month by an average household was 19 kilogram.[32]

TABLE 4.17

Monthly Per Capita Expenditure on Major Food Items as Percentage of Total Food Expenditure in India

(Per cent)

Item / Year	*1972-73*	*1977-78*	*1983*	*1987-88*	*1993-94*
Rural					
Rice	28.4	28.6	28.5	24.7	24.4
Wheat	12.5	11.9	12.1	11.4	10.3
Coarse Cereal	14.8	10.4	8.6	4.9	3.6
Total Cereals	55.7	51.0	49.2	41.0	38.3
Pulses	5.9	5.9	5.4	6.2	6.0
Urban					
Rice	18.9	18.9	19.2	15.3	15.3
Wheat	13.0	12.4	11.5	9.8	9.5
Coarse Cereal	5.9	3.6	3.2	2.0	1.4
Total Cereals	36.2	34.1	33.0	26.5	25.7
Pulses	5.3	6.0	5.5	6.0	5.6

Source: P.D. Joshi, Changing Pattern of Consumption Expenditure in India and Some Selected States, Sarvekshana Analytical Report No. 2, National Sample Survey Organisation, , Government of India, New Delhi, 1998, p. 32.

There are differences in the pattern of food consumption in India, more so in cereals. Apart from the two major cereals - rice and wheat - there are other cereals, i.e. maize, jowar and bajra, which are produced and consumed in India. However, rice and wheat appear to have received major emphasis at the cost of coarse grains. The problem of food scarcity is viewed quite seriously considering fluctuations in the production, income and intake of required food.

Per Capita Food Expenditure in Sri Lanka

Table 4.18 provides monthly per capita expenditure on major food items by sectors during 1986-87 and 1996-

97 socio-economic surveys in Sri Lanka. Per capita expenditure on food was highest in urban sector and lowest in rural sector in 1986-87 and 1996-97. In 1986-87, the proportion of food expenditure for rice was, however, the highest in rural sector, accounting 26.2 per cent of the food expenditure, compared to 25.4 per cent in the estate sector and 16.3 per cent in the urban sector. The sectoral differences of food expenditure indicate that the total per capita expenditure on food was the highest at Rs.1189 for urban households, while it was Rs.942 and Rs.948 for the rural and estate sectors respectively in 1996-97. In the rural and estate sectors the proportion of food expenditure for rice was over 20 per cent while in the urban sector it was 14 per cent. Per capita expenditure on wheat flour amounted to Rs. 34.1 in 1986-87 and Rs.102 in 1996-97 in the estate sector representing 11.5 and 10.8 per cent of the total food expenditure respectively while it was relatively low for the rural and urban sectors. The proportion of per capita expenditure spent on pulses was highest in estate sector during 1986-87 and 1996-97. This is a reflection of the dietary pattern of estate households; the same trend has been reflected in previous surveys as well.[33]

The share of rice consumption in total food expenditure in 1996-97 declined to 20 per cent from 24 per cent in 1986-87, but the per capita consumption increased from 8.6 kilogram in 1986-87 to 8.8 kilogram in 1996-97. The fall in the per capita rice consumption in the urban sector was supplemented by a significant increase in bread consumption. The major determining factor was the convenience of bread as readymade food item. The differences in the structure of expenditure patterns observed in the urban, rural and estate sectors mainly reflect the differences in income levels, dietary patterns and to some extent a difference in prices.

TABLE 4.18

Monthly Per Capita Expenditure on Major Food Items as Percentage of Total Food Expenditure in Sri Lanka

Item	*1980-81*	*1985-86*	*1990-91*	*1995-96*
All Sectors				
Rice	31.5	22.4	25.3	19.9
Wheat	7.1	5.6	7.9	5.2
Pulses	2.4	3.6	4.4	3.7
Urban				
Rice	23.2	18.5	17.6	14.4
Wheat	9.1	8.6	7.1	5.2
Pulses	2.3	3.3	4.4	3.2
Rural				
Rice	33.9	27.9	23.9	21.0
Wheat	5.8	6.8	4.6	4.8
Pulses	2.4	3.6	4.2	3.8
Estate				
Rice	33.5	25.7	23.6	22.8
Wheat	14.4	16.4	11.3	14.0
Pulses	3.0	4.9	5.4	5.9

Source: Department of Census and Statistics, Household Income and Expenditure Survey – 1995-96, Preliminary Report, Ministry of Finance and Planning, Sri Lanka, Colombo, 1999.

Consumption of Cereals in India

The major objective of this section is to review the consumption quantities of major food commodities in Indian households such as rice and wheat over the time. The changes in real income, relative prices, tastes and preferences could be taken as the determinants of changes in quantity-wise consumption.

Table 4.19 presents per capita quantity consumption of major cereals, i.e., rice and wheat, in the rural and urban areas. It has been observed that the per capita consumption of rice has increased during the period 1972-73 to 1993-94 in rural urban areas. The percentage increase was 43 and 52 per cent in rural and urban areas respectively during the same period.

TABLE 4.19

Monthly Per Capita Consumption of Rice and Wheat in India

(Kg)

Item	*1972-73*	*1977-78*	*1983*	*1987-88*	*1993-94*
Rural					
Rice	6.59	7.12	6.63	7.04	7.02
Wheat	3.88	4.05	4.46	4.94	4.40
Urban					
Rice	4.94	5.48	5.32	5.35	5.28
Wheat	4.83	4.87	4.82	4.98	4.72

Source: P.D. Joshi, Changing Pattern of Consumption Expenditure in India and Some Selected States, Sarvekshana Analytical Report No. 2, National Sample Survey Organisation, Government of India, New Delhi, 1998, pp. 75-76.

In the rural sector, the average per capita consumption of wheat had increased from 3.88 kilograms in 1972-73 to 4.94 kilograms in 1987-88 and declined to 4.40 kilograms in 1993-94. In urban areas, the quantity consumption of wheat was 4.83 kilograms in 1972-73 and increased to 4.98 kilograms in 1987-88 and declined to 4.72 kilograms in 1993-94. The changes in the age distribution of population over the time could have a bearing on the increase in per capita consumption levels. In fact it indicates that when foodgrain prices continuously increase over the period, the expenditure pattern also tends to change, but the quantity of cereal consumption is more or less same.

Quantity Consumption in Sri Lanka

A salient feature observed in the per capita consumption of major cereals in Sri Lanka in 1995-96, was the decline in case of rice, and an increase in regard to wheat, especially when compared to previous periods. The per capita consumption of rice in 1995-96 was estimated to be 8.49 kilograms. The sector-wise data indicates that in all sectors per capita rice consumption had declined in 1995-96 substantially in comparison to the consumption levels recorded in previous periods. The per capita consumption of wheat in 1995-96 was computed at 3.38 kilograms. It may be observed from Table 4.20 that the per capita wheat consumption had increased precisely during the period

TABLE 4.20

Monthly Per Capita Consumption of Rice and Wheat in Sri Lanka

(Kg)

Item	*1980-81*	*1985-86*	*1990-91*	*1995-96*
All Sectors				
Rice	10.38	10.04	9.84	8.49
Wheat	2.53	2.96	2.78	3.38
Urban				
Rice	8.31	7.73	7.35	6.37
Wheat	3.69	3.75	3.84	4.15
Rural				
Rice	11.07	10.73	10.57	8.91
Wheat	2.06	2.43	2.23	3.09
Estate				
Rice	8.89	10.02	9.98	8.54
Wheat	3.00	5.74	4.78	7.72

Source: Department of Census and Statistics, Household Income and Expenditure Survey – 1995-96, Preliminary Report, Ministry of Finance and Planning, Sri Lanka, Colombo, 1999.

from 1980-81 to 1995-96 in all sectors. Wheat flour occupies an important place as a major source of cereal intake after rice. A substantial increase in wheat consumption in the estate sector is explained by the fact that the estate household's diet mainly comprised of wheat flour preparations.[34] The fall in per capita rice consumption was supplemented by the significant increase in wheat and wheat products, like bread, in all the sectors.

Food aid programmes that led to changes in relative prices of commodities have also influenced consumption pattern, especially where the subsidized imports have been widely distributed. In Sri Lanka, low-priced imported wheat has displaced domestically produced rice and coarse grains.[35] After a considerable drop in paddy production in 1996, and the uncertainties experienced in the rice trade in 1997, a supply shortage was evident in the market, which caused significant price variations in the rice market.

Therefore, the dominance of cereals, especially rice and wheat, as the main staple for most populations in India and Sri Lanka should not conceal the importance of other food sources either because of differences in food consumption across different sectors or because of the need for diversified foods in respect of healthy food and nutrition security.

Nutritional Intake in India and Sri Lanka

One of the important objectives of food policy both in India and Sri Lanka is to ensure that all citizens have an adequate diet or at least a diet adequate to meet basic needs. Nutritional intake using calorie criteria is considered as an important indicator of food security. The increase in productivity in agriculture has allowed consumers to improve their diets in terms of both calories consumed and the variety of food eaten. The standards recommended by the

Graph 4.4: Calorie Intake in India and Sri Lanka

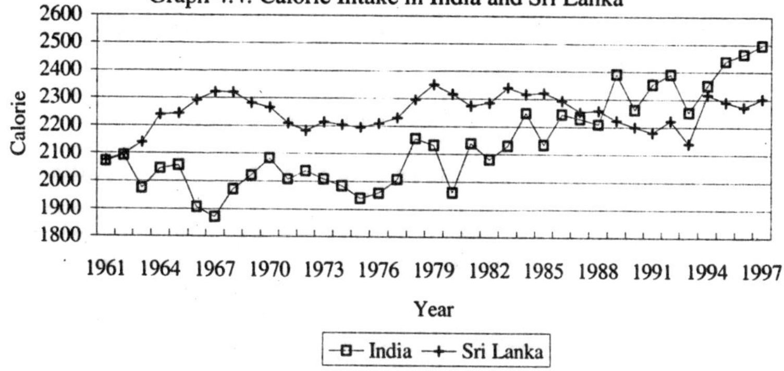

Food and Agricultural Organisation, at a minimum required calorie intake, is 2260 calorie per person. Those persons whose daily calorie intake falls below the required minimum are reckoned to be nutritionally deficient. As rice and wheat production and consumption have grown, production and consumption of important protein rich foods have fallen.[36] As a result, a reasonable proportion of population in both the countries is short of energy requirements and remains malnourished. It is an established fact that calorie requirements per individual, per day, vary depending on factors such as age, sex, physique, extent of physical activity, health and the climate in which individuals live and work. However, the adequacy of any supply of food depends on the composition of individual diets. The main nutrition disorders commonly found in India and Sri Lanka are related to deficiencies in protein, energy malnutrition and micro-nutrient deficiencies such as iron, iodine and vitamins. Although India and Sri Lanka have shown a remarkable leap in other social indicators compared with other countries in South Asia the improvement in nutritional status has not been significant. The nutritional wastage of children has been increasing due to under-nourishment associated with poverty and lower purchasing power. Under-nutrition is also due to a number of other factors, such as food availability, food affordability, food consumption behaviour, cultural patterns, and socio-economic factors.

TABLE 4.21

Daily Calorie and Protein Intake in India and Sri Lanka

(Per day)

Year	*Calorie*		*Protein*	
	India	*Sri Lanka*	*India*	*Sri Lanka*
1961	2070	2075	53	43
1971	2007	2208	50	43
1981	2138	2274	52	46
1991	2354	2180	57	48
1997	2496	2302	59	52

Source: http://www.apps.fao.org.

Table 4.21 shows the development of food supply measured in calories per capita per day for both India and Sri Lanka. While the progress made towards increasing food security, especially as indicative by average daily calorie availability per capita, has been impressive, it has been uneven from 1961 to 1997 both in India and Sri Lanka. Between 1961 and 1997 average calories intake in India rose from 2,070 per person per day to about 2,496 per person per day, while in the case of Sri Lanka it increased from 2,075 to 2,302 per person per day during the same period. The calorie and protein intake has been showing an increasing trend both in India and Sri Lanka; both of them have attained the minimum calorie requirement of 2,200-2,300 as recommended by Food and Agricultural Organisation. In India, the per capita calorie intake was lower than Sri Lanka from 1962 to 1988. Since 1989 the per capita calorie availability in India was higher than Sri Lanka (Graph 4.4).

Graph 4.5: Protein Intake in India and Sri Lanka

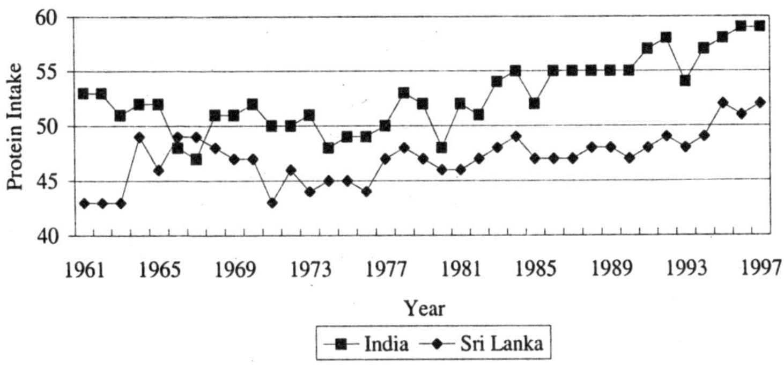

The protein intake has increased from 53 kilo calorie in 1961 to 59 kilo calorie in 1997 in India, where as during the same period in Sri Lanka the increase was from 43 to 52. During the period 1961-97, the average protein intake in India was higher than Sri Lanka except in 1966 and 1967 (Graph 4.5).

Even though Sri Lanka has been following the "minimum needs" strategy for its development process, yet a massive proportion of population has remained unacceptably poor. Nearly half of the country's households have been facing calorie inadequacy for many decades; the proportion of such households is even higher in the urban sector. However, during the past decade, considerable improvement in adequate supply of calories has been reported from the estate sector. But the other two sectors have recorded only a marginal improvement. Nevertheless, the overall quality of life in Sri Lanka has been higher than in any other country in South Asia because of its food distribution programmes, and social welfare measures like free education and free health services.[37]

TABLE 4.22

Average Calorie Intake and Percentage of Calorie from Different Food Items in India

Category / Year	*1971-72*	*1983*	*1993-94*
Rural			
Calorie	2168	2221	2153
Cereals	82.43	82.43	78.48
Pulses, Nuts	7.34	4.46	4.92
Milk, Fish, Meat, etc.	4.56	4.28	6.83
Fruits, Vegetables, etc.	2.21	4.42	4.43
Edible Oil, etc.	3.46	4.41	5.34
Urban			
Calorie	2179	2089	2071
Cereals	71.08	69.43	67.28
Pulses, Nuts	6.38	5.51	6.05
Milk, Fish, Meat, etc.	7.43	6.96	9.02
Fruits, Vegetables, etc.	8.57	10.16	8.86
Edible Oil, etc.	6.54	7.94	8.79

Source: P.D. Joshi, Changing Pattern of Consumption Expenditure in India and Some Selected States, Sarvekshana Analytical Report No. 2, National Sample Survey Organisation, , Government of India, New Delhi, 1998, p. 92.

The relationship between food consumption patterns and energy is an important indicator of food security. Food items that are considered high in nutrition value may be low in calorie value. Table 4.22 presents the average per capita per diem intake of calorie in different food groups in the rural and urban areas of India. It reveals that percentage of calorie intake in both the sectors has declined in respect of cereals and its substitutes. In India the declining trend in the calorie intake from cereals in rural and urban areas may be attributed to diversified consumption patterns towards nutritious milk, egg, meat, fish, etc. It also reveals that the intake has increased by about 45 kilo calorie during 1972-73 to 1983 and further gone down by 68 kilo calorie during 1983 to 1993-94 in the rural areas. Whereas the decrease was 90 and 18 kilo calorie during the same periods in urban areas. The inequality in the size distribution of calorie intake over the years has also come down which is in conformity with the declining trend in the incidence of poverty.

In India, the variations in calorie intake across different sectors could be explained by the levels of food availability and disparities in the levels of per capita income. The rural-urban price and income differentials faced by the marginalised population, especially landless labourers, and the small and marginal farmers in rural segments, can be an important determinant of variations in calorie intake. Besides, the rural land distribution is also crucial in explaining variations in the rural per capita calorie intake.

In Sri Lanka, sources of calorie intake differed markedly across different sectors during the period from 1986-87 to 1996-97. Overall, cereal accounted for 55.98 per cent of total daily calorie intake in 1986-87 and it had increased to 57.9 per cent in 1996-97. But rice was the dominant source of energy accounting for 44 per cent in 1996-97. In the estate sector, wheat flour was the second largest source of daily energy provider. On the other hand, in the urban sector, bread accounted for the major part of daily energy provider apart from rice.[38] Urban households derive a comparatively higher proportion of energy from meat, fish and milk products. This indicates that urban food basket contains more of these items compared to the other two sectors.

TABLE 4.23

Average Calorie Intake and Percentage of Calorie from Different Food Items in Sri Lanka

Item	*Urban*	*Rural*	*Estate*	*All Sectors*
1986-87				
Calorie	2093	2194	2554	2204
Cereals	52.02	55.81	64.83	55.98
Milk, Fish, Meat, etc.	6.26	3.09	2.44	3.57
Fruits, Vegetables, etc.	1.30	1.21	1.10	1.22
Edible Oil, etc.	16.08	18.20	12.51	17.31
Others	24.34	21.69	19.12	21.92
1996-97				
Calorie	2195	2336	2674	2337
Cereals	55.80	57.90	67.90	57.90
Milk, Fish, Meat, etc.	8.10	5.00	3.00	5.20
Fruits, Vegetables, etc.	1.80	1.80	1.20	1.70
Edible Oil, etc.	10.10	12.40	8.60	11.90
Others	27.10	23.00	19.30	23.00

Source: Central Bank of Sri Lanka, Report on Consumer Finances and Socio Economic Survey: Sri Lanka,1986-87 and 1996-97, Part I, Colombo, 1999.

The increased per capita food consumption, which became possible owing to increased real incomes, greater availability of food items and changing dietary habits, may have led to the increased energy intake during this period. In Sri Lanka the calorie consumption rose in all the three sectors between 1986-87 and 1996-97.

The largest increase in calorie was observed in the rural sector (142) followed by the estate sector (120). The corresponding increase for the urban sector was 102. The increased consumption of rice, bread, wheat flour, fish and milk was the major source of increased energy intake in the rural sector.

In Sri Lanka, the changing household consumption patterns are also having impact on national food security. Wheat is gradually becoming a more important component of the Sri Lanka diet encouraged by the government through subsidies on wheat price and tariffs on rice imports. Thus, the maintenance of rice output at 85-90 per cent of the domestic needs as well as improvement in per capita wheat consumption through rise in imports, has proved to be an acceptable food security strategy in recent years in Sri Lanka. The prices of rice and wheat have remained relatively stable and supplies readily accessible to all segments of the economy.

Even though at the national level the minimum calorie requirement of 2,260 is attained in India and Sri Lanka to meet the basic needs of the their population continuously there is a demand for an efficient food transferring system of food from the surplus area to the deficit areas. The size of such a transfer to meet basic needs depends on the extent of the calorie deficiencies among the affected population. If there are no transfers of foodgrain to calorie-deficit areas then there will have to be a substantial increase in the supply of calories to accommodate existing shortfalls and to take account of the needs of the growing population. In this context the public distribution system plays an effective role in India, like the earlier food stamp programme in Sri Lanka. Currently, Sri Lanka relies on market mechanism to distribute food; in India also the market plays a vital role to a certain extent. In this context, even if output grows to meet basic needs, such an increase in supplies would not be sufficient condition to ensure that all consumers would be able to satisfy their needs. An additional condition is that people must have the means to acquire their food in the market. Consequently, both in India and Sri Lanka it is not only important to meet the basic needs but substantial increases in the incomes of the poor calorie-deficient population is also necessary to enable them to purchase according to their needs.

Summary

In both the countries, India and Sri Lanka the overall pattern of demand would be heavily influenced by population growth, increase in the income and price variations. The increase in average household income and the population growth are two significant factors that determine the future food security at the national level. The rate of urbanisation in Sri Lanka is comparatively lower than India. The rise in per capita income is unlikely to create much additional demand for cereals. Nevertheless, the population growth and increase in per capita income will be more dominant determinants of the growth in cereal demand in coming years. Therefore, this study considers the demographic basis of growth as of primary importance in future cereal demand to ensure sustained food security. The demographic growth can indirectly influence the quantum of food demand through its effects on national income distribution. The annual rate of population growth in India has been higher than that of in Sri Lanka. As expected, the crude birth and death rates were reported to be higher in India in comparison to Sri Lanka. The population migration from rural to urban areas in India is increasing but in Sri Lanka it shows a declining trend.

The low level of per capita food supply in India and Sri Lanka are determined by rapid demographic growth. Therefore, if the focus is shifted from these average levels of per capita food availability to the numbers of people who are poorly supplied with food then, without doubt, rapid population growth is contributing to the total quantum of human hunger. Conversely, however, it is very doubtful whether the problem of human hunger is having a major independent influence upon contemporary death rates and thereby on the rates of population growth. There is no doubt that death rates would be somewhat lower in India and Sri Lanka if level of food availability are improved. But, in the present days, a great many factors such as lifestyle changes, improvements in medical supplies, immunisation programmes, transportation developments and increased levels of education help reduce mortality.

The average income has risen both in India and Sri Lanka since the 1950s, and hence the structure of demand for food has become much more diverse. As incomes increase there tends to be lower relative consumption of rice and increased preference for wheat and its products like bread, and also increased demand for vegetables, fruits, fish and meat. Such developments have been also influenced by increased urbanisation, growing communications and changing employment patterns. In India, rural households received the highest percentage (46 per cent) of household income from agricultural and allied activities whereas in Sri Lanka it was a mere 9.5 per cent. In India, the share of income from wages and salaries (57 per cent) was the highest source of urban households whereas in Sri Lanka it was 49.4 per cent. In Sri Lanka, rural households received 2.9 per cent of the household income as transfer payments made by the government under the *Janasaviya* and *Samurdhi* programmes.

In India, there is no official estimate on household income but the National Sample Survey Organisation for the first time computed the average household monthly income by using consumption data along with estimates of savings and income data. Generally, the average household expenditure is used as proxy for household income. But in Sri Lanka, Central Bank of Sri Lanka since 1953 is estimating average household income through its Consumer and Socio-Economic Surveys.

Besides, the prices of foodgrains determine the demand for food both the countries. According to Yudelman the rate of increase in demand for food in South Asia as a whole is expected to fall steadily from an average of 3.1 per cent in 1990-2000 to 3.0 per cent between the years 2000 and 2010, and further to 2.5 per cent during the period of 2010-25, before falling even further to 1.9 per cent per year during the period 2025-50. This rather sharp decline in the rate of increase in demand is attributable largely to the declining population growth and change in consumption pattern. Both in India and Sri Lanka the price of rice is higher than wheat or wheat flour.

The food consumption patterns in Sri Lanka have changed over the years due to several factors, e.g., changes in consumer preferences, relative price variations, changing demographic composition, policy measures, and variation in supply conditions. The share of expenditure on basic items like rice and wheat flour declined steadily while that on fish increased. The diversification of food expenditure in India and Sri Lanka clearly indicates a shift towards more nutritious food security. However, these changes in expenditure could also be the result of changing relative prices. It could be argued that a sharp reduction in the administered prices of wheat flour and bread would have contributed to a shift from rice to bread and wheat flour. Even though the Sri Lankan government removed the flour subsidy, the per capita consumption rose moderately possibly due to its relative price advantage over rice. Bread is considered an important food item in the cereal group and a major substitute for rice and wheat flour. Changes in the relative price of rice and wheat flour and bread between 1986-87 to 1996-97 seem to have a significant impact on the shift from rice and wheat flour to bread.

Thus, changing consumption patterns could increase the amount of calories available for meeting basic needs in India and Sri Lanka. In fact, per capita income has increased in both the countries. The demand for meat and dairy products and the derived demand for foodgrain are rising much more rapidly than the demand for foodgrain for direct consumption. The most pronounced effects on shifts in demand for individual cereals come from changing tastes as incomes. This is most evident in the growth of 'derived' demand for cereals used as cattle feed. Most of cereals are used as cattle feeds depending on local availability, tradition and relative prices.

Although India and Sri Lanka have shown a remarkable leap in other social indicators, compared with other countries in South Asia, the improvement in nutritional status has not been significant. The increase in per capita calorie availability in India and Sri Lanka has been rising - from 2070 and 2075 in 1961, to 2496 and 2302 in 1997, respectively. In India the per capita calorie was lower than Sri Lanka between 1962 to 1988, but from 1989 onwards the per capita calorie availability in India has been higher than that of Sri Lanka.

In the rural areas in India cereals accounted for 82.43 per cent of daily total calorie intake in 1983, but' it had declined to 78.48 per cent in 1993-94 while in urban areas the daily calorie intake of cereals had declined from 69.43 to 67.28 during the same period. In Sri Lanka, cereals

accounted for 55.98 per cent of daily total calorie intake in 1986-87 but it had increased to 57.9 per cent in 1996-97. In Sri Lanka rice was the dominant source of energy accounting for 44 per cent of the total calorie intake in 1996-97. In the estate sector of Sri Lanka, wheat flour was the second largest source of daily energy requirement.

REFERENCES

1. G.M. Meier, Leading Issues in Economic Development, (Oxford, 1984), p. 48.
2. D. Grigg, The World Food Problem, (Oxford, 1993), pp. 7-9.
3. Food and Agricultural Organization, The Fifth World Food Survey, (Rome, 1982), p. 70.
4. P.L. Kutzner, World Hunger: A Reference Handbook, (Oxford, 1991), pp. 170-173.
5. K. Blaxter, People Food and Resources, (Cambridge, 1986), p. 31.
6. Radha Sinha, Food and Poverty, (New York, 1976), p. 7.
7. P.R. Brahmanand, "The Economy Since Independence", Indian Horizons, Vol. XXXXV, nos.3 & 4, (1998), p. 105.
8. Michael Lipton, "Urban Bias", In G.M.Meier ed. Leading Issues in Economic Development, (Oxford, 1984), p. 437.
9. Central Bank of Sri Lanka, Report on Consumer Finances and Socio Economic Survey 1996-97, Part – I, (Colombo, 1999), p. 21.
10. G.S. Bhalla and Peter Hazell, "Foodgrains Demand in India to 2020: A preliminary Exercise", Economic and Political Weekly, (December 27, 1999), p. A154.
11. National Council of Applied Economic Research, India Human Development Report, (New Delhi, 1999), p.26.
12. National Sample Survey Organisation, Report of the Pilot Survey of Income, Consumption and Savings – Part II, Report No. 398, (New Delhi, 1993), p. 1.
13. National Council of Applied Economic Research, n.11, p. 32.
14. Department of Census and Statistics, Household Income and Expenditure Survey – 1995-96, Preliminary Report, (Colombo, 1999), p. 12.

15.
16.
17. Central Bank of Sri Lanka, Report on Consumer Finances and Socio Economic Survey 1996-97, Part – I, (Colombo, 1999), pp. 78-80.
18. Cairns Group comprises Argentina, Australia, Brazil, Canada, Chile, Columbia, Fiji, Indonesia, Malaysia, New Zealand, Paraguay, Philippines, South Africa, Thailand and Uruguay.
19. World Trade Scanner, 4 March, (New Delhi,1999), p. 235.
20. R.O. Oslen, "Impact and Implications of Foreign Surplus Disposal on Underdeveloped Economies," Journal of Farm Economies, Vol. 42, (1960), pp. 1042-51.
21. Dodla Sai Prasada Rao, Kailash Chandra Sharma and William Sheperd, "A Reassessment of Agricultural Price Policy in Developing Countries", In Antonio Jorge and Jorge Salazar-Carrillo, ed. Price Policies and Economic Growth, (London,1997), p. 152.
22. Johnston and Mellor J.W, "Role of Agriculture in Economic Development", American Economic Review, (March 1961), p. 571.
23. The NSS Rounds are 27th (1972-73), 32nd (1977-78), 38th (1983), 43rd (1987-88), and 50th (1993-94).
24. Central Bank of Sri Lanka, Economic Progress of Independent Sri Lanka, (Colombo, 1998), p. 44.
25. The World Bank, Sri Lanka: Recent Economic Developments and Prospects', Poverty Reduction and Economic Management – South Asian Region, Report No. 17761-CE, (Colombo, 1998), p. 6.
26. National Council of Applied Economic Research, n11, p. 97.
27. *Ibid.*, p. 97.
28. Department of Census and Statistics, n.14, p. 14.
29. P.D. Joshi, Changing Pattern of Consumption Expenditure in India and Some Selected States, (New Delhi, 1998), p. 7.
30. National Council of Applied Economic Research, n.11, p. 86.
31. National Council of Applied Economic Research, n.11, p. 89.
32.
33. Central Bank of Sri Lanka, n.17, p. 102.

34. Central Bank of Sri Lanka, Report on Consumer Finances and Socio Economic Survey, Part I 1986-87, (Colombo, 1999), p. 105.
35. Central Bank of Sri Lanka, n.17, p. 112.
36. C.Ford Runge and Benjamin Senauer, "A Removable Feast", Foreign Affairs, Vol. 79. No. 3, (2000) p. 44.
37. Pradeep Bhargava, Political Economy of Sri Lanka, (New Delhi, 1987), p. 45.
38. Central Bank of Sri Lanka, No.17, p. 119.

5

Distribution and Access to Food

Households constitute the central social unit to access food through a Public Distribution System (PDS). An efficient food distribution system in a country plays a major role in ensuring food security. An adequate food supply could provide national food security in any nation. But, if food supply does not guarantee household and individual food security, the population could face the threat of food insecurity. Food distribution ensures the physical and economic accessibility to food. A proper food distribution system is needed for all the households, so that food items become available to them at affordable prices. The search for household food security must start by making food accessible to the population, especially to the vulnerable segments.

The primary role of food distribution is to supply adequate food and ensure that the population has physical access to food by transferring it from the producer to the consumer. Therefore, the food transfer cost has to be kept at a minimum, which depends on the efficiency of such transfers. Much of the food produced in a country or area may not be consumed locally. In such a situation either it should be shifted from surplus areas to deficit areas or be exported. Farmers have to market their produce to meet their other needs through an organised trading system. If the domestically produced food is not sufficient to feed the entire population the balance has to be maintained through imports.

Since the population in every country is growing, there is an increase in the demand for food. As the development process unfolds a larger share of food is consumed in places far away from where it is produced. This process demands better distribution of food because people become more dependent on markets for their food. Consequently, they need an efficient and guaranteed food distribution system. The efficiency of any distribution system depends on the efficiency of the marketing system. The access of farmers to the market crucially depends on the infrastructure like, for example, a good network of roads. Poor infrastructure slows down transportation and increases the transport costs of food.

One of the major objectives of India and Sri Lanka, since independence, has been to provide a minimum level of living to everyone. This requires the provision of not only the needed quantum of foodgrains but also the required quality of food. Since independence, both the countries have been experiencing a mismatch between supply and demand for food. This situation has led planners to introduce a mechanism to ensure food security. The governments considered that the PDS could be an efficient tool to control food scarcities. Food distribution in both India and Sri Lanka could be viewed either as a tool of macro economic management or as an anti poverty measure. In the former, the main concern of the policymakers is the management of scarcities through buffer stocking, rationing and imports. This ensures food availability in the face of fluctuations in output. As an anti poverty measure, public foodgrain distribution aims at transferring incomes to low income groups. It also aims to raise nutritional standards of vulnerable groups and ensure household food security. Food security in India and Sri Lanka has to do more with physical access to food than with economic access.

Although the government's policies and programmes in India and Sri Lanka have changed over the years, but both the governments have taken steps to ensure that staple food is available to the people at affordable prices. The production as well as the distribution of foodgrains have had a major impact on the country's post-independence history. Therefore, both the governments try to handle food production and distribution cautiously. Food security should ensure the accessibility of food to the poor by a social welfare system and a proper distribution system.

Marketing in India

Efficient food distribution is not possible without an effective agricultural marketing system, which is needed to co-ordinate production and consumption. According to the National Commission on Agriculture, agricultural marketing is a process, which starts with a decision to produce a saleable farm commodity and involves all aspects of market structure, both functional and institutional, based on technical and economic considerations. It includes pre and post-harvest operations, assembling, grading and sorting, packing, storage, transportation, and distribution.[1] Marketing channels, on the other hand, involve a number of market intermediaries that can be grouped into three major sectors: Government (Food Corporation of India, Warehousing Corporations, Fair Price Shops and Ration Shops), private sector (commission agents, wholesalers, rice and roller flour mills, bakeries and retailers) and co-operative/farmers association. The government's involvement in food marketing basically entails the provision of overall policy direction and major market infrastructure and, in the case of important staple commodities like rice and wheat, the implementation of specific market intervention measures such as price support and commodity procurement programmes. Procurement of foodgrains is undertaken by specialised government agencies primarily to support buffer stock operations for stabilizing supply and the price of the foodgrains.

India has entered a stage of development where marketing become a serious constraint both in the sale of foodgrains and in the supply of inputs. Despite major efforts of the government, the food marketing systems continue to be sub-optimal. There are major constraints, which hamper the improvement of marketing performance. The first has to do with the preponderance of various Marketing Acts and Trading Practices, which vary from State to State. The second major constraint is infrastructure. The number of regulated markets is small (22 per cent of the total) and the existing capacity of the markets is not sufficient to accommodate the market arrivals during the glut.[2] The third major constraint is institutional. The Food Corporation of India (FCI) is suffering from huge losses on account of poor storage, transportation, handling, buffer stocking operations, etc. Although it has a welfare function in that it is mandated to provide cheap food to the poor through Fair Price Shops and to provide support price operations in far-flung areas, FCI nevertheless operates at higher costs than private trade and its administrative setup is top-heavy. The last major constraint is quality management. The foodgrain price policies shape the marketing systems. The operational efficiency of government corporations is relatively better than private traders.[3] In the private sector there are more than two lakh wholesale dealers and about four million retailers operating in the marketing of foodgrains.[4] In the face of growing economic costs of foodgrain procurement and distribution, the government's involvement in marketing can be sustained only through high subsidies.[5]

The commodity is brought to the village market over a period of about 6 to 8 weeks after the commencement of harvesting. This period may be called the peak marketing period of the harvested crop. Prices received by the farmer during this period are farm harvest prices. Farm harvest prices are defined as "the average wholesale price at which the commodity is disposed of by the producer at the village site during the specified harvesting period".[6] The peak marketing periods for rice, wheat and gram are shown in Table 5.1.

TABLE 5.1

Marketing Season of Agricultural Commodities in India

Sl. No.	*Item*	*Season*	*Period*
1	Rice	Winter	December – May
		Autumn	September – December
		Summer	April – June
2	Wheat	—	April – June
3	Gram	—	April – June

Source: Ministry of Agriculture, Indian Crop Calendar, Directorate of Economics and Statistics, Government of India, New Delhi, 1967, p. 29.

In 2000, there were 7,289 Wholesale Assembling Markets, 2,349 Principal Markets, and 4,778 Sub-Markets in India. The arrival of rice, wheat, gram and jowar to wholesale markets showed an increasing trend during the period from 1970-71 to 1999-2000.The market arrival of rice had increased from 25.2 per cent to 44.5 per cent during the same period. At the same time jowar's market arrival increased from 12.2 per cent to 18.1 per cent during the same period, even though jowar production is mostly for self-consumption (Table 5.2). In India, the National Agricultural Co-operative Marketing Federation is an apex co-operative organisation dealing with procurement, distribution, export and import of selected agricultural commodities. The Government of India has established the Small Farmers' Agriculture Business Consortium to solve the problems of poor marketing in rural areas.

TABLE 5.2

Arrivals of Rice, Wheat and Gram from Villages into Wholesale Assembling Markets as Percentage of Production in India

(per cent)

Year	*Rice*	*Wheat*	*Gram*	*Jowar*
1970-71	25.2	29.8	28.2	12.2
1975-76	15.2	30.5	33.6	11.2
1981-82	30.7	25.7	29.2	15.2
1982-83	32.8	28.0	33.0	12.5
1983-84	30.3	26.7	30.7	11.8
1984-85	31.6	24.9	30.8	10.2
1985-86	31.2	20.2	29.5	12.0
1986-87	32.3	28.7	30.3	12.1
1987-88	32.9	26.2	31.2	14.0
1988-89	29.7	27.1	32.9	10.3
1989-90	30.7	27.0	30.6	10.5
1990-91	30.9	29.5	32.3	11.0
1991-92	29.8	27.8	32.0	10.3
1992-93	38.9	29.3	36.3	11.5
1993-94	44.8	32.2	37.4	9.3
1994-95	37.7	32.4	39.6	9.9
1995-96	39.7	31.3	37.4	10.7
1996-97	42.3	30.3	40.9	10.4

1997-98	41.1	32.4	38.7	17.3
1998-99	39.0	34.7	35.7	18.2
1999-2000	44.5	35.3	45.1	18.1

Source: Directorate of Economics and Statistics, Bulletin on Food Statistics, (various issues) Ministry of Agriculture, Government of India, New Delhi.

Marketing in Sri Lanka

Since Independence the successive governments in Sri Lanka have intervened in rice distribution through domestic procurement, imports, processing, transportation, storage, distribution, and financing.[7] Until 1978 the government intervention affected the rice market in a variety of ways. The government determined the level of rice imports and the quantities to be issued to the market under the subsidised rice-rationing scheme. Sri Lanka also determined the guaranteed floor price to be paid to the farmers for paddy and the level of imports and the price of the closet substitute for rice: wheat flour. Since 1978 along with the economic liberalisation some of these policies were terminated but the guaranteed price and manipulation of wheat flour prices remained. The post-1977 regime was characterized by a decrease in government involvement in agricultural marketing with the private sector assuming dominant role in both produce and input marketing. In 1993, the private sector was allowed to import rice under licenses issued by the government. Prior to 1977 the coarse cereals had a good market since the imports of these commodities and their substitutes were banned at that time. However, with the resumption of imports of some of these commodities after 1977 farmers ran into serious marketing problems. Though the government interventions decreased significantly, much of the institutional structure established to support the rice sector continued to remain at a less active level.

In Sri Lanka, there are two channels of paddy marketing systems, i.e., private (collector, miller, wholesaler, retailer) and public (Paddy Marketing Board, Co-operative Wholesale Establishment and Co-operative Societies). The traders who collect paddy are called primary traders. A primary trader may be the trader who buys and sells to paddy millers or a miller who buys directly from farmers. The Paddy Marketing Board (PMB) is a public marketing agency. The functions of the PMB are procurement, storage, and distribution to different co-operative stores, in accordance with the guidelines of Food Commissioner of Sri Lanka. According to Wikramasinghe,[8] there are 20,000 rice mills operating in Sri Lanka of which 9,000 are medium and large-scale commercial mills located in major paddy producing districts of Ampara, Kurungala, Anuradhpura, Polonnaruwa and Hambantota.[9] The wholesalers buy rice from the millers. The principal retailers are the grocery traders who sell to consumers. In the public marketing system, the PMB purchases paddy through its own purchasing centres and multi-purpose co-operative societies[10] at a guaranteed price. After milling at its own or private mills, it sells rice through co-operative wholesale establishments, multi-purpose co-operative societies and army co-operative wholesale establishments to consumers at their respective retail shops. The contribution of private traders in rice marketing is about 90-95 per cent of the total marketing in Sri Lanka.[11] The wheat flour marketing is handled by multi-purpose co-operative societies.

Regulated Markets in India

The role of the government is limited to protecting the supply of wage goods, mass consumption goods and essential goods. The government tries to promote an organised marketing of agricultural commodities through regulated markets. A regulated market aims at eliminating malpractices, reducing market charges and providing fair and reasonable prices to producers and consumers respectively by facilitating efficient informal competition through private trade.

TABLE 5.3

Progress of Regulated Markets in India

Year	*No. of Regulated Markets*	*Growth Rate*
1951	236	—
1961	715	11.7
1973	2754	14.4
1981	4605	5.3
1990	6217	3.0
1994	6809	0.9
1998	7062	0.9
1999	7075	0.2
2000	7127	0.7

Source: Directorate of Economics and Statistics, Bulletin on Food Statistics, (various issues), Ministry of Agriculture, Government of India, New Delhi.

The Marketing Committees – the main enforcing institutions – have been instrumental for orderly marketing. As marketed surpluses increase, more markets are brought under regulation (Table 5.3). The number of regulated markets was 236 in 1951, which increased to 7,127 by 2000. The number of regulated markets has increased sharply, from 715 to 2754 between 1961 and 1973, immediately after the green revolution. The compound growth rate increased from 11.7 to 14.4 per cent from 1951-61 to 1961-73. The average area served by a regulated market varied from 900km^2 to 33km^2 across states, but the National Commission on Agriculture has recommended a radius of 5 km^2. In the case of wheat and rice public agencies buy about 30-40 per cent, co-operatives handle about 10 per cent of the assembled produce, and private traders operate the rest. However, this constitutes about 12-16 per cent of the total production of wheat and rice.[12] In India, the regulated markets have succeeded mainly in the states of Haryana and Punjab.[13]

The co-operation of producers, consumers, market middlemen, and very importantly the existence of rural infrastructure are highly essential for an efficient marketing system. Foodgrain production needs to be geographically dispersed through a flexible and viable transportation network. The familiar mode of transportation in the Indian village primary markets are bullock and camel carts, tractors, and mini-trucks, but the dominant means of transport, i.e., tractor alone carries 65 per cent of the total produce. The railways carry about 15 per cent of the total foodgrains produced.[14] In the context of the economic liberalisation, therefore, it is the responsibility of the state to facilitate an improvement in post-harvest marketing and services to farmers for the better distribution, availability and accessibility of food. These include providing a rural marketing infrastructure, maintaining roads, and strengthening the marketing system, including market information. The government has the social obligation to distribute food equitably regardless of the costs.

Procurement of Foodgrains in India

The procurement of foodgrains is one of the essential aspects of food security. It serves the objective of providing price security to farmers, which in turn induces the farmers to sustain production levels. The procurement prices depend on support prices. The Central and State governments are responsible for ensuring the smooth functioning of the PDS; while Food Corporation of India (FCI) procures, stores and transports the stocks; the state governments lift and distribute these stocks through ration/fair price shops. The ratio of procurement price to open-market price positively influences procurement.

The minimum support price may not necessarily play an effective role; on the other hand it may play a supportive role in technology improvement for agriculture. Over the years public distribution has come to depend heavily on the procurement of foodgrains.

Procurement prices are based on support prices determined by the Department of Agriculture and Co-operation. In keeping with the policy of providing price support to major foodgrains (wheat, paddy and coarse grains), the government continues to procure foodgrains conforming to prescribed specifications offered by farmers at the minimum support prices. The procurement of foodgrains under the price support scheme is largely concentrated in a few states. In a good crop year, purchases by the FCI may be substantially higher, whereas in a poor crop year when market prices are high purchases may be small.

The Department of Food and Civil Supplies ensures food security through the procurement of foodgrains by building up and maintaining food stocks, besides monitoring their quality, storage, movement and delivery to distributing agencies. The procurement operations of wheat, paddy and coarse grains are totally voluntary. The farmers have the option to sell their produce to the FCI / State agencies at support prices, or in the open market, whichever is beneficial to them. Rice is collected by way of a statutory levy on rice millers and rice dealers. The state governments with the approval of the Central Government fix the percentage of levy. The procurement of rice depends on the quantum of paddy milled by rice millers/dealers. Therefore, no targets for the procurement of foodgrains can be fixed. The percentage share of the central pool procurement of rice and wheat since 1971 is presented in Table 5.4.

TABLE 5.4

Percentage of Rice and Wheat Procurement to Production in India

Year	*Production (Million Tons)*		*Procurement as % of Production*	
	Rice	*Wheat*	*Rice*	*Wheat*
1971	42.23	23.83	8.19	21.36
1976	48.74	28.85	12.31	22.95
1981	53.63	36.31	11.56	18.15
1986	63.83	47.05	14.32	22.38
1987	60.56	44.32	12.76	17.73
1988	56.86	46.17	12.91	14.21
1989	70.49	54.11	14.03	16.52
1990	73.57	49.85	17.40	22.21
1991	74.29	54.52	15.72	14.06
1992	74.68	55.13	15.21	11.46
1993	72.87	57.21	19.88	22.44
1994	80.30	59.84	17.52	19.84
1995	81.16	65.47	12.62	18.83
1996	76.98	62.10	15.11	13.14
1997	81.74	69.35	17.49	13.41
1998	82.53	66.35	16.58	19.07
1999	86.08	71.29	19.32	19.83
2000	89.48	75.52	21.22	21.65

Source: Directorate of Economics and Statistics, Bulletin on Food Statistics, (various issues) Ministry of Agriculture, Government of India, New Delhi.

The production of rice had increased from 42.23 million tons in 1971 to 89.48 million tons in 2000. Similarly the procurement of rice has increased from 3.46 million tons to 18.99 million tons during the same period. The procurement of rice had constantly remained more than 10 per cent of the production of except 1971. The procurement of rice has increased from 8.19 per cent in 1971 to 21.22 in 2000.

In the case of wheat the production had increased from 23.83 million tons in 1971 to 75.52 million tons in 2000, and its procurement had increased from 5.09 million tons to 16.36 million tons during the same period. The procurement of wheat has increased from 21.36 per cent in 1971 to 21.65 in 2000 but the highest of 22.95 per cent was procured in 1976. The FCI procures roughly 12-15 per cent of rice production and 15-20 per cent wheat production each year. The procurement of rice shows an increasing trend from 1971 to 2000.

A state-wise data shows that a little more than half of the total procurement of foodgrains was from Punjab followed by Uttar Pradesh and Haryana with about 15 per cent each. With the addition of Andhra Pradesh, the four states shared around 90 per cent of total procurement in 1985. However, nearly 60 per cent of the total wheat and 45 per cent of the total rice procured in the country came from Punjab alone in that year.

In the early 1950s, domestic procurement accounted for a little less than 50 per cent of the total public distribution of foodgrains. Subsequently, except in good crop years, major reliance was placed on imports for meeting domestic requirements. During 1961-63, domestic procurement represented around one-eighth of the public distribution. Until 1964, procurement was confined to surplus states. It was extended to deficit states as well during the drought years and thereafter. In a situation of shortage or scarcity, unregulated purchase and movement of foodgrains by private trade at times leads to indiscriminate and speculative rise in prices by movement of surpluses of the producing regions to areas of high purchasing power. Thus, the objective of procurement till the mid-1960s was to redistribute the limited supplies from producers to consumers through government agencies within a crop year: its purpose was not to even out supplies between good and bad years. The situation began to change after 1967-68, as the output of foodgrains, particularly wheat, increased with the adoption of new technology based on high-yielding varieties of seeds. In most of the subsequent years, requirements were met entirely from domestic procurement and stocks. In this sense the country achieved self-sufficiency, even though the per capita consumption of the poorest sections of the population was far below the desired nutritional level.

The four main systems of procurement are monopoly procurement, graded levy on producers, levy on millers and traders, and preemptive/open market purchases.[15] The choice of a particular system depends upon the structure of production, the development of the infrastructure including the marketing system, the nature of the food situation, and above all, the administrative organization and experience of the state government. Imposition of interstate movement restriction is a prerequisite to successful procurement operations.

The procurement system also varies with time and by commodity. For example, procurement of wheat and coarse grains is done through preemptive/open market purchases (except in Maharashtra for jowar), which is facilitated by the existence of regulated markets for these commodities.[16] For paddy, which is traded in milled form, a levy on millers and traders is operationally more convenient. When the food situation was more acute during the 1960s, monopoly procurement and graded levy (i.e., levy at progressive rates) were imposed in many of the rice-producing states, particularly those with a deficit. Currently, only Kerala State has a graded levy on producers of paddy. Cereals are procured mostly by the field staffs of the FCI, the state civil supplies corporations or departments, cooperative marketing agencies, etc.

The PDS has to supply reasonable quantities of foodgrains at reasonable prices, particularly to vulnerable sections of the population. Procurement from domestic production must also be done at reasonable prices, which may have to be lower than the ruling market prices in some years, particularly in the years of food shortage. In such cases, the remainder of the marketable surplus is sold in the open market at prices higher than the ones which would have been had there been no procurement. It is argued that the weighted average price received by the producer from the sale of the levy and the non-levy portions of marketable surplus may not be less than the price he would have received in the absence of the levy and would be high enough to avoid any disincentive to farmers.[17]

Storage and Buffer Stock in India

The buffer stocks of foodgrains are maintained to moderate both seasonal and annual price variability in India. It is presumed that the average requirement and stocks could be higher in periods of good harvests and *vice versa*. The respective governments maintain food stocks commensurate with the requirements of the minimum operational stocks for monthly releases for public distribution. Since globalisation the actual stocks have shrunk, even though the governments have allotted a fixed quantity of foodgrains for their distribution. According to

Brown, the world carry-over foodgrain stock declined to a new low of 52 days of consumption in 1996, more than 100 days of consumption in 1987, 56 days in 1973, and around 90 days in 1960.[18]

TABLE 5.5

Percentage of Rice and Wheat Stock to Production in India

Year	*Production (Million Tons)*		*Stock as % of Production*	
	Rice	*Wheat*	*Rice*	*Wheat*
1971	42.23	23.83	5.68	21.78
1976	48.74	28.85	11.76	43.15
1981	53.63	36.31	11.58	14.24
1986	63.83	47.05	14.80	30.05
1987	60.56	44.32	10.63	17.15
1988	56.86	46.17	8.14	10.27
1989	70.49	54.11	8.68	11.03
1990	73.57	49.85	12.94	18.90
1991	74.29	54.52	12.51	9.85
1992	74.68	55.13	12.72	6.30
1993	72.87	57.21	16.40	19.40
1994	80.30	59.84	22.42	21.69
1995	81.16	65.47	19.68	20.24
1996	76.98	62.10	16.81	11.40
1997	81.74	69.35	14.06	9.75
1998	82.53	66.35	14.15	19.14
1999	86.08	71.29	17.10	24.08
2000	89.48	75.52	23.13	33.13

Source: Directorate of Economics and Statistics, Bulletin on Food Statistics, (various issues) Ministry of Agriculture, Government of India, New Delhi.

The stock of rice had increased from 2.40 million tons in 1971 to 20.70 million tons in 2000. Similarly, the stock of wheat has increased from 5.19 million tons to 25.04 million tons during the same period. However, there had been variations in the stocks of rice and wheat during the period. For example, the percentage share of stock to production of rice had increased from 5.68 per cent in 1971 to 23.13 in 2000. Correspondingly the stock of wheat increased from 21.78 per cent in 1971 to 33.13 in 2000 but the highest amount of 43.15 per cent was reported in 1976. The percentage share of stocks to production of rice showed an increasing trend from 1971 to 2000.

Storage in villages is restricted generally to a minimum period when the produce is needed for personal consumption as food, feed and seeds by farmers or by way of non-availability of transport in villages. In India, there are two types of storage structures: namely cover and plinth, and scientific storage. The first type in general is economical and is used only for shorter duration with high risk of quality deterioration due to weather. The second type of storage has been mainly adopted by FCI, Central Warehousing Corporation (CWC) and State Warehousing Corporations (SWCs), with the storage losses of less than one per cent.

There are three types of stocking systems in India. The base level stocks are lying in storage at various depots in small quantities, or are in transit and, therefore, not available for issue. The food security stocks are intended to fill the gap between procurement and distribution in a bad year. The operational stocks are required for month-to-month distribution during a year. The first two stocks combined together are termed as *buffer stock*. These stocks are intended to fill the gaps arising from shortfalls in procurement, the requirements of distribution, and crop failures due to drought. These stocks would normally get built up from the surplus of procurement in good years though occasional imports to meet the overall shortfalls may also be required. The availability of adequate buffer stocks not only provides an insurance against scarcity in bad years, but also helps to even out fluctuations in output and in prices.

The importance of building up a buffer stock of foodgrains to stabilise the food economy of the country has been recognised ever since the great Bengal Famine in 1943. The three agencies engaged in storing and warehousing are FCI, CWC and SWCs. The utilisation of the storage capacity of the FCI as of February 1999 was 67 per cent.[19] The FCI is the sole Central Government agency, which purchases, stores, transports and distributes foodgrains. But, since 1980, the FCI has confined its procurement to rice and wheat, while the National Agricultural Co-operative Marketing Federation handles coarse cereals.

Procurement, Storage and Buffer Stock in Sri Lanka

The buffer stock ensures the adequacy and availability of food supply to overcome any scarcities or emergencies. Sri Lanka's policy with regard to buffer stocking aims to maintain a minimum of one month's requirement in essential food –such as rice, flour and sugar – for distribution at times of scarcity.[20] Even though Sri Lanka is self-sufficient in rice, seasonal fluctuations in paddy production necessitate a proper buffer stock system to stabilise supplies and prices.

With the process of trade liberalisation under way, the responsibility for buffer stocking has shifted partly from the public sector to the private sector in Sri Lanka. The Food Commissioner's Department handles the stocking and distribution of wheat flour, while the private sector maintains rice and sugar. The government monitors the levels of buffer stock and the imports of rice, wheat flour, and sugar. Sri Lanka introduced Customs Bonded Warehouse System in 1989 to ensure an uninterrupted availability of rice and to maintain the reliability of food security through the private sector.[21]

TABLE 5.6

Percentage of Rice Procurement and Off-Ration Sales to Production in Sri Lanka

Year	*Production $*	*Procure-$ ment$*	*Percen-tage#*	*Off-Ration Sales$*	*Percen-tage#*
1971	9.49	6.81	71.79	—	—
1972	8.92	5.50	61.63	—	—
1973	8.92	4.78	53.58	0.04	0.73
1974	10.90	4.36	39.98	0.07	1.70
1975	7.85	2.42	30.79	0.06	2.37
1976	8.52	2.69	31.54	0.01	0.42
1977	11.40	5.12	44.94	0.03	0.61
1978	12.86	6.75	52.51	0.04	0.65
1979	13.04	5.41	41.52	0.15	2.69
1980	14.51	2.11	14.57	0.55	26.00
1981	15.16	1.97	13.00	0.64	32.26
1982	14.66	8.34	56.87	0.45	5.43
1983	16.89	8.04	47.63	0.78	9.70
1984	16.41	1.69	10.28	0.40	23.71
1985	18.06	0.98	5.44	0.09	8.81
1986	17.60	1.45	8.23	0.23	15.89
1987	14.47	1.53	10.57	0.21	13.44
1988	16.84	1.05	6.24	0.04	4.13
1989	14.03	0.50	3.60	—	0
1990	17.26	0.31	1.82	—	0

Note: # - Procurement as a percentage of Production, $ - Lakh Tons and * - Off-ration sales as a percentage of total procurement by PMB.

Source: Nutrition and Janasaviya Division, Food and Nutrition Statistics 1950-90, Ministry of Policy Planning & Implementation, Sri Lanka, Colombo, 1992.

In Sri Lanka, the production of rice has increased from 9.49 lakh metric tons in 1971 to 17.26 lakh metric tons in 1990. On the other hand procurement of rice has declined from 6.81 metric tons to 0.31 lakh metric tons during the same period. The procurement of rice has declined from 71.79 per cent in 1971 to 1.82 per cent in 1990. The procurement of rice has constantly declined over a period of time.

The off-ration sale of rice has gradually increased from 0.04 lakh metric tons in 1973 to 0.78 lakh metric tons in 1983, and thereafter declined to 0.04 metric tons in 1988. However, the off-ration sale of rice has increased sharply immediately after economic liberalisation in Sri Lanka. The targeting of rationing system has forced the PMB to sell a certain amount of its share of rice procured through co-operative outlets under off-ration sales up to 1987.

Public Distribution System in India

The necessity of launching the PDS at the all-India level was first considered in the wake of the Great Bengal Famine of 1943. But at regional level the PDS was initiated in 1939 for the first time in Bombay, when the famine came to be identified more with the prevalence of chronic hunger and under-nourishment. The PDS was, in fact, planned to tackle such a situation. Rationing was abolished immediately after Independence but was reintroduced in 1950 as shortage of foodgrain led to increase in prices.[22]

The PDS has developed through three different phases. The first phase (since Independence till the beginning of the Green Revolution in 1966) was concerned with safeguarding adequate supplies for urban people and the overall management of shortages through rationing and imports. In the second phase (1966-1980) supplies became comfortable, and the PDS was perceived as the consumer-oriented counterpart of public procurement programmes. In the third phase (since 1980's), the government launched wage-employment programmes or food for work programmes to ensure economic access to food.

The ration system, introduced as a result of food scarcity during this period evolved into the present PDS in the mid-1960s. It was characterised by near self-sufficiency in foodgrains production, the holding of huge buffer-stocks by the government, and the rapid expansion of the distribution outlets deep into rural areas of the country. The PDS has become a significant instrument of the government's policy of ensuring the availability of foodgrains to the public at affordable prices by regulating the open market prices of essential commodities and enhancing food security at the household level. The Fair Price Shops (FPS) and Ration Shops (RS) play a meaningful role in delivering household food and nutrition security. There were 50,523 FPSs and RSs in 1961 and this number had increased to 4,35,375 by 1996. The number of rations shops has been increased according to increase in the number of households. The PDS in India has a network of over 4 lakh fair price/ ration shops which serve 160 million families and is, perhaps, the largest such distribution network in the world. PDS is intended to translate the macro level self-sufficiency in foodgrains to micro level by ensuring access to food and other essential items to poor families. However, the PDS, as it was being implemented, has been widely criticised for its failure to reach the poor effectively, for urban bias and lack of transparency and accountability.

The food shortages result in high prices, which make it difficult for the poor to purchase adequate supplies. So the government's responsibility lies in the stabilisation of prices through the PDS. The PDS has emerged as an indispensable mechanism to ensure the availability of foodgrains at subsidised and affordable prices. This system is regarded as a safety net to compensate, to some extent, the loss in real incomes due to price rise during the initial periods of the Structural Adjustment Programme. Different phases of the PDS in India have been discussed in following sections.

TABLE 5.7

Number of Fair Price Shops / Ration Shops in India

Year	*Fair Price Shops/Ration Shops*	*Year*	*Fair Price Shops/Ration Shops*
1961	50523	1989	351802
1966	142815	1990	358490
1971	122038	1991	374799
1976	240210	1992	388500
1981	283560	1993	408596
1986	325081	1994	424865
1987	333467	1995	429557
1988	345191	1996	435375

Source: Directorate of Economics and Statistics, Bulletin on Food Statistics 1994-95, Ministry of Agriculture, Government of India, New Delhi, 1996.

The sale of rice under PDS had increased from 3.23 million tons in 1971 to 8.99 million tons in 2000. The share of PDS sale of rice had also increased from 7.65 per cent in 1971 to 10.05 in 2000, but the highest sale of 17.06 per cent was recorded in the year 1988. However, the PDS sale of wheat had declined from 18.72 per cent in 1971 to 9.71 per cent in 2000. There was a considerable difference between the share of rice and wheat distribution to the total production in India. Gradually the gap has narrowed down due to the fact that some states also started subsidised distribution of rice and wheat. Till 1992 the share of wheat distribution was higher than rice and there after rice, but after 1992 the distribution of rice under PDS has been higher than wheat. But, interestingly, over the period of time the overall distribution of rice and wheat under PDS, has marked a decline.

TABLE 5.8

Percentage of Rice and Wheat Distributed under PDS to Total Production in India

Year	*Production (Million Tons)*		*PDS as % of Production*	
	Rice	*Wheat*	*Rice*	*Wheat*
1971	42.23	23.83	7.65	18.72
1976	48.74	28.85	7.47	17.40
1981	53.63	36.31	11.93	17.71
1986	63.83	47.05	13.25	18.07
1987	60.56	44.32	16.23	19.81
1988	56.86	46.17	17.06	18.89
1989	70.49	54.11	12.34	14.14
1990	73.57	49.85	12.27	13.82
1991	74.29	54.52	15.22	16.76
1992	74.68	55.13	14.24	15.14
1993	72.87	57.21	14.23	10.22
1994	80.30	59.84	10.64	9.01
1995	81.16	65.47	12.11	8.60
1996	76.98	62.10	15.39	21.19
1997	81.74	69.35	14.23	14.17
1998	82.53	66.35	14.03	13.04
1999	86.08	71.29	14.20	12.20
2000	89.48	75.52	10.05	9.71

Source: Directorate of Economics and Statistics, Bulletin on Food Statistics, (various issues) Ministry of Agriculture, Government of India, New Delhi, 1996.

Integrated Tribal Development Project in India

In 1985, a scheme for the distribution of foodgrains at specially subsidised prices for the people living in Integrated Tribal Development Project areas and tribal-majority states was introduced. The FCI has since been supplying wheat and rice to these areas at special concessional prices, which are substantially below the PDS prices.

Revamped Public Distribution System in India

However, due to the unsatisfactory performance of foodgrains distribution and general concern about the welfare of people in neglected areas of India, the government was tempted to inaugurate the Revamped Public Distribution System (RPDS) in 1992. This programme covered in 1,775 Blocks under the Integrated Tribal Development Programme, Draught Prone Area Programme, Designated Hill Area, and Desert Development Programme. Under this programme, the state governments were to undertake the distribution of rice, wheat, sugar and kerosene, and some other items like tea, soap, pulses and iodised salt. In order to guarantee the increased availability of foodgrains in areas notified under the RPDS, an extra quantity of two million tonnes of foodgrains (rice and wheat) was allocated to states/union territories from the Central pool. The foodgrains distributed in RPDS areas are issued at prices, which are lower, by Rs.50 per quintal than the Central Issue Price (CIP) of the normal PDS. In these areas, foodgrains were released at a price held at a rupee per kilogram lower than the CPI to all families. The RPDS was launched in all the backward areas, irrespective of their economic status. The state governments have been advised to ensure that the retail prices of commodities in these blocks are not higher than the CIP by more than 25 paise/kg.

However, the RPDS could not fully achieve its objectives due to various reasons. It is also observed that the PDS is mostly urban-biased.[23] However, a study by Mahendra Dev and Suryanarayana shows that there are differences in urban bias across states and also in respect of commodities like rice and coarse cereals.[24] It was found to be rural-biased in the case of rice-producing states like Andhra Pradesh, Bihar, Gujarat, Kerala, Himachal Pradesh, Tamil Nadu and Tripura. Whether or not it served the rural or urban poor, in recent times its role as a safety net has narrowed due to increase in the issue prices of PDS commodities. The PDS suffers from poor targeting and the leakage of supplies to the open market, and subsidy to non-deserving beneficiaries to great extent.[25]

Targeted Public Distribution System (TPDS)

The importance of an effective PDS that ensures the availability of food at affordable prices at the household level for the poor can hardly be over emphasised. However, the PDS, as it stood earlier, was widely criticised for its failure to serve the population below the poverty line, its urban bias, negligible coverage in states with the highest concentration of the rural poor and the lack of transparent and accountable arrangements for delivery. Realising this, since 1997 the government had streamlined the PDS by issuing special cards to families to Below Poverty Line (BPL) and selling foodgrains under the PDS to them at specially subsidised prices.

The TPDS covers the really poor and vulnerable sections of society, such as landless agricultural labourers, marginal farmers, rural artisans/craftsmen – potters, tappers, weavers, blacksmiths, and carpenters. In rural areas it covers slum-dwellers and persons earning their livelihood on a daily basis in the informal sector like porters, rickshaw-pullers and hand-cart pullers, while in the urban areas it covers people like fruit and flower sellers on the pavements, etc. The TPDS is meant to cover the entire population falling below the poverty line.

Open Market Sale Scheme (Domestic) in India

The open-market sale of wheat and rice is undertaken by the government through the FCI, if considered necessary, in order to exert moderating influence on the open-market prices of wheat and rice without jeopardising the PDS. The important objectives of the scheme are to release the much-needed storage space in procurement season for rice and wheat; to reduce the transport costs of stocks held by the FCI; to control the open-market prices of rice and wheat; and, to reduce to some extent the food subsidy.

TABLE 5.9

Open Market Sale of FCI in India

(lakh ton)

Year	*Wheat*	*Rice*
1993-94	28.56	0.17
1994-95	50.29	4.54
1995-96	63.38	6.36
1996-97	41.65	2.54

Source: Lok Sabha Secretariat, Ninth Report, Standing Committee on Food, Civil Supplies and Public Distribution 1998-99, Government of India, New Delhi, 1999.

Import/Export of Foodgrains in India

The import/export policy of foodgrains is guided by a constant review of stock position of foodgrains *vis-à-vis* prescribed buffer stock norms, production, procurement trends, requirement for the PDS, and open market prices. The noteworthy objective of the FCI is to building up and maintains sizeable buffer stocks from imports and internal procurement as a measure of national food security. The sale of foodgrains by the FCI for export purposes is generally undertaken when the stocks are in excess of the requirements for the PDS and other welfare schemes. The import of foodgrains is discouraged to save foreign exchange and farmers are given incentives to produce more to gain self-sufficiency. The Department of Food and Civil Supplies and the Ministry of Commerce generally formulate a long-term export-import policy for foodgrains consistent with national food security.

Other Programmes

Besides the PDS, foodgrains are also released under Jawahar Rozgar Yojna, Employment Assurance Scheme, Employment Generation Scheme, Wheat-based Nutrition Programmes, supply of foodgrains at concessional rates to Scheduled Caste and Tribe / Other Backward Class hostels, and Mid-Day Meals Scheme. In recent years the Government of India launched new schemes. Under the *Antyodaya Anna Yojana*[26] programme 10 million poorest families would be identified out of 65.2 million BPL populations. They would be provided with 25 Kilogram of foodgrains per family per month at Rs.2 per Kilogram for wheat and Rs.3 per Kilogram for rice. The estimated annual allocation of foodgrains for *Antyodaya* families would be 30 lakh tonnes, involving a subsidy of Rs.2315 crores. *Annapurna Scheme*[27]provides 10 kilograms of foodgrains per person per month free of cost to Indigent senior citizens or persons under the National Old Age Pension Scheme. *Sampoorna Gramin Rozgar Yojana*[28] provides 5 million tonnes of foodgrains annually by the Centre free of cost for undertaking work programmes. Some of the other programmes of the Central Government are Food for Work Programme, Wheat Based Nutrition Programme, Scheme for Supply of Foodgrains to Scheduled

Caste / Scheduled Tribe / Other Backward Classes Hostels, Scheme for Supply of Foodgrains to Indigent Population living in Welfare Institutions, etc.[29]

Allocation and Off-take of Foodgrains

The Central Government maintains food stocks commensurate with the requirements of the minimum buffer stocks and operational stocks needed for the monthly release of foodgrains for PDS supplies. However, the system seems to be miserably failing as is evident from the off-take of foodgrains from the PDS (Table 5.10).

TABLE 5.10

Allocation and Off-take of Foodgrains Under PDS/TPDS in India

(Million Tons)

Year	*Rice*		*Wheat*	
	Allocation	*Off-take*	*Allocation*	*Off-take*
1991-92	11.36	10.17	10.36	8.83
1992-93	11.48	9.69	9.25	7.85
1993-94	12.41	9.10	9.56	6.09
1994-95	13.32	8.01	10.91	5.11
1995-96	14.61	9.75	11.32	5.81
1996-97	15.10	12.04	10.71	9.35
1997-98	12.83	9.90	10.11	7.08
1998-99	12.93	10.74	10.11	7.95
1999-00	13.84	11.31	10.37	5.76
2000-01	16.26	7.74	12.29	3.98

Source: Ministry of Finance, Economic Survey 2000-2001, Government of India, New Delhi.

The fall in the off-take of foodgrains in the PDS is due to an exorbitant rise in the Central Issue Price. The

Government has been fixing the Central Issue Price for rice and wheat from time to time to safeguard the interests of vulnerable sections. The term "issue price" refers to the ex-godown price for bagged grains issued from the Central Government stocks. The wholesale issue prices of rice and wheat are fixed by the Government after taking into account the procurement price, the consumer ability to pay, the impact on general price level, the prevailing open-market prices, the availability of the budgetary subsidies, and the cost of imported foodgrains. The state governments fix the retail issue prices through a network of FPS/RS to the end consumers. There is a great deal of spatial variation on retail prices for rice and wheat.

Table 5.11

Reason for Not / Part Purchase of Rice and Wheat from PDS in India

Reason	*Rural*		*Urban*	
	Rice	*Wheat*	*Rice*	*Wheat*
Not entitled/no ration card	7.76	4.32	16.76	11.18
Not required	35.69	60.91	14.95	39.96
Not available in ration shop	25.46	22.35	19.35	21.13
Quantity not satisfactory	5.30	2.35	19.55	15.85
Not available in sufficient quantity	14.84	1.79	22.28	4.68
Not available in sufficient small quantity	0.34	0.10	0.57	0.21
Credit purchase not possible	1.46	0.87	0.88	0.86
Others	8.40	6.18	4.92	5.05

Source: National sample Survey Organisation, Sarvekhana, Issue No. 43, Ministry of Statistics and Planning and Programme Implementation, Government of India, New Delhi, Vol. XIII, No.4, April-June 1990.

The main reason for the low off-take from the PDS is

that most households do not have the ration cards. Even in villages where every household has the ration card they have not been renewed for many years, thus lowering the entitlement of households. Now people are generally not interested in getting the ration cards, as most often the ration shops are closed or supplies not available. Even so, many of the households, despite having the ration cards are not getting their full quota as it is not being supplied. A drastic targeting of beneficiaries in both rural and urban areas is needed (Table 5.11).

Issue Prices in India

The Government of India fixes issue prices for releasing grain stocks from the central pool held by the FCI. The prices are usually subsidised to serve a social purpose by giving food to the vulnerable sections of society at cheaper rates. During the 1990s the FCI has been looking for profits, instead of running on "no profit no loss" basis. The subsidy arises from the fact that the total pooled expenditure including storage costs, interest, transport, and handling charges in public distribution are not fully recovered through sales at issue prices. These prices are designed to provide food to the vulnerable sections of the population at a rate cheaper than the prevailing market rate.

The issue price of rice had increased from Rs.150 per quintal in 1979 to Rs. 700 in 1999, while the issue price of wheat (PDS) had increased from Rs.130 per quintal to Rs. 650 during the same period. The percentage changes have not been showing any definite trend for rice and wheat. The issue price was increased around 30 per cent for rice in 1990-91 and 1997-99 and the highest of 44.44 per cent for wheat during 1997-99. The increase in issue price is another reason for reduced off-take in recent years.

TABLE 5.12

Issue Prices of Rice and Wheat in India

(Rs. per Quintal)

W.e.f.	*Rice*	*% Change*	*W.e.f.*	*PDS Wheat*	*% Change*
25.10.1979	150	—	01.12.1978	130	—
01.01.1981	165	10.00	01.12.1978	130	0.00
01.10.1981	175	6.06	01.04.1981	145	11.54
01.10.1982	188	7.43	01.08.1982	160	10.34
16.01.1984	208	10.64	15.04.1983	172	7.50
10.10.1985	217	4.33	10.08.1984	172	0.00
01.02.1986	231	6.45	01.02.1986	190	10.47
01.10.1986	239	3.46	01.04.1986	190	0.00
01.10.1987	239	0.00	16.17.1986	190	0.00
25.01.1989	244	2.09	25.03.1988	204	7.37
25.06.1990	289	18.44	01.05.1990	234	14.71
28.12.1991	377	30.45	28.12.1991	280	19.66
11.01.1993	437	15.92	11.01.1993	330	17.86
01.02.1994	537	22.88	01.02.1994	402	21.82
01.06.1997	537	0.00	01.06.1997	450	11.94
20.01.1999	700	30.35	20.01.1999	650	44.44

Source: Directorate of Economics and Statistics, Agricultural Statistics at a Glance 2000, Ministry of Agriculture, Government of India, New Delhi.

Food Distribution System in Sri Lanka

After Independence, the successive governments in Sri Lanka relied on different schemes to ensure food availability and accessibility at affordable prices to the whole population, namely Rationing Scheme, Guaranteed Price Scheme, Government Distribution System, Government Buffer Stocking System, Food Stamp Scheme (FSS), Poor Relief Scheme, etc. The essential feature of a proper food distribution scheme is the timely distribution of food items to locations where they are most needed and make this accessible to the needy people. In this regard the co-operatives play a major role in Sri Lanka.

The government food distribution system and the co-operative movement in Sri Lanka are inseparable. Until about 1977 the Food Commissioner's Department, with its countrywide wholesale supply centres, had distributed all food commodities through a network of retail co-operative outlets and private dealers registered with the Food Commissioner. The Food Commissioner's Department built up considerable food stocks through imports and from local procurement, and distributed them through the co-operative network of around 9,000 retail outlets spread across the country. Nearly 80 per cent of rice distributed in the country in 1976 was sold through the co-operatives and about 3,900 private distributors were authorised by the Food Commissioner. There was at least one private authorised distributor or one co-operative retail outlet for every 300 families in 1977 in the country, which ensured easy physical accessibility. Approximately 75 per cent of the income of the co-operatives was derived from the distribution of rice.

The importance of the co-operative distribution system has, however, been declining since liberalisation in Sri Lanka (Table 5.13). Only the number of Co-operative Wholesale Establishments increased from 87 to 109 during 1980-90. The disruption of food availability (mainly imports[30]) during World War II forced the then Sri Lankan government to establish the Food Commissioner's Department in 1942 and entrust it with the tasks of procurement, imports, storing and distribution of main food items such as rice, wheat flour, sugar, dhal, and milk. Essential food items were distributed equitably through the rationing scheme throughout the country. As the situation demanded, essential food items imported by the private sector were requisitioned and distributed through the co-operative network. Every household of the country was supplied with sufficient rations of grain and pulses through the organised co-operative network. The main objective of the co-operative distribution scheme was to ensure that food was made available to the people in a war situation.

TABLE 5.13

Number of Marketing Outlets of the Public Sector in Sri Lanka

Source / Year	*1980*	*1990*	*Growth Rate*
Co-operatives	8678*	289	-28.84
Retail Outlet	—	7488	—
Marketing Department Selling Centre	239	156	-4.18
Co-operative Wholesale Establishment	87	109	2.28
Markfed Selling Centres	9	9	0.00
Milk Board Branches	1167	706	-4.90
Total	10180	8468	-1.82

Note: *Multipurpose Co-operative Society includes retail outlet.

Source: Nutrition and Janasaviya Division, Food and Nutrition Statistics 1950-90, Ministry of Policy Planning & Implementation, Sri Lanka, Colombo, 1992.

In this situation of inadequate rice supplies, the guaranteed price scheme was implemented through the Marketing Department, which was established in 1935. The subsidisation of the consumer prices of food began in 1943 and the first commodity subsidised was rice; the subsidy was extended to other commodities. Further, in order to maintain the nutritional level of pre-school children the milk-feeding scheme was introduced in 1944.

The total availability of rice had increased from 12.88 lakh tons in 1971 to 18.98 lakh metric tons in 1990. However, rice distributed through Food Commissioner of Sri Lanka, under rationing scheme had declined from 8.81 lakh metric tons to 2.07 lakh metric tons during the same period. The share of distribution to total rice availability has declined gradually from 68.35 per cent in 1971 to 10.89 in 1990.

TABLE 5.14

Percentage of Rice Distributed under Ration to Total Availability in Sri Lanka

Year	*Availability (Lakh Ton)*	*Distribution (Lakh Ton)*	*Distribution as % of Availability*
1971	12.88	8.81	68.35
1972	11.58	7.93	68.46
1973	12.36	6.86	55.54
1974	13.91	5.59	40.18
1975	12.44	6.16	49.48
1976	12.77	6.12	47.89
1977	16.83	6.77	40.20
1978	14.55	5.73	39.40
1979	15.15	4.47	29.52
1980	16.40	2.80	17.05
1981	16.73	1.62	9.67
1982	16.27	1.55	9.53
1983	18.12	1.40	7.74
1984	16.67	1.68	10.08
1985	19.88	1.80	9.06
1986	19.80	1.74	8.77
1987	15.49	2.47	15.94
1988	17.20	2.25	13.06
1989	14.46	2.76	19.07
1990	18.98	2.07	10.89

Source: Nutrition and Janasaviya Division, Food and Nutrition Statistics 1950-90, Ministry of Policy Planning & Implementation, Sri Lanka, Colombo, 1992.

The policy of the government in the post-Independence period was to increase domestic food production and meet the deficit by imports. The distribution system was introduced to ensure that food was available to every household through a rationing scheme to maintain nutritional status. All the households, irrespective of income levels, were provided with ration books and rice was issued at subsidised prices. Many food items[31] were brought under the guaranteed price scheme; their prices were raised several times to encourage an increase in production with a view to reducing the imports.

TABLE 5.15

Government Expenditure on Subsidies and Transfers as a Percentage of Gross Domestic Product in Sri Lanka

Year	*Subsidies & Transfers*		
	*Household**	*Pensions*	*Total*
1988	4.0	1.9	5.8
1989	4.8	1.9	6.8
1990	4.6	1.4	6.5
1991	5.4	2.4	6.9
1992	4.5	1.9	5.6
1993	4.5	2.1	5.4
1994	4.9	2.3	5.9
1995	4.4	2.2	6.1
1996	4.2	2.0	6.0

Note: * Includes wheat subsidy.

Source: Central Bank of Sri Lanka, Review of Economy (various issues).

The policy of food subsidy underwent its first change after the introduction of income criteria to determine the eligibility for ration rice. The provision of free ration rice was withdrawn for income tax payers and dependants, and most middle-level wage earners came into this category. A scheme to cross subsidise rice with wheat flour and sugar was also introduced. The government expenditure on household subsidy almost remained stable at around 4.5 per cent of the GDP except in 1991 (5.4 per cent), mostly involving wheat (Table 5.15).

The growing domestic paddy production warranted the need for an organisation to handle the procurement and distribution of paddy and rice. It resulted in the creation of the PMB in 1971 empowered to procure paddy from farmers at guaranteed price through Multi-purpose Co-operative Societies and deliver it after milling to the Food Commissioner for the release of rice under the rationing scheme. The primary objective of the PMB is to improve paddy production through guaranteed price, purchase more rice for the rationing scheme, reduce rice imports, and save public funds by cutting imports.

Early in 1978, the 35 year-old government monopoly on the distribution of rice, sugar and wheat flour underwent a change, and private imports and distribution were permitted. The private sector was entrusted to play a major role in food distribution. It was encouraged to engage in food commodities business including purchasing, processing and food marketing. The buffer stock maintenance of essential commodities, hitherto a government responsibility, was transferred to the private sector under the Customs Bonded Warehouse Scheme. However, the Food Commissioner was entrusted with the task of monitoring the quantities imported and the maintenance of minimum stock levels. With the launch of the Customs Bonded Warehouse Scheme, consumers turned to the private distribution system. In 1990, the private sector was allowed to import the total requirement of rice under the Customs Bonded Scheme.

Food Stamp Scheme in Sri Lanka

The rice rationing in Sri Lanka remained in force until 1978. After 1978, the government decided to replace rationing with an eligibility criterion. This criterion stipulated that only households of five persons or more, earning less than Rs 300 per month, would be eligible for rice subsidies under the Food Stamp Scheme (FSS). The value of a food stamp was about Rs.18 per capita per month.[32] (Their nominal value was kept constant and thus their real value was somewhat less). With the shift from rice rationing to food stamps, the distinction between the market price of rice and the equivalent consumer cost virtually disappeared. And because of the steep fall in the international price of rice between 1982 and 1986, the non-poor consumers (or, more accurately, those who did not qualify for food stamps) paid more than the international price of rice. In 1987, the government adopted a sliding scale based on family size to determine eligibility. All members of a household received stamps if the family income was below Rs 300 per month, but only two members received stamps if the income fell in the range of Rs 600-700 per month. According to the World Bank country report for 1988 the number of stamp recipients has stayed approximately the same (about 7.3 million) although targeting appears to have improved somewhat.

In 1978, a significant reduction in the number of beneficiaries was effected through the revalidation of ration books by withdrawing the free ration from families whose incomes crossed the cut-off point. A further modification in the FSS was introduced in September 1979, enabling eligible households to purchase one or more of a basket of commodities consisting of rice, paddy, flour, bread, sugar, locally produced pulses, lakspray, vitamilk, parakum condensed milk, dried fish and kerosene[33]. A major change under this system was that the entitlement of subsidy was based on rupee term instead of commodity term as implemented earlier. This proved to be disadvantageous to beneficiaries in the context of rising prices, as it drastically reduced the benefit to poorer segments of the population and hit the food distribution pattern.

The introduction of FSS was based on total household incomes. Those households consisting of five or less members receiving an income of Rs.300 or less per month were entitled to food stamps. The value of the food stamps was initially fixed at Rs.25 per month for children aged below eight, Rs.20 for each child over eight and below 12 and Rs.15 for a household member above 12 years. Each individual family eligible for food stamps also received kerosene stamps at the rate of Rs.9.50 per month. Food and kerosene stamps were issued every three months except for the sixth issue, which was issued for a period of six months. Table 5.16 shows the number of food stamps issued from 1979 to 1990. In the first issue 72.21 lakh food stamps were distributed of which 70.35 per cent have been given to age 12 years and above. The lowest of 66.11 lakh food stamps were distributed in the 10th Issue as compared to the highest of 80.52 lakhs in 1989 (20th Issue). The percentage share of beneficiaries in the age group 8-12 years were more or less constant from First issue to 21st Issue. The percentage share of beneficiaries has fluctuated among the age groups below 8 years and above 12 years during the period 1979-90.

TABLE 5.16

Number of Food Stamps Issued in Sri Lanka

Issue No.	*Period*	*No. of Stamps Issued (lakh)*	*Percentage of Stamps Issued*		
			Age <8 years	*Age 8-12 years*	*Age 12+ years*
1st Issue	1.09.1979	72.21	18.64	11.51	70.35
2nd Issue	1.12.1979	72.77	20.84	11.17	68.00
3rd Issue	1.03.1980	75.80	20.30	10.40	66.67
4th Issue	1.06.1980	74.01	20.46	10.56	69.11
5th Issue	1.09.1980	74.41	20.07	10.49	69.44
6th Issue	1.12.1980	74.20	19.64	10.49	69.86
7th Issue	1.06.1981	73.57	18.50	10.45	71.05
8th Issue	1.12.1981	73.28	17.08	10.41	77.97
9th Issue	1.06.1982	72.13	15.35	10.45	74.20
10th Issue	1.11.1982	66.11	14.54	11.43	81.76
11th Issue	1.06.1983	71.18	12.42	10.61	76.97
12th Issue	1.12.1983	70.59	11.11	10.62	79.68
13th Issue	1.06.1984	70.01	9.71	10.39	79.80
14th Issue	1.12.1984	69.53	8.48	10.54	80.87
15th Issue	1.06.1985	68.96	7.10	10.45	82.46
16th Issue	1.12.1985	68.54	5.78	10.56	83.64
17th Issue	1986	70.25	24.53	10.45	69.31
18th Issue	1987	73.63	21.21	13.59	67.92
19th Issue	1988	77.04	19.97	10.77	68.21
20th Issue	1989	80.52	17.42	10.52	70.58
21st Issue	1990	70.03	16.26	11.45	72.26

Source: Nutrition and Janasaviya Division, Food and Nutrition Statistics 1950-90, Ministry of Policy Planning & Implementation, Sri Lanka, Colombo, 1992.

The government distribution system ensured the availability of basic food only to food stamp recipients. As the food stamp subsidy was based on rupee term the value of food stamps dropped annually in terms of food prices. This seriously affected the nutritional health of the poor. Therefore, in order to help the food stamp recipients to cope the adverse inflationary trends, the government introduced a new scheme *viz.* the Poor Relief Scheme, and the administration of this scheme was subsequently transferred from the Food Commissioner's Department to the Social Service Department. Under the Poor Relief Scheme the poverty line cut-off point was raised from Rs. 300 to Rs.700.

Despite the coverage of half the population by food stamps, the government's decision not to index the value of these stamps to prices made the programme ineffective as a "safety net". In periods of sharp price increases (such as in the early 1980s) the per capita calorie consumption of the lowest decile fell to an unprecedented level of 1,221 calories in 1980-81 and 1,181 calories in 1981-82. The contrast was sharp: the consumption level for this decile stood at 1,335 calories per capita in 1978-79 at the inception of the food stamps programme, against 2,013 calories per capita in 1969-70 during the ration programme.[34] Overall, the impact of the social policy for the poor was rather complex. Starting from a relatively favourable base year of 1970, a sharp deterioration evidently took place in the 1973-75 period.

Death rates increased in 1974-1975 – perhaps resulting from acute food shortages and high food prices caused by drought, which could not be ameliorated fully by the ration system. The estate sector as a whole in which living standards have been traditionally much low was particularly affected by food shortages and rising mortality, particularly in the context of a disruption caused by the land reforms in 1972 and 1975.[35] The food stamps and other nutritional programmes contributed only 20 per cent of the low per capita daily consumption of the poor at 1,865 calories in 1982 compared with 44 per cent of 2,072 calories in 1973.[36]

The targeting of services to beneficiaries was attempted for the first time and the 'in kind' food transfer was converted into a non-indexed food stamps scheme. This removed the 'safety net' from the poor whose incomes did not keep pace with the contemporary high level of inflation.[37]

As part of its general emphasis on restricting current expenditures, the adjustment strategy focused on the benefit to be derived from targeting; it confined food subsidies, which had reached 5.4 per cent of the GDP by 1979 to the poor and those adversely affected by the adjustment process. In January 1978 the rice ration, which had been freely available to the entire population for 36 years was restricted to 6,857 million persons in households with annual incomes of less than Rs.3,600 per annum. Since 1986 food stamps have been issued under the Poor Relief Scheme on a scale graded according to family incomes with an upper limit of Rs.8,400 per annum.

The value of stamps was initially determined to provide the same basket of goods as ration holders had been receiving at the time of the conversion. However, in January 1980, as part of the structural adjustment strategy's emphasis on the correction of price distortions, the price of basic commodities was allowed to rise in accordance with market forces.

The gradual rise in prices thereafter eroded the real value of the income transfers. This reduced the food subsidy burden on the Budget from 13.9 per cent in 1979 to 4.6 per cent in 1982 and 2.1 per cent in 1990. The share of social expenditure in general, and food subsidy in particular, in the government Budget declined in the first half of the 1980s – from 26 per cent in 1980 to 17 per cent in 1984.

Summary

The extensive public distribution system, employment generation, food for work and nutritious noon meal programmes play an important role in India and Sri Lanka ensuring food security at the household level. Rural works programmes are probably the most popular measures aiming directly to improve the welfare of the poorest segments of the agricultural population.

In Sri Lanka, '*in kind*' food transfer was converted into food stamps scheme in 1978, which removed the safety net from the consumption of the poor whose income did not keep pace with high levels of inflation. The Tamil insurgency in Sri Lanka has prompted a further evolution of social policy towards combining social and economic aspects of development within the purview of one targeted, time-bound programme, the *Janasaviya (*income supporting programme*)*.

Finally, all programmes have been integrated into the *Samurdhi* package since 1995. The safety net programmes should be seen as a package because of the complementarities of programmes. The eligibility criteria and amounts of entitlements as part of the "transfers to the truly needy" should be reviewed and the amounts, possibly raised.

In India, the subsidised public food distribution system still functions, attaining certain targets. But the best way to protect the most vulnerable sections is through safety nets based on targeting. Thus, the objective of resource transfer to the needy through supply of subsidised essential items has not been fully achieved in India. Targeting or limiting the beneficiaries of the subsidised programme and confining it to the poor and nutritionally vulnerable have to be made administratively and politically feasible. Over the past five decades, both India and Sri Lanka have provided fairly consistent financial support to the public food distribution programmes. This has led to a relatively better availability of nutrition to the population.

The buffer stock plays a principal consumer price stabilisation role to defend retail foodgrain prices in both the countries. In India, Food Corporation of India plays an important role to procure, store and distribute the foodgrains. In Sri Lanka, Paddy Marketing Board procures the paddy and the Food Commissioner Office distributes the rice.

In India, ration system has been changed into revamped public distribution system and subsequently into targeted food distribution system for the population below poverty line. The policy implication of this research is that ideally targeted public distribution system should be delivered through Panchayats or Co-operative Societies or Non-Governmental Organisations, which should deal with goods of common use also at reasonable prices if the system is preferred to continue as a poverty alleviation programme in India. This will ensure the opening of the ration/fair price shops every day, and also making them more viable. This will reduce the dependence of the weaker sections upon the market. In India, in the light of the experience gained during the implementation of TPDS, various programmes, such as identification of the beneficiaries, functioning of the fair price / ration shops, and effectiveness of the vigil by panchayats need to be scrutinised at the level of implementation to bring out their policy implications. However, in Sri Lanka, the free ration system has been changed into income subsidy through food stamps and subsequently into a cash income transfer scheme to the poor population.

Economic development and a food distribution system that reach the broadest possible spectrum of India and Sri

Lanka's population are essential to achieving sustainable national food security. By and large, however, achieving national food security will depend on a large private sector, and a free market that brings variety of nutritious food to the widest possible number of people at the lowest possible cost. This will require a good marketing network that underpins economic development, provides widespread, reliable access to food. Public sector assistance, therefore, must be effectively targeted to stimulate and facilitate private sector activity and to address pockets of poverty in India and Sri Lanka that are being left behind by the upswing in free market activity.

In India, an increase in the proportion of households reporting availability of adequate food, throughout the year, has been observed for the period 1983 to 1993-94, in both rural and urban areas. During this period, the proportion of such households has increased from 81.1 per cent to 94.5 per cent for rural and from 93.3 per cent to 98.1 per cent for urban India respectively. Safety net systems are needed for those sections, which absolutely cannot function for themselves within the social and economic environment in which they exit. Where applicable, forest-based livelihoods can combine income generation, food supplies, and multiple services to human communities with environmental protection based on sustainable management. The strengthening of the markets should reduce price margins between consumers and farmers.

REFERENCES

1. Government of India, Report of the National Commission on Agriculture Part II-Policy and Strategy, (New Delhi, 1976), p. 81.
2. D.S.Sidhu, "Measures to Enhance the Efficiency of Agricultural Marketing Systems: Case of India", In Asian Productivity

Organisation, Seminar Report, Marketing Systems for Agricultural Products, (Tokyo, 1997), p. 13.

3. R.W. Cummings Jr, Pricing Efficiency in the Indian Wheat Market, (New Delhi, 1967), p. 45.
4. A.C. Juneja, "India", In Asian Productivity Organisation, Seminar Report, Marketing Systems for Agricultural Products, (Tokyo, 1997), p. 187.
5. D.S. Tyagi, Managing India's Food Economy, (New Delhi, 1990), p. 240.
6. Ministry of Agriculture, Report of the Enquiry Committee, Collection of Agricultural Prices in India, (New Delhi, 1954), p. 15.
7. In Sri Lanka, Paddy Marketing Board and Department of Food involve in procurement, storage, milling , transportation and distribution of foodgrains.
8. W.D. Wickramasinghe, "Government Intervention in Rice Market", Economic Review, Vol. 24, nos. 10-12, (1999), p. 12.
9. These districts produce more than 50 per cent of the total paddy production in Sri Lanka.
10. The Multi-purpose Co-operative Societies of Sri Lanka was started in 1957.
11. T. A. Dharmaratne and others, "Paddy/Rice Marketing: Perspectives and Prospects in 90s", EconomicRreview, Vol. 24, nos. 10-12, (1999), p. 9.
12. D. S. Sidhu, n.2, p. 112.
13. G. Parthasarathy, "Rural Markets: Pricing of Agricultural Products and Regulation of Markets", Indian Journal of Agricultural Marketing, Vol. 8, No. 2. (New Delhi, 1994).
14. D.S. Sidhu, n.2, p. 116.
15. Ram Saran, "Recent Changes in Food Policy", Agricultural Situation in India, (New Delhi,1971), p. 17.
16. Pre-emptive purchases of wheat are made when procurement tends to be extremely low as a result of two or three successive years of low production. The general approach is that most procurement, particularly of wheat, is voluntary.

17. P.S. George, Government Interventions in Foodgrains Markets, (Ahmedabad, 1985), p. 13.
18. Lester R. Brown, The Agricultural Link: How Environmental Deterioration Could Disrupt Economic Progress, (Washington, 1997), p. 16.
19. Lok Sabha Secretariat, Ninth Report, Standing Committee on Food, Civil Supplies and Public Distribution, (New Delhi, 1999), p. 33.
20. N.B. Liyanarachchi, "Food security and Food distribution", Economic Review, Vol. 23, nos.1 & 2, (1997), p. 8.
21. Food Commissioner's Department, Annual Report 1990, Colombo, 1991), p. 5.
22. Lok Sabha Secretariat, n.19, p. 56.
23. D.S.Tyagi, n.5, p. 216.
24. S.M. Dev and M.H Suryanarayana, "Is PDS Urban Biased and Pro-rich: An Evaluation", Economic and Political Weekly, Vol. 26, No. 4, (1991), pp. 2357-66.
25. D.S. Sidhu, n.2, p. 112.
26. Antyodaya Anna Yojana was launched in December 2000.
27. Annapurna Scheme was launched in 2000-01.
28. Sampoorna Gramin Rozgar Yojana was launched in August 2001.
29. Economic Survey 2001-2002, Government of India, Ministry of Finance, New Delhi, p. 128.
30. Rice imports from Burma and Japan, and Wheat from India, Egypt and Brazil.
31. The GPS covers Paddy, Maize, Gingelly, Sorghum, Mustard, Chillies, Green Gram, Tamarind, Black Pepper, Coffee.
32. Neville, Edirisinghe, The Food Stamp Program in Sri Lanka: Costs, Benefits, and Policy Options for Modifications, Research Report 58, (Washington, D.C., 1985), p. 17.
33. Ministry of Policy and Planning and Implementation, Food and Nutrition Statistics,1950-1990, (Colombo, 1992), p. 97.
34. W.D. Lakshman, ed., Dilemmas of Development; Fifty Years of Economic Change in Sri Lanka, (Colombo, 1997), p. 165.

35. *Ibid.*, p. 170.
36. P. Alailima, Evolution of Government Policies and Expenditure on Social Welfare in Sri Lanka during the 20th Century, (Colombo, 1985), p. 5.
37. W.D. Lakshman, n.30, p. 170.

6

Conclusion

This study attempted to piece together a comparative analysis of food security issues in South Asia in general, and India and Sri Lanka in particular. The achievement and maintenance of self-sufficiency in major food crops still continues as the main objective in South Asian region.

South Asian countries have shown a fair agricultural performance since 1961. A comparison of data on cropped area shows that Sri Lanka has increased its area by 0.18 per cent per annum as against 0.15 per cent in India during 1961 to 1997. Among the major inputs, irrigated coverage shows a relatively steady increase in all South Asian countries. Nepal's growth level of irrigated area during 1961 to 1997 has been quite impressive. Pakistan has better coverage of irrigation than all other SAARC nations since 1961. Thus, the intensification of production in irrigated agriculture played an important role in achieving and maintaining national food security in the past, and must continue to do so in future. India has attained the level of self-sufficiency in domestic production of foodgrains, while Sri Lanka is about to attain it. The possible solution to ensure and sustain the future food security, i.e., the watershed development in rainfed areas, is suited as the best alternative rather than "high-cost-low-benefit" irrigation projects.

The cropping pattern is also an important element of food security in South Asia. The share of area under cereal cultivation had shown an increase from 1961 to 2000. However, the area under coarse cereal had shrunk during the same period in India, Maldives, Pakistan and Sri Lanka. This is a matter of concern due to the fact that coarse cereals are the main food items of the poor people in rainfed areas in South Asia. Similarly, the share of area under pulses production has been declining in Bhutan, India and Pakistan. Only Sri Lanka was able to increase the area under pulse cultivation at the rate of 5.43 per cent annually. However, the production of coarse cereals has been declining over the years because of the changing crop composition of foodgrain output and consumption in favour of superior or costlier cereals and against coarse cereals.

It has been observed that all South Asian countries have increased their areas under cultivation of food crops from 1961 to 2000. It has proved the hypothesis, a higher diversification of food crops in agriculture is positively correlated with food security. The growth level variations of harvested area are not as impressive as production and yield of major crops in South Asia. Smaller countries such as Bhutan and Nepal have performed relatively better than the economically better off nations like India, Pakistan and Sri Lanka. The population explosion has had a negative impact on per capita cropland in all countries, except Sri Lanka which has been following comparatively better and more effective family planning programmes.

Going by conventional measures of food security, namely physical and economic access, there has been a substantial improvement in food security in all South Asian countries. A comparison of the growth rate between the pre-green revolution period (1961-65) and post-green revolution period (1966 to 2000) shows a modest variation in acceleration in production and productivity. Analysis shows that most of the yield-based growth came from wheat and rice, and particularly wheat, the average yield of which increased between the pre and post-green revolution periods. India registered a higher growth rate in cereal and paddy production than all other countries. The increasing trend in per capita paddy production has been registered only in India, Pakistan and Sri Lanka during 1961 to 2000. However, in case of paddy Sri Lanka recorded a better per capita production than India during the same period. The level of per capita food production has risen significantly in India and Pakistan. It indicates that higher food production per capita is positively related to food security in India, Pakistan and Sri Lanka.

India has food self-sufficiency in cereals as compared to other countries in the sub-continent. This is amply reflected in smaller volume of cereal imports, equivalent to 1.03 per cent of the domestic supply.

The Green Revolution technologies have been remarkably successful in creating new high yielding varieties of rice in India and Sri Lanka, and wheat in India grown on irrigated land. Interestingly, the Green Revolution has not shown similar success with improved varieties of coarse cereals applicable to rainfed areas in India and Sri Lanka. Thus, given the diversity of crops grown in India and Sri Lanka on rainfed land, a standard technological package is required to enhance productivity of such crops.

In India and Sri Lanka, several incentives were offered to farmers with a view to increase the food production. These were improved seed distribution through agriculture extension workers, fertiliser at subsidised rates and agricultural credit to facilitate farmers to adopt improved methods of management of their crops. India, which provides substantial subsidies to wheat and rice production, has now become the second largest rice and wheat producer in the world.

Agricultural policies in general and food policy in particular, therefore, should be designed to facilitate food security by providing guidance for positive adjustment. The conventional supply-side food policy instruments are broadly classified into self-sufficiency and price stability. A range of policies, including size of holdings, producer prices, inputs, credit, fertilisers, marketing, processing and agro-industries, research, and irrigation promotes domestic food production. The important instrument of price stability is the buffer stock system to control retail prices. The major policies of demand side are nutritional status and policy instruments. The important component of the nutritional status is the construction of a national food balance-sheet through household income-expenditure surveys. The policy instruments to provide entitlements are food subsidies, employment generation, food-for work programmes, and cash transfers.

In India and Sri Lanka there are different sets of policies to ensure food security. The agricultural supply policies are related to food production which includes subsidised inputs – irrigation, fertilisers, seeds, and credit. The demand factor includes poverty alleviation programmes and income generation programmes.

The food policy in India evolved since the Bengal famine of 1943, and in Sri Lanka since the introduction of rationing scheme in 1942, has proved successful and enhanced national food security with the help of different policies. In fact, both India and Sri Lanka are managing food economy reasonably well, looking after the lean years of production as well as years of surplus, through the buildup maintenance and timely utilisation of a sizable buffer-stock of rice and wheat in a manner which could bring credit to the Food Corporation of India in India, and to Paddy Marketing Board in Sri Lanka, in terms of magnitude of the task, in both physical and financial terms.

Several policy measures have been enacted in India and Sri Lanka to reduce adverse effects of weather on farm incomes. These include comprehensive crop insurance schemes, the advance payment plan, foodgrain reserves, and income support measures.

Incentive prices in the form of Minimum Support Prices in India and Guaranteed Price Scheme in Sri Lanka were very important instruments to control the open market prices and ensure food security. However, in Sri Lanka the Guaranteed Price Scheme's importance has declined considerably due to liberalisation, while in India, the Commission for Agricultural Costs and Prices and Food Corporation of India provide institutional support for implementation of price policy.

Market-oriented policies provide an environment for economic growth, which is the major instrument of poverty alleviation and increased food security. It can be an intensification of the "food for work" programmes, targeted programmes, and emergency relief to cover only urban non-farm labourers, small and marginal farmers and landless agricultural workers. The important income generation programmes in India are Integrated Rural Development Programme, National Rural Employment Programme, Rural Landless Employment Guarantee Programme, Jawahar Rozgar Yojana, Employment Assurance Scheme, etc. In Sri Lanka the programmes are

Integrated Rural Development Programme, Janasaviya Samurdhi, etc. The Mid-Day Meals Scheme also provides individual (School Children) food security in both the countries. As a step forward in this direction, India and Sri Lanka should develop research on promotional and regulatory services and economic programmes to ensure household and individual food security rather than national food security.

The overall pattern of demand for foodgrains will be heavily influenced by population growth, increases in income and price variation both in India and Sri Lanka. The rise in per capita income is unlikely to create much additional demand for cereals. Nevertheless, population growth and per capita income will be dominant determinants of the growth in cereal demand in the coming years. Therefore, this study considers the demographic basis of growth in future cereal demand as of primary importance. The annual rate of population growth in India has been higher than in Sri Lanka. The rate of urbanisation is comparatively lower in Sri Lanka than in India. As expected, the crude birth and death rates were reported to be higher in India than in Sri Lanka. The population migration from rural to urban areas in India is increasing, but in Sri Lanka it shows a declining trend.

The average household income has risen in India and Sri Lanka since the 1950s, as a result of which the structure of demand for food has become much more diverse. As income rises there tends to be lower relative consumption of rice, increased preference for wheat and its products like bread, and increased demand for vegetables, fruits, fish and meat. Such developments are the result of increased urbanisation, growing communications, and changing employment patterns.

In India, rural households receive the highest percentage (46 per cent) of household income from agricultural and allied activities whereas in Sri Lanka it is only 9.5 per cent. In India, the share of income from wages and salaries (57 per cent) is the highest source of urban households. In Sri Lanka 44.1 per cent of rural households receive income from wages and salaries as compared to 49.4 per cent urban households. In Sri Lanka, rural households receive 2.9 per cent of the household income as transfer payments made by the government under the Janasaviya and Samurdhi programmes. It is the difference in household income composition that ultimately determines the consumption pattern in rural and urban areas both in India and Sri Lanka.

The share of expenditure on basic items like rice and wheat flour declined steadily while that on fish increased. The diversification of food expenditure in both the countries clearly indicates a shift towards more nutritious food security. However, these changes in expenditure could also be the result of changing relative prices. The prices of foodgrains determine the demand for food in India and Sri Lanka.

In the case of Sri Lanka, it could be argued that a sharp reduction in the administered prices of wheat flour and bread have contributed to a shift from rice to bread and also wheat flour. Even though the Sri Lankan government has removed the flour subsidy, the per capita consumption rose moderately, possibly due to its relative price advantage over rice.

Thus, a shift in consumption patterns away from rice could in principle add substantially to the amount of calories available for meeting basic needs in India and Sri Lanka. The most pronounced effects on shifts in demand for individual cereals come from changing tastes as income rise. This is most evident in the growth of 'derived' demand for cereals used as cattle feed. Most of cereals are used as cattle feeds depending on local availability, tradition and relative prices.

Although India and Sri Lanka have shown a remarkable progress in other social indicators, the increase in per capita calorie availability had risen from 2,070 and 2,075 for India and Sri Lanka in 1961 to 2,496 and 2,302 in 1997 respectively. In India the per capita calorie was lower than Sri Lanka from 1962 to 1988. But after 1989 the per capita calorie availability in India was higher than Sri Lanka.

In India, cereal accounted for 82.43 per cent of daily total calorie intake in 1983 but it declined to 78.48 per cent in 1993-94 in rural areas; in urban areas the daily calorie intake from cereals have declined from 69.43 to 67.28 during the same period. In Sri Lanka, cereal accounted for 55.98 per cent of daily total calorie intake in 1986-87 and it increased to 57.90 per cent by 1996-97. In Sri Lanka, rice was the dominant source of energy accounting for 44 per cent of the total calorie intake in 1996-97. In the estate sector of Sri Lanka, wheat flour was the second largest source of daily energy requirement. But the urban households in both the countries derive a comparatively higher proportion of energy from meat, fish and milk products.

The per capita consumption is a realistic indicator of rice and wheat. It provides a reasonable assessment of household food security in India and Sri Lanka, where the per capita quantity consumption of cereals, especially rice and wheat. has been gradually increasing over a period of time.

Further, in both India and Sri Lanka there has been an improvement in total income and expenditure which is amply reflected in increases in their per capita consumption. However, even though income or consumption-expenditure shows an increase in income and economic access, this has not been so in reality with increased market dependence and changing consumption patterns in favour of costlier superior cereals which is dictated largely by availability rather than by choice.

Over the past five decades, both India and Sri Lanka have provided fairly consistent financial support to the public food distribution programmes. This has led to a relatively better nutrition to the population which is largely due to free and subsidised access in both countries. It depicts that the better targeting of food distribution system in both countries, and hence increases food security. The extensive public distribution system, employment generation, food for work and nutritious noon meal programmes play an important role, ensuring food security at the household level. Rural works programmes are probably the most popular measure aiming directly to improve the welfare of the poorest segments of the agricultural population.

Buffer stock operations play a major role in price stabilisation at the retail level both in India and Sri Lanka. In India, Food Corporation of India plays an important role to procure, store and distribute the foodgrains. In Sri Lanka, Paddy Marketing Board procures the paddy and the Food Commissioner Office distributes the rice.

In India the public distribution system still functions, but with more focus on target groups. Targeting or limiting beneficiaries of the subsidised programme to the poor and nutritionally vulnerable has to be made administratively and politically feasible. Besides ration system has been changed into revamped public distribution system and subsequently into targeted food distribution system for the population below poverty line. The policy implication of this study is that ideally targeted public distribution system should be delivered through panchayats or co-operative societies or non-governmental organizations or self-help groups, which should deal with goods of common use at reasonable prices if it is preferred to continue as a poverty alleviation programme in India. This will ensure the opening of the ration/fair price shops every day and also making these shops more viable. This will reduce the market dependence of the weaker sections. In India, in the light of the experience gained during the implementation of Public Distribution System, various other programmes, such as identification of the beneficiaries, functioning of the fair price/ration shops, and effectiveness of the vigil by panchayats need to be scrutinised at the level of implementation. The mounting excessive stocks of foodgrains much above the levels required for distribution, have led to elimination of private trade and higher commitments for food subsidy. One of the reasons for excessive stocks was due to higher procurement and poor off-take under Targeted Public Distribution System in recent years. Higher procurement prices edge out private trade thus causing Food Corporation of India to procure more than what is required. The Below Poverty Level quota should be increased from the existing 20 kg. per family. Employment generation should be expanded for creating an effective demand for foodgrains. Foodgrain management policy requires both short-term as well as long-term policy changes to meet the situation of emerging surpluses and wastage.

But in Sri Lanka, the free ration system has been converted into income subsidy through food stamp scheme and subsequently into a cash income transfer scheme to the poor population. In Sri Lanka, "*in kind*" food transfer was converted into food stamps scheme in 1978. This removed the safety net from the consumption of the poor, whose incomes did not keep pace with high levels of inflation. Further, evolution of social policy towards combining social and economic aspects of development within the purview of one targeted, time-bound programme, the *Janasaviya* (income supporting programme) has been in operation. Finally, since 1995 all programmes have been integrated into the *Samurdhi* package. The safety net programmes should be seen as a package because of the complimentarities of programmes

Economic development and a food distribution system which can reach the broadest possible spectrum of India and Sri Lanka's population are essential to achieving sustainable national food security. By and large, however, achieving national food security will depend on a large private sector and a free market that bring variety of nutritious food to the maximum possible number of people at the lowest possible cost. This will require a good marketing network that underpins economic development, provides widespread and reliable access to food. South Asian countries should assist each other by giving priority of acquisition in respect of foodgrains by strengthening the Food Reserve System to reduce the malnourished population.

India and Sri Lanka should formulate village subsidy programmes to stimulate economic activities in the rural areas by improving rural infrastructures or rural public works such as roads, and small irrigation dams and bridges, in order to ensure food security. Effective and efficient utilisation of food is also considered an essential component of food security today. Addressing food security in both these countries, therefore, requires comprehensive measures that integrate ongoing assistance in several areas: land reform, application of new research including biotechnology and modern farming methods to increase yield and reduce losses; empowerment of women, stabilisation of population, improvement of health and nutrition, education and technological training and assurance of adequate safety nets for periods of adjustment.

The food prospects of India and Sri Lanka are not without some limited promise. Population growth rates are generally falling, while production of foodgrain and irrigation capacity can be utilised effectively especially by undertaking watershed projects in rainfed areas. There seems to be greater diversity in the of expenditure pattern, i.e., the increase in the spending of marginal income on non-food items which previously would have been spent on food. The major concern of food security is that food may not be fairly distributed between all needy households and individual especially malnourished children, lactating and pregnant women, etc. This could be rationalised through supplementary income schemes to increase the purchasing power of the deprived households in the rural and urban areas to secure more food and calorie requirement.

The role of the governments in relation to food supply during the last five decades reflects some of the more important aspects of policy formulation, and the broad objectives towards which welfare policies in India and Sri Lanka have continued to be directed. It seems clear, for instance, that since independence food policy in both the countries was, to a large extent, guided directly by electoral considerations. Food policy could not be easily ignored in policy formulation due to the fact that the concept of food security has become a priority expectation of the people.

Thus, in the wider context of intensifying poverty, food subsidy reappeared at the forefront of political issues. It becomes evident that a food subsidy programme as a policy may be good for the present population but bad for economic growth and hence for the welfare of the future population.

Appendices

APPENDIX I

Food Production Index in South Asia (1989-91=100)

Year	*South Asia*	*Bangla-desh*	*Bhutan*	*India*	*Maldi-ves*	*Nepal*	*Pakis-tan*	*Sri Lanka*
1961	46	56	50	46	47	47	34	54
1962	45	54	53	46	49	48	36	58
1963	47	61	55	47	50	48	37	60
1964	47	61	56	47	52	49	38	64
1965	46	61	57	45	53	51	40	58
1966	45	59	59	45	58	49	39	58
1967	48	67	60	47	60	50	42	64
1968	52	68	61	51	61	52	46	68
1969	53	72	63	52	62	54	47	67
1970	56	69	64	56	65	55	49	72
1971	56	64	66	56	67	55	49	72
1972	54	63	67	53	64	54	51	73
1973	58	69	69	58	67	59	53	70
1974	56	67	70	55	67	61	55	75
1975	62	74	72	62	76	63	56	78
1976	62	72	74	62	73	62	58	78
1977	66	77	75	66	78	61	61	79
1978	68	80	77	68	75	63	61	85
1979	66	79	79	65	73	61	65	95
1980	68	80	84	67	81	67	66	100
1981	73	79	89	72	82	70	69	100
1982	73	82	90	72	85	65	71	97
1983	80	84	93	81	91	79	74	108
1984	82	84	100	82	93	79	76	103

1985	84	88	96	84	95	80	79	110
1986	86	88	98	85	96	78	86	110
1987	85	88	108	84	94	87	86	96
1988	92	90	96	93	95	93	89	100
1989	99	98	97	99	93	98	97	96
1990	100	100	101	100	104	102	100	105
1991	102	102	102	101	103	100	104	99
1992	105	104	101	105	107	96	106	101
1993	109	104	105	109	109	107	113	106
1994	112	100	110	113	110	104	117	114
1995	116	104	113	116	113	113	127	119
1996	119	110	115	119	112	115	133	105
1997	123	111	117	122	115	119	135	108
1998	123	115	117	122	120	119	142	113
1999	128	126	114	126	131	121	144	117
2000	128	128	114	125	131	124	145	115

Source: http://www.fao.apps.org

APPENDIX II

PRODUCER PRICES OF RICE IN SOUTH ASIA (LOCAL CURRENCY)

Year	*Bangladesh*	*Bhutan*	*India*	*Nepal*	*Pakistan*	*Sri Lanka*
1966	555	591	591	960	396	529
1967	486	722	722	990	491	652
1968	586	702	702	1080	492	760
1969	552	709	709	1180	494	729
1970	532	728	728	1130	488	712
1971	579	769	769	1270	527	693
1972	1039	884	884	1480	770	712
1973	1028	1058	1058	1580	1054	1162
1974	1481	1400	1400	1610	1465	1975
1975	3334	1510	1508	1570	1195	2005
1976	1905	1240	1241	1239	1393	1791
1977	1890	1310	1310	1477	1487	1688
1978	2129	1270	1274	1422	1608	1952
1979	2502	1400	1404	1689	1608	2014
1980	2757	1620	1615	1735	1875	2455
1981	3112	1770	1765	1545	2125	3229
1982	3603	1950	1860	1922	2200	3407
1983	3458	2160	1950	2512	2250	3542
1984	4033	2390	2104	2534	2250	3600
1985	4659	2640	1735	3030	2325	3900
1986	4248	2920	1941	3580	2550	3960
1987	5368	3240	2068	3580	3250	4160
1988	6255	3580	2183	3820	3375	4250
1989	6110	3960	2275	4470	3587	5660
1990	5520	4380	2165	4820	3750	7330
1991	6330	4700	3583	4840	3875	7230
1992	6310	5000	3927	5000	4375	8060
1993	5560	5300	3948	5300	4625	8200
1994	6160	5600	3980	5600	5250	7980
1995	7070	N®.52	6.46	6.78	9.27	10.35
GR	10.36	8.52	6.46	6.78	9.27	10.35

Source: http://www.apps.fao.org.

Bibliography

Books

Acharya, K.C.S., *Food Security System of India* (New Delhi: Concept Publishing Company, 1983).

Ahmed, R., *Foodgrain Supply, Distribution, and Consumption Policies within a Dual Pricing Mechanism: A Case Study of Bangladesh, Research Report No. 8* (Washington D.C.: IFPRI, 1979).

Alailima, P. and Sanderatne, N., *Trends and Future Prospects for Food Supply and Consumption: Implication for Food Policy in Sri Lanka* (Colombo, 1982)

Alailima, P., *Evolution of Government Policies and Expenditure on Social Welfare in Sri Lanka during the 20th Century* (Colombo, 1985).

Alamgir, M. and Arora, Poonam, *Providing Food Security for All* (London: Intermediate, 1991).

Alderman, H., and Braun, Joachim von, *The Effects of the Egyptian Food Ration and Subsidy System on Income Distribution and Welfare, Research Report No. 45* (Washington D.C.: IFPRI, 1984).

Alderman, H., and others, *Egypt's Food Subsidy and Rationing System: A Description, Research Report No. 34* (Washington D.C.: IFPRI, 1982).

Alderman, H., *The Effect of Income and Food Price Changes on the Acquisition of Food by Low-Income Households* (Washington D.C.: IFPRI, 1986).

Antonio, Jorge and Carrillo, Jorge Salazar, ed., *Price Policies and Economic Growth* (London: 1997).

Asian Development Bank, *Industry Sector Policy Review* (Manila:1995).

Asian Productivity Organisation, *Marketing Systems for Agricultural Products* (Tokyo: APO, 1997).

Asian Productivity Organisation, *Sustainable Agriculture Development in Asia* (Tokyo: APO, 1994).

Bangladesh Institute of Development Studies and I.F.P.R.I., *Development Impact of the Food-For-Work Program in Bangladesh, Technical paper submitted to the World Food Programme* (Dhaka & Washington D.C.: BIDS & IFPRI, 1985).

Bansil, P.C., *Ceylon Agriculture: A Perspective* (Delhi: Dhanpat Raj, 1971).

Barbara, Huddleston, *Food Security and Food Assistance, World Food Summit: Technical Background Paper 13* (Rome:1996).

Basu, K., and others, (ed.), *Choice, Welfare and Development: A Festschrift in Honour of Amartya K. Sen* (Oxford: Clarendon Press, 1995).

Bhalla, G.S.and Tyagi, D.S., *Patterns in Indian Agriculture Development: A District Level Study* (New Delhi: Institute for Studies in Industrial Development, 1989).

Bhargava, Pradeep, *Political Economy of Sri Lanka* (New Delhi: IAAS, 1987).

Bhatia, B.M., *India's food Problem and Policy Since Independence* (Bombay: Somaiya, 1970).

Binswanger, H., and Landell-Mills P., *The World Bank's Strategy for Reducing Poverty and Hunger: A Report to the Developing Community* (Washington D.C.: World Bank, 1995).

Blaxter, K., *People Food and Resources* (Cambridge: 1986).

Brown, R. Lester, *The Agricultural Link: How Environmental Deterioration Could Disrupt Economic Progress, Paper 136* (Washington D.C.: Worldwatch, 1997).

Central Bank of Sri Lanka, *Consumer Finance Survey 1981/82* (Colombo: 1983).

Central Bank of Sri Lanka, *Review of the Economy 1985* (Colombo: 1986).

Central Bank of Sri Lanka, *Economic Progress of Independence Sri Lanka* (Colombo: 1998).

Central Bank of Sri Lanka, *Report on Consumer Finances and Socio Economic Survey, Part I 1986-87* (Colombo: 1989).

Central Bank of Sri Lanka, *Annual Report 1978* (Colombo: 1989).

Central Bank of Sri Lanka, *Annual Report 1998* (Colombo: 1999).

Central Bank of Sri Lanka, *Report on Consumer Finances and Socio Economic Survey, Part I 1996-97* (Colombo, 1999).

Central Bank of Sri Lanka, *State of the Economy – 2000* (Colombo: 2001).

Central Statistical Organisation, *Selected Socio-Economic Statistics* (New Delhi: Government of India, various years).

Chaturvedi, Pradeep ed., *Sustainable Agriculture in India* (New Delhi: IAAS, 1990).

Chopra, R.N., *Evolution of Food Policy in India* (New Delhi: Macmillan, 1981).

Chopra, R.N., *Food Policy in India: A Survey* (New Delhi: Intellectual Publishing House, 1988).

Clark, Cal and Roy, K.C., *Comparing Development Patterns in Asia* (London: Lynne Rienner Publishers, 1997).

Crosson, P. and Anderson, J.R., *Resources and Global Food Prospects* (Washington D.C.: 1992).

Cummings, R.W. Jr., *Pricing Efficiency in the Indian Wheat Market* (New Delhi: 1967).

David, E. Bell and Michael R. Reich, ed., *Health Nutrition, and Economic Crisis: Approaches to Policy in the Third World* (Dover: 1988).

Davut, Aris, *Guide to agricultural Extension in Sri Lanka* (Peradeniya: 1976).

Department of Census and Statistics, *Household Income and Expenditure Survey: 1995-96, Preliminary Report* (Colombo: Government of Sri Lanka, 1999).

Dreze, J., and Sen, A. ed., *The Political Economy of Hunger* (Oxford: Clarendon, 1990).

Dreze, J., and Sen, A., *Hunger and Public Action* (Oxford: Clarendon Press, 1989).

Dyson, Tim. *Population and Food: Global trends and future prospects* (London: Routledge, 1996).

Dyson, Tim., *Global Environmental Change Programme* (London: Routledge, 1996).

Edirisinghe, Neville, *The Food Stamp Program in Sri Lanka: Costs, Benefits, and Policy Options for Modifications, Research Report 58* (Washington, D.C.: IFPRI, 1985).

Esman, J. Milton, *Landlessness and Near-Landlessness in Developing Countries* (Ithaca: Cornell University Press, 1978).

Fernando, N.A., *The Political Economy of Agricultural Pricing Policies in Sri Lanka since Independence* (Colombo: 1987).

Fonseca, A. J., *Food Aid for Relief and Development: An Evaluation,* (New Delhi: Indian Social Institute, 1983).

Food and Agricultural Organisation, *The Fifth World Food Survey* (Rome: 1982).

Food and Agricultural Organisation, *Food Security: still Far From the Goal* (Quebec City: FAO, 1995).

Food and Agricultural Organisation, *World Food Summit Plan of Action: World Food Summit, Report of the World Food Summit, 13-17 November 1996* (Rome: FAO, 1996).

Food Commissioner Department, *Annual Report 1990* (Colombo: Government of Sri Lanka, 1991).

Frank, Ellis, *Agricultural Policies in Developing Countries* (Cambridge: Cambrigde University Press, 1992).

Gavan, James and Chandrasekera, Indrani Sri, *The Impact of Public Foodgrain Distribution on Food Consumption and Welfare in Sri Lanka, Research Report No. 13* (Washington D.C.: IFPRI, 1982).

George P.S., *Public Distribution in Kerala: Income Distribution Implications and Effectiveness, Research Report No. 7* (Washington D.C.: IFPRI, 1979).

George P.S., *Some Aspects of Procurement and Distribution of Foodgrains in India, Food Subsidies, Working Paper No. 1* (Washington D.C.: IFPRI, 1985).

George, P.S., *Government Interventions in Foodgrains Markets* (Ahmedabad: IIM, 1985).

George, P.S., *Some aspects of Procurement and Distribution of Foodgrain in India, Working Paper on Food Subsidies No. 1* (Washington, D.C.: IFPRI, 1985).

Gillespie, S., and McNeill, G., *Food, Health and Survival in India and Developing Countries* (Delhi: Oxford University Press, 1992).

Gittinger, J., and others, ed., *Food Policy: Integrating Supply, Distribution and Consumption* (Baltimore: John Hopkins University Press, 1987).

Gooneratne, W. and Gunawardena.P.L.J, ed., *Poverty and Inequality in Rural Asia* (Bangkok: ILO/ARTEP, 1984).

Gopalan, C., *Towards India's Food and Nutrition Security, Key Note Address at the National Symposium on Food Security for the Poor* (New Delhi: FAO and IAAS, 1995).

Government of India, *The Famine Enquiry Commission, Final Report* (New Delhi: 1945).

Government of India, *Report of the Agricultural Prices Commission on Price Policy for Kharif Cereals for 1965-66 Season* (New Delhi: 1965).

Government of India, *Report of the Jha Committee of Foodgrain Prices for 1964-65* (New Delhi: 1965).

Government of India, *Interim Report on Agricultural Price Policy* (New Delhi: 1975).

Government of India, *Report of the National Commission on Agriculture Part II-Policy and Strategy* (New Delhi: 1976).

Government of India, *Report on the Operations of the Food Corporation of India* (New Delhi: Bureau of Industrial Costs and Prices, 1991).

Government of India, *Technical Cooperation among Developing Countries, What India can offer* (New Delhi: n.d).

Government of India, *Ninth-Five Year Plan, 1997-2002,* Vol. II (New Delhi: 2000).

Griffin, Keith, *The Political Economy of Agrarian Change* (Cambridge: Macmillan, 1974).

Grigg, D., *The World Food Problem* (Oxford: Basil Blackwell, 1985).

Haq, Mahbub ul, *Human Development in South Asia 1997* (Karachi: Oxford University Press, 1997)

Hayami, Yujiro and others, ed., *Agricultural Development: An International Perspective* (Baltimore and London: 1985).

Hubbard, M., *Improving Food Security: A Guide for Rural Development Managers* (London: IT Publications, 1995).

Joshi, P.D., *Changing Pattern of Consumption Expenditure in India and Some Selected States* (New Delhi: NSSO, 1998).

Kabra, Kamal Nayan, and Ittyerah, Anil Chandy, *The Public Distribution System in India* (New Delhi: Eastern, 1992).

Kabra, Kamal Nayan, *Political Economy of Public Distribution of Food in India* (New Delhi: Ajanta, 1990).

Kahlon, A.S. and Tyagi, D.S., *Agricultural Price Policy in India* (New Delhi: Allied Publishers, 1983).

Kapila, Uma, ed., *Indian Agriculture: Emerging Perspectives and Policy Issues After four years of Economic Reforms* (New Delhi: Academic Foundation, 1995).

Krishna, Raj and Raychaudhuri, *Some Aspects of Wheat and Rice Price Policy in India* (Washington, D. C.: IFPRI, 1980).

Krueger, O. Anne and others, (ed.), *The Political Economy of Agricultural Pricing Policy: Asia,* Vol. 2 (Washington D.C.: The World Bank, 1991).

Kumar, S. Suba., *Impact of Subsidized Rice on Food*

Consumption and Nutrition in Kerala, Research Report 5 (Washington, D.C.: IFPRI, 1979).

Kutzner, P.L., *World Hunger: A Reference Handbook* (Oxford, 1991).

Lakshman, W.D. ed., *Dilemmas of Development; Fifty Years of Economic Change in Sri Lanka* (Colombo: Sri Lanka Association of Economists, 1997).

Lappe, Francis Moore. and Collins, Joseph, *Food First: The Myth of Scarcity* (London: Earthscan Publishers, 1980).

Lok Sabha Secretariat, *Ninth Report, Standing Committee on Food, Civil Supplies and Public Distribution* (New Delhi: Government of India, 1999).

Lustig, Nora., *Food Subsidy Programs in Mexico, Food Subsidies Working Paper 3* (Washington, D.C.: IFPRI, 1986).

Maunder, Allen and Ohkawa, Kazushi. ed., *Growth and Equity in Agricultural Development* (London and Hampshire: Gower, 1983).

Maxwell, S. and Frankenberger T., *Household Food Security; Concepts, Indicators, Measurements: A Technical Review* (New York & Rome: UNICEF & IFAD, 1992).

Maxwell, S., *Food Security in Africa: Priorities for Reducing Hunger Africa Recovery Briefing Paper 6* (New York: The United Nations, 1992).

Meier, G.M., *Leading Issues in Economic Development* (Oxford: Oxford University Press, 1984).

Mellor, J.W., *The New Economics of Growth: A strategy for India and the Developing Countries* (Baltimore and London: The Johns Hopkins University Press, 1988).

Mellor, J.W., and Ahmed Raisuddin, (ed.), *Agricultural*

Price Policy for Developing Countries (Baltimore and London: The Johns Hopkins University Press, 1988).

Ministry of Agriculture and Irrigation, *Report of the National Commission on Agriculture* (New Delhi: Government of India, 1976).

Ministry of Agriculture, *Bulletin on Food Statistics, 1994-95* (New Delhi: Government of India, 1996).

Ministry of Agriculture and Cooperation, *Agricultural Statistics at a Glance* (New Delhi: Government of India, 2000).

Ministry of Civil Supplies, Consumer Affairs and Public Distribution, *Focus on the Poor* (New Delhi: Government of India, 1997).

Ministry of Finance and Planning, *Statistical Profile of Sri Lanka* (Colombo: Government of Sri Lanka, 1998).

Ministry of Finance, *Economic Survey* (New Delhi: Government of India, various years).

Ministry of Finance, *Government Subsidies, Discussion Paper 9,* (New Delhi: Government of India, 1997).

Ministry of Plan Implementation, *Agricultural Statistics of Sri Lanka* (Colombo: Government of Sri Lanka, various years).

Ministry of Policy Planning and Implementation, *Food and Nutrition Statistics, 1950-1990* (Colombo: Government of Sri Lanka, 1992).

Mukherjee, Amitava, *Structural Adjustment Programme and Food Security* (Aldershot: Avebury, 1994).

Narayanan, S., *Demand-Supply Gap and Public Distribution of Foodgrain in India* (New Delhi: Agricole, 1986).

National Council of Applied Economic Research, *India Human Development Report,* (New Delhi: Oxford University Press, 1999).

National Sample Survey Organisation, *Report of the Pilot Survey of Income, Consumption and Savings – Part II, Report No. 398* (New Delhi: Government of India, 1993).

National Sample Survey Organisation, *Reported Adequacy of Food Intake in India: 1993-94, Report No. 415* (New Delhi: Government of India, 1997).

Nawani, N.P., *Towards Food for all Ideas for a New Public Distribution System* (New Delhi: Ministry of Information and Broadcasting, Government of India, 1995).

Paul, A. Groves, ed., *Economic Development and Social Change in Sri Lanka: A Spatial and Policy Analysis* (New Delhi: Manohar, 1996).

Pinstrup-Anderson, P., ed., *Consumer-Oriented Food Subsidies: Benefits, Costs and Policy Options* (Washington D.C.: IFPRI, 1987).

Pinstrup-Anderson, Per *Agricultural Research and Technology in Economic Development* (London: 1982).

Planning, Ministry of Finance and, *Statistical Abstract of Sri Lanka 1999* (Colombo: Government of Sri Lanka, 1999).

Postal, S., *Last Oasis, Facing Water Scarcity* (New York: 1992).

Postal, S., *Water for Agriculture: Facing the limits, Worldwatch Paper 93* (Washington D.C.: *Worldwatch,* 1989).

Price, J. Gittinger, and others, ed., *Food Policy: Integrating Supply, Distribution and Consumption* (Washington D.C.: IBRD, 1987).

Price, J. Gittinger, and Others., *Household Food Security and Role of Women* (Washington D.C.: IBRD, 1990).

Radhakrishna, R. and Rao, K. Hanumantha., *Food Security, Public Distribution and Price, UNDP Research Project, Policy Discussion Paper No. 4* (Thiruvananthapuram: Centre for Development Studies, 1994).

Rastgannikov, G. Victor., *Economic Development and Food Problem: A study of Eastern Countries* (New Delhi: Agrcole, 1993).

Ravallion, M., *Reaching the Poor through Rural Public Employment: A Survey of Theory and Evidence, Discussion Paper 94* (Washington D.C.: The World Bank, 1990).

Riches, Graham, ed., *First World Hunger: Food security and Welfare Policies* (London: 1997).

Rudra, Ashok, *Political Economy of Indian Agriculture* (Calcutta: K.P. Bagchi & Company, 1992).

Ruttan, V. ed., *Why Food Aid?* (Baltimore: Johns Hopkins University Press, 1993).

Sahn, E. David., *Food Consumption Patterns and Parameters in Sri Lanka (mimeo)* (Washington D. C.: IFPRI, 1986).

Sen, A., *Poverty and Famines: An Essay on Entitlement and Deprivation* (New Delhi: Oxford University Press, 1982).

Sen, Sudhir, *Reaping the Green Revolution* (New York: 1972).

Sharma, J.S. and Gandhi P. Varant., *Production and Consumption of Foodgrains in India: Implications of Accelerated Economic Growth and Poverty Alleviation, Research Report 81* (Washington D.C.: IFPRI, July 1990).

Singer, H. others, *Food Aid: The Challenge and the Opportunity* (Oxford: Clarendon Press, 1987).

Sinha, Radha, *Food and Poverty* (New York, 1976).

Suryanarayana, G., *Public Distribution in India* (Allahabad: Chugh, 1985).

The World Bank, *Poverty and Hunger: Issues and Options for Food Security in Developing Countries* (Washington D.C.: 1986).

The World Bank, *Sri Lanka Country Economic Update: Public Sector Rationalisation for Private Sector Development and Poverty Alleviation, Report No. 11862-CE* (New York: 1993).

The World Bank, *Sri Lanka: Nonplantation Crop Sector Policy Alternatives* (Washington D.C.: 1996).

The World Bank, *Sri Lanka: Recent Economic Developments and Prospects, Poverty Reduction and Economic Management – South Asian Region, Report No. 17761-CE* (New York: 1998).

Thorbecke, Erick, and Svejnar, J, *Economic Policies and Agricultural Performance in Sri Lanka 1960-84* (Paris: OECD, 1987).

Timmer, C., *Getting Prices Right: The Scope and Limits of Agricultural Price Policy* (Ithaca: Cornell University Press, 1986).

Tyagi, D.S. and Vyas V.S., ed., *Increasing Access to Food: The Asian Experience* (New Delhi: Sage, 1990).

Valdes, Alberto, ed., *Food Security for Developing Countries* (Colorado: Westview, 1981).

Venugopal, K.R., *Deliverance from Hunger: The Public Distribution System in India* (New Delhi: Sage, 1992).

Von J. Braun, and Kennedy E. ed., *Agricultural Commercialization: Economic Development and Nutrition* (Baltimore: Johns Hopkins University Press, 1994).

Von J. Braun, and Kennedy E., *Commercialization of Agriculture and Household Food Security: Policy Implications of Programs in The Gambia, Rwanda, and Ethiopia in Structural Change in African Agriculture, IFPRI Policy Briefings 5* (Washington D.C.: IFPRI, 1990).

Von J. Braun, and others, ed., *Improving Food Security of the Poor Concept, Policy and Programs* (Washington D.C.: IFPRI, 1992).

Von, J. Braun, and Hartwig de Haen., *The Effects of Food Price and Subsidy Policies on Egyptian Agriculture* (Washington D.C.: IFPRI, 1983).

Wanigaratne, R.D. *Intra-Regional disintegration effects of Frontier Land Settlement in Sri Lanka,* (Colombo: 1987).

Wiliamson, Gray Cheryl., *Food Consumption Parameters for Brazil and Their Application to Food Policy, Research Report 32* (Washington D.C.: IFPRI, 1982).

World Food Programme, *Annual Report 1998* (Rome: 1999).

Young, H., *Food Scarcity and Famine: Assessment and Response* (Oxford: Oxfam Publications, 1992).

Yudelman, M., *Demand and Supply of Foodstuffs upto 2050 with special reference to Irrigation* (Colombo: IIMI, 1993).

Articles

Alderman, H. and Braun J. von, "Egypt's Food Subsidy Policy: Lessons from the Past and Options for the Future", *Food Policy,* Vol. 3, No. 11, August 1986, pp. 223-237.

Barker, Randolf and Samad, M., " Irrigation Development and Food Security in Sri Lanka", *Economic Review,* Vol. 23, No. 12, 1998.

Bhalla, G.S., and Hazell, Peter, "Food grains Demand in India to 2020: A preliminary Exercise", *Economic and Political Weekly,* December 27, 1999.

Bhalla, G.S., and Singh, G., "Recent Developments in Indian Agriculture: A State Level Analysis", *Economic and Political Weekly,* Vol. 32, No. 13, 1997.

Brahmanand, P.R., "The Economy Since Independence", *Indian Horizons,* Vol. XXXXV, No. 3 & 4, (1998), pp. 101-115.

Braun, von, "Effects of Technological Change in Agriculture on Food Consumption and Nutrition: Rice in a West African Setting", *World Development,* Vol. 6, No. 9, 1988, pp. 1083-1098.

Chakrabarti, Sibaji, "In Search of Growth Pattern for Foodgrains Production in India", *Economic and Political Weekly,* Review of Agriculture, (Mumbai), December 1982, pp. A122-A126.

Chaudhuri, G.S. Roy, and Krishna, Raj "Some Aspects of Wheat Price Policy in India", *Indian Economic Review,* Vol. XIV, No. 2, October 1979, pp. 101-125.

Chellaraj, G., Wade B. Brorsen, and Paul L. Farris, "Impact of Rice Subsidy on Food Consumption in India", *Indian Journal of Agricultural Economics,* (Pune), Vol. 47, No. 2, 1992, pp. 215-223.

Corbett, J., "Famine and Household Coping Strategies", *World Development,* Vol. 16, No. 9, 1988, pp. 1099-1112.

Dahanayaka, P.A.S., "Disincentive effects of Food Aid on Food Production in Sri Lanka", *Staff-Studies,* Vol. 8, No. 2, 1978, pp. 29-38.

Dandekar, V.M., "Minimum Support Prices for Foodgrains: Guidelines for a Policy and a Programme", *Artha Vijnana,* Vol. 7, No. 4, December 1965, pp. 273-283.

Dantwala, M.L., "Agricultural Policy: Prices and Public Distribution System: A Review", *Indian Journal of Agricultural Economics,* Vol. 48, No. 2, 1993, pp. 173-186.

Dantwala, M.L., "Agricultural Price Policy: Reply", *Economic and Political Weekly,* Vol. III, No. 11, March 16, 1968, pp. 459-460.

Dantwala, M.L., "My Academic Dialogues: Agricultural Price Policy and the Green Revolution", *Indian Journal of Agricultural Economics,* Vol. 51, No. 1 & 2, January-June 1996, pp. 51-59.

Dantwala, M.L., "Problems of Buffer Stocks", *Economic and Political Weekly,* Review of Agriculture, March 1969, pp. A63-A67.

Desai, D.K. and Ramachandran, V., "Working Capital and Credit Needs of Foodgrains Distribution in India", *Economic and Political Weekly,* Vol. IX, No. 29, 1974, pp. 1150-1165.

Dev, S. Mahendra, and Suryanarayan M.H., "Is PDS Urban Biased and Pro-Rich?", *Economic and Political Weekly,* Vol. XXVI, No. 41, 1991, pp. 2357-2366.

Dev, S. Mahendra., "Food Security: PDS vs EGS: A Tale of Two States", *Economic and Political Weekly,* Vol. XXXI, No. 27, 1996, pp. 1752-1764.

Devereux, S., "Entitlements, Availability and Famine: A Revisionist View of Wollo, 1972-74", *Food Policy,* Vol. 13, No. 3, 1988, pp. 270-282.

Dharmaratne, T.A., and others, "Paddy/Rice Marketing: Perspectives and Prospects in '90s", *Economic Review,* Vol. 24, nos.10-12, 1999, pp. 6-11

George, P. S., "Public Distribution System, Food Subsidy and Production Incentives", *Economic and Political Weekly,* Vol. XXXI, No. 39, 1996, pp. A140-A144.

Ghose, Arabinda, "Agriculture: Future Challenges", *Indian Horizons,* Vol. XXXXV, No. 3 & 4, 1998, p. 139-150.

Gupta, S.C. and Sethi, J.D., "Food Policy: Objectives and Instruments", *Economic and Political Weekly,* Vol. II, No. 14, 1967, pp. 683-693.

Hay, R.W., "Famine Incomes and Employment: Has Botswana Anything to Teach Africa", *World Development,* Vol. 16, No. 9, 1988, pp. 1113-1125.

Hay, R.W., and Rukuni, M., "SADCC Food Security Strategies: Evolution and Role", *World Development,* Vol. 16, No. 9, 1988, pp. 1012-1024.

Holst, Willem, "Planning for Self-Sufficiency in Foodgrains", *Economic and Political Weekly,* Vol. II, No. 27, 1967, pp. 1211-1227.

Howes, Stephen, and Jha, Shikha., "Urban Bias in Indian Public Distribution System", *Economic and Political Weekly,* Vol. XXVII, No. 19, 1992, pp. 1022-1030.

John, R. Tarrant, "World Food Prospects for the 1990s", *Journal of Geography,* November-December 1990, pp. 234-238.

Johnston, and Mellor, J.W., "Role of Agriculture in Economic Development", *American Economic Review,* March 1961.

Joshi, P.K. and Kaneda, Hiromitsu, "Variability of Yields in Foodgrains Production since Mid-Sixties", *Economic and Political Weekly,* Review of Agriculture, March 1982.

Kannan, R. and Chakrabarty, T.K., "Demand Projections for Selected Food Items in India, 1985-86 to 2000-01", *Economic and Political Weekly,* Review of Agriculture, December 1983, pp. A135-A142.

Kennedy, E. and Cogill, B., "The Commercialization of

Agriculture and Household-level Food Security: The case of Southwestern Kenya", *World Development,* Vol. 16, No. 9, 1988, pp. 1075-1082.

Khadka, Narayan., "Regional Food Security in South Asia", *Asian Profile,* Vol. 18, No. 5, 1990.

Krishna, Daya, "Government Operations in Foodgrains: A Comment", *Economic and Political Weekly,* Vol. II, No. 48, 1967, pp. 2131-2132.

Krishna, Rao I.Y.R., "An Experiment in Food Security", *Economic and Political Weekly,* Vol. XXVII, No. 37, September 11, 1993, pp. 1911-1993.

Kumar, Praduman, and Mathur, V.C., "Structural Changes in the Demand for Food in India", *Indian Journal of Agricultural Economics,* Vol. 51, No. 4, 1996, pp. 664-673.

Kumar, S. Subha., "Effect of Seasonal Food Shortage on Agricultural Production in Zambia", *World Development,* Vol. 16, No. 9, 1988, pp. 1051-1064.

Kundu, Amitab, "Urban Bias in PDS: Re-examination of NSS Data", *Economic and Political Weekly,* Vol. XXVII, No. 26, 1992, pp. 1340-1341.

Laxminarayan, H., "Doing without a Food Policy", *Economic and Political Weekly,* Vol. V, No. 24, 1967, pp. 949-951.

Liyanarachchi, N.B, "Food Security and Food Distribution", *Economic Review,* Vol. 23, nos.1& 2, 1997, pp. 7-11.

Mellor, W. John, "The Functions of Agricultural Prices in Economic Development", *Indian Journal of Agricultural Economics,* Vol. XXIII, No. 1, January-March 1968.

Minhas, B.S., "Towards National Food Security", *Indian Journal of Agricultural Economics,* Vol. XXXI, No. 4, October-December, 1976, pp. 8-19.

Misra, S.N., "Capital Formation and Accumulation in Indian Agriculture Since Independence" *Indian Journal of Agricultural Economics,* Vol. 51, No. 1 & 2, 1997.

Mittal, and Krishnan S. Anantha, "Politics of Hunger and Right to Food", *Economic and Political Weekly,* Vol. XXXII, No. 5, 1997, pp. 201-204.

Mujumdar, N. A., "Food Security, Price Stability and the Budget", *Economic and Political Weekly,* Vol. XXXII, nos.20 & 21, 1997, pp. 1201-1203.

Mukherjee, Neela and Mukherjee, Amitava, "Rural Women and Food Insecurity: What a Food Calendar Reveals", *Economic and Political Weekly,* Vol. XXIX, No. 11, 1994, pp. 597-599.

Rath, Nilakantha, "On fixation of Price in Agriculture on the basis of Cost of Production", *Artha Vijnana,* Vol. 7, No. 4, December 1965, pp. 321-329.

Rath, Nilakantha, "Poverty in India Revisited", *Indian Journal of Agricultural Economics,* Vol. 51, No. 1 & 2, January-June 1996, pp. 76-108.

Rath, Nilakantha, "Prices, Costs of Production and Terms of Trade of Indian Agriculture", *Indian Journal of Agricultural Economics,* Vol. XL, No. 4, October-December 1985, pp. 451-464.

Oslen, R.O. "Impact and Implications of Foreign Surplus Disposal on Underdeveloped Economies," *Journal of Farm Economies,* Vol. 42, 1960, pp. 1042-51.

Paarlberg, Robert, "The Global Food Fight", *Foreign Affair,* Vol. 79, No. 3, 2000, pp. 35.

Pandey V.K. and K.C. Sharma, " Crop Diversification and Self-Sufficiency in Foodgrains", *Indian Journal of Agricultural Economics,* Vol. 51, No. 4, October-December, 1996, pp. 644-651.

Panse, V.G., and others, "A Plan for Improvement of Nutrition of India's Population", *India Journal of Agricultural Economics,* Vol. XIX, 1964.

Parthasarathy, G., "Rural Markets: Pricing of Agricultural Products and Regulation of Markets", *Indian Journal of Agricultural Marketing,* (New Delhi), Vol. 8, No. 2, 1994.

Parthasarthy, G. and Mohinder S. Mudahar, "Foodgrain Prices and Economic Growth", *Indian Journal of Agricultural Economics,* Vol. XXXI, No. 2, April-June, 1976, pp. 16-30.

Patnaik, Usta, "Export-Oriented Agriculture and Food Security in Developing Countries and India", *Economic and Political Weekly,* Special Number, September, 1996, pp. 2429-2449.

Peoples Bank, "Peasant Agriculture", *Economic Review,* (Colombo), Vol. 3, No. 10, 1978.

Pinckney, T.C. and Valdes, A., "Short-run Supply Management and Food Security: Results from Pakistan and Kenya", *World Development,* Vol. 16, No. 9, pp. 1025-1034.

Radhakrishna, R.,"Food Trends, Public Distribution System and Food Security Concerns", *Indian Journal of Agricultural Economics,* Vol. 51, No. 1-2, 1996, pp. 168-183.

Raj, K.N., "Regional Variations in Foodgrain Prices", *Economic and Political Weekly,* Vol. I, No. 1, August 20, 1966, pp. 49-52.

Rao C.H. Hanumantha and Subbarao K., "Marketing of Rice in India: An Analysis of the Impact of Producers' Prices on Small Farmers", *Indian Journal of Agricultural Economics,* Vol. 24, No. 3, July-September, 1969, pp. 1-15.

Rao V.M., "Beyond 'Surpluses': Food Security in Changing Context", *Economic and Political Weekly,* Vol. XXX, No. 4, January 28, 1995, pp. 215-219.

Rao, V.M., "How Secure Is Food Security?", *Economic and Political Weekly,* Vol. XXVII, No. 48, November 28, 1992, pp. 2598-99.

Ray S.K., "Effects of Consumption Availability Fluctuations on Foodgrains Prices", *Economic and Political Weekly,* Review of Agriculture, June 1972, pp. A86-A92.

Ray S.K., "Foodgrains Demand and Supply: Projections of Regional Imbalances", *Economic and Political Weekly,* Review of Agriculture, June 1971, pp. A59-A74.

Ray S.K., "Weather and Reserve Stocks for Foodgrains", *Economic and Political Weekly,* Review of Agriculture, September 1971, pp. A131-A142.

Reardon T, and others, "Coping with Household-level Food Security in Drought-affected Areas of Burkina Faso", *World Development,* Vol. 16, No. 9, 1988, pp. 1065-1074.

Runge, C. Ford, and Senauer, Benjamin, "A Removable Feast", *Foreign Affairs,* Vol. 79, No. 3, May-June 2000, pp. 39-51.

Sanderatne, N., "A Profile of the Informal Rural Credit Market in the Mid-Seventies", *Staff Studies* Vol. 11, No. 2&3, 1981, pp. 70-81.

Saran, Ram, "Recent Changes in Food Policy", *Agricultural Situation in India,* 1971.

Satyasai, K.J.S. and K.U., Viswanathan, "Diversification of Indian Agriculture and Food Security", *Indian Journal of Agricultural Economics,* Vol. 51, No. 4, 1996, pp. 674-679.

Sawant, S.D. and Achuthan, C.V., "Public Distribution

System in India: Why to Revamp it?", *Agricultural Situation in India,* Vol. LII, No. 4, July 1995, pp. 199-205.

Shah, Amita, "Food Security and Access to National Resources: A Review of Recent Trends", *Economic and Political Weekly,* Vol. XXXII, No. 26, 1997, pp. A46-A54.

Shah, C.H., "Essentials of a National Food Policy: A Critique of the Foodgrains Policy Committee's Report", *Economic and Political Weekly,* Vol. I, No. 8, 1966, pp. 322-326.

Shankar, Kripa, "Revamped Public Distribution System: Who Benefits and How Much?", *Economic and Political Weekly,* Vol. XXXII, No. 13, 1997, pp. 629-630.

Shaw, J. and Singer, H., "Food Policy, Food and Economic Adjustment", *Food Policy* (special issue), Vol. 13, No. 1, February 1988.

Shaw, Robert, "Development Reconsidered: Gap Between Government and People", *Health,* 1972, pp. 60-67.

Sirisena, L.N., "An Evaluation of Agricultural Policy on the Paddy Sector, 1950-85", *Sri Lanka Economic Journal,* Vol. 1, No. 1, 1986.

Sunando, Roy, "Public Distribution of Cereals: An Alternative Model", *Economic and Political Weekly,* Vol. XXVII, No. 23, 1992, pp. 1209-1213.

Suryanarayana, M.H., "PDS Reform and Scope for Commodity-Based Targeting", *Economic and Political Weekly,* Vol. XXX, No. 13, 1995, pp. 687-695.

Suryanarayana, M.H., "PDS: beyond Implicit Subsidy and Urban Bias – the Indian Experience", *Food Policy,* Vol. 20, No. 4, 1995, pp. 445-463.

Suryanarayana, M.H., "Uruguay Round and Global Food Security", *Economic and Political Weekly,* Vol. XXXII, No. 43, 1997, pp. 2821-2828.

Swaminathan, M.S. and Balaji, V.,"Food Security for the Poor-What Does it Take?", *IASSI Quarterly,* Vol. 16, No. 1, 1997, pp. 17-35.

Swaminathan, M.S., "Science and Technology for Sustainable Food Security", *Indian Journal of Agricultural Economics,* Vol. 51, No. 1-2, 1996, pp. 60-75.

Swaminathan, M.S., "Science and Technology for Sustainable Food Security", *Indian Journal of Agricultural Economics,* Vol. 51, No. 1 & 2, January-June 1996, pp. 60-75.

Swaminathan, Mathura, "Structural Adjustment, Food Security and System of Public Distribution of Food", *Economic and Political Weekly,* Vol. XXXI, No. 26, 1996, pp. 1665-1672.

Timmer, C., "Food Price Policy: The Rationale for Government Intervention", *Food Policy,* February 1989, pp. 17-27.

Vyas, V.S., "Diversification in Agriculture: Concept, Rationale and Approaches", *Indian Journal of Agricultural Economics,* Vol. 51, No. 4, October-December 1996, pp. 636-643.

Vyas, V.S., and Bandyopadhyay, S.C.,"National Food Policy in the Framework of a National Food Budget", *Economic and Political Weekly,* Review of Agriculture, March 1975, pp. A2-A18.

Wade, Nicholas, "Green Revolution I: A Just Technology Often Unjust in Use," *Science,* December. 1974.

Wendy, S. Ayres, and McCalla, F. Alex, "Rural Development, Agriculture, and Food Security", *Finance and Development,* Vol. 33, No. 4, December 1996, pp. 8-11.

Wickramasinghe, W.D., "Government Intervention in Rice Market", *Economic Review,* Vol. 24, nos.10-12, 1999, pp. 12-13.

Young, H., and Jaspars, S., "Nutritional Assessments, Food Security and Famine", *Disasters,* Vol. 19, No. 1, 1995.

Index

Z

■■■